ELECTIONS FOR SALE

ELECTIONS FOR SALE

The Causes and Consequences of Vote Buying

edited by
Frederic Charles Schaffer

LYNNE
RIENNER
PUBLISHERS

BOULDER
LONDON

Published in the United States of America in 2007 by
Lynne Rienner Publishers, Inc.
1800 30th Street, Boulder, Colorado 80301
www.rienner.com

and in the United Kingdom by
Lynne Rienner Publishers, Inc.
3 Henrietta Street, Covent Garden, London WC2E 8LU

Library of Congress Cataloging-in-Publication Data
Elections for sale : the causes and consequences of vote buying / edited by
Frederic Charles Schaffer.
   p. cm.
   Includes bibliographical references and index.
   ISBN-13: 978-1-58826-434-3 (hardcover : alk. paper)
   1. Elections—Corrupt practices. 2. Voting. I. Schaffer, Frederic Charles.
   JF1083.E54 2006
   364.1'324—dc22

                                                        2006022544

British Cataloguing in Publication Data
A Cataloguing in Publication record for this book
is available from the British Library.

Printed and bound in the United States of America

The paper used in this publication meets the requirements
of the American National Standard for Permanence of
Paper for Printed Library Materials Z39.48-1992.

5   4   3   2   1

3/07

Contents

Part 4 Conclusion

Tables and Figures

Tables

Figures

Acknowledgments

The idea for this book grew out of a conference that I co-organized with Andreas Schedler on the topic of vote buying. We were intrigued that in many new democracies and semiauthoritarian regimes, political parties, civic associations, and members of the mass media regularly denounce efforts to control electoral outcomes by buying votes. Yet, we also noticed that systematic knowledge about the comparative politics of vote buying is surprisingly scarce.

To learn more, we invited a handful of experts from around the world to address the following questions: How can one observe the retail trade in votes? How do citizens perceive the commercialization of suffrage rights? How do political entrepreneurs purchase votes under different circumstances? How successful are different techniques of vote buying? How well do economic, cultural, and institutional theories explain the marketization of votes? How effective have different counterstrategies been in neutralizing practices of vote buying?

Both the seminal conference and the book project received generous backing from the Center for International Studies at the Massachusetts Institute of Technology. I would like to single out for thanks the director of the center, Richard Samuels, for his ongoing and enthusiastic support. I am deeply grateful as well to Andreas Schedler, who played a key role in bringing this book to life. I also owe him a much more personal debt, since many of my own ideas about vote buying took shape in the course of our many conversations and e-mail exchanges, and in cowriting one of the chapters for this book. I learned much, too, from the other contributors to this volume, and I thank them as well. Recognition is also due to John Gerring of Boston University for his many constructive suggestions, and to Marilyn Grobschmidt at Lynne Rienner Publishers for her wise editorial advice. I offer, finally, special thanks to my family for all the ways that they have helped, both large and small.

—*Frederic Charles Schaffer*

1

Why Study Vote Buying?

Frederic Charles Schaffer

Vote buying, sometimes regarded as a phenomenon of olden times and backward places, is making an impressive comeback. As more and more countries introduce competitive elections, reports of vote buying are multiplying. In many corners of the world, it seems, a blossoming market for votes has emerged as an epiphenomenon of democratization. Struggling for votes in places where party labels and electoral platforms may not mean much, political parties and candidates are trying to sway voters by offering them particularistic material rewards.

Vote buying campaigns have met with bitter complaints by political activists and election observers, and they have been the target of multiple efforts at legal reform and voter education. The controversy and action sparked in the world of politics, however, have not been matched by systematic research in the academic world. This volume, on the comparative politics of vote buying, sets out to narrow the glaring gap between political relevance and scholarly attention.

Varieties of Vote Buying

Vote buying, in its barest sense, involves the exchange of money, goods, or services for votes. While instances of vote buying have reportedly taken place within the International Whaling Commission, among members of the US Congress, and between shareholders of large corporations (among other contexts), the focus of this book is the purchase of votes in popular elections. Even such a narrow focus on electoral exchanges covers a remarkable phenomenological variety of activities.

For one, there is a dizzying array of material inducements that parties and candidates have offered to voters in exchange for their votes: soap, tires, chairs, sarongs, watches, chickens, shingles, cement, whisky, coffins,

1

haircuts, cigarettes, fertilizer, bicycles, funerals, vasectomies, dictionaries, fumigators, Viagra, Oxycontin, television sets, free rent, rugby balls, dried meat, mobile phones, birthday cakes, electric fans, cooking oil, bags of rice, barbed wire, corn grinders, plastic sheeting, washing machines, plastic surgery, teeth cleaning, and the list goes on.

The amount of money distributed can also vary widely. On the low end, individuals from one poor neighborhood of Metro Manila received only 30 pesos (US 60 cents) during a relatively noncompetitive 2002 local race. On the high end, the price of a vote in Kuwait's 1996 parliamentary elections reportedly surpassed 3,000 dinar (US$10,000) (*Agence-France Press* 1996). In Thailand, the average offer per household in the 1996 general election was 678 baht (US$27)—though Bangkok residents were likely to be given twice as much as rural dwellers (Pasuk et al. 2000). Gypsies in the Greek city of Sofades receive about US$16 per vote (Marantzidis and Mavrommatis 1999, 448). In Russia, voters were offered 50–100 rubles (US$2–4) for their votes in the 2000 election (Borisova 2000). That same year, many Mexican voters received 250–500 pesos (US$25–50) per vote.

There is even great diversity in how benefits are distributed. In Cambodia, canvassers sneak from house to house in election-eve darkness on "the night of the barking dogs," while in one Malaysian election, voters were openly showered with money from a helicopter above. In Thailand, vote buyers made lavish "donations" at weddings. In other places, money has been dispensed as conditional loans, sent as postal orders, or paid out in generous lottery schemes and bingo games.

The Reach of Vote Buying

Vote buying is not, of course, a new phenomenon. It was common in ancient Rome, especially during the late republic, where it was called *ambitus* (from the verb *ambire,* to "go around" or "canvass support") (Lintott 1990). In England, candidates "treated" voters to food and drink as far back as the 1660s (Kishlansky 1986, 192–197). Vote buying was also present at the birth of US democracy. Even before the Declaration of Independence, votes were bought, often with intoxicating drinks, a practice then known as "swilling the planters with bumbo." Among those who swilled voters was George Washington. In his first race, for the Virginia House of Burgesses in 1758, he bought 160 gallons of rum, wine, beer, and cider to treat 391 voters and their hangers-on (Sydnor 1984 [1952], 51–54).

Today, after three decades of global democratization—as almost all political regimes, be they democratic or authoritarian, are holding some kind of elections—vote buying has turned into a worldwide phenomenon. In recent years, credible reports of vote buying have come from all regions of the world: from Asia (India, Taiwan, Japan, Thailand, Malaysia, Cambodia, Mongolia, Indonesia, the Philippines, South Korea) to Africa (Benin, Niger, Kenya, Zambia, Senegal, Morocco, Zimbabwe, Nigeria, São Tomé and Principe) to Europe and the successor states of the former Soviet Union (Greece, Russia, Ukraine, Armenia, Bulgaria, Macedonia) to the Middle East (Yemen, Kuwait, Lebanon) to South and Central America (Peru, Belize, Brazil, Chile, Panama, Guatemala, Columbia, Venezuela, Argentina) to North America (Mexico, the provinces of Quebec and Nova Scotia in Canada, and the US states of Georgia, Florida, Michigan, Kentucky, Indiana, Illinois, Mississippi, and West Virginia).

Sometimes, efforts at vote buying are sporadic and isolated. In several countries, however, vote buying campaigns have been massive. In the Philippines, an estimated 3 million people nationwide were offered some form of payment in the 2002 *barangay* (community-level) elections—about 7 percent of all voting-aged adults (Social Weather Stations 2002). In Thailand, 30 percent of household heads surveyed in a national sample said that they were offered money during the 1996 general election (Pasuk et al. 2000). In Taiwan's third largest city, Taichung, and its surrounding county, 27 percent of a random sample of eligible voters reported in 1999 that they accepted cash during electoral campaigns past (Cheng, Wang, and Chen 2000). In Cambodia, 40 percent of respondents in a 1999 national survey stated that someone in their household had received a gift to vote for the party of the gift giver (Collins et al. 2000, 30–31). In the Ukraine, almost 70 percent of the people surveyed nationwide in 2002 believed that vote buying occurred "always" or "sometimes" (Sharma 2003, 13). In the Armenian city of Yerevan, 75 percent of a random sample of citizens reported that an electoral bribe had been offered to them, their friends, or their relatives during the 2003 parliamentary elections (Transparency International Armenia 2003). In Brazil, an estimated 6 million people nationwide were offered money for their votes in the 2000 municipal elections, about 6 percent of all voting-aged adults (Speck and Abramo 2001). In Argentina, 12 percent of low-income adults surveyed in the provinces of Buenos Aires, Córdoba, and Misiones reported receiving something from a candidate or party during the 2001 electoral campaign (Brusco, Nazareno, and Stokes 2004, 70). In Mexico, a nationwide exit poll following the 2000 election found that almost 5 percent of voters received from a party some form of particularistic reward, while a national postelection survey found that about 15 percent of respondents received from a party either a gift or assistance (Cornelius 2004, 50–52). While these numbers—all derived from mass surveys—must be treated with care, they do provide a conservative, if rough, gauge of just how widespread the practice is in certain countries.

Though the amount of money offered to individual voters varies greatly depending on the competitiveness of the election and the local level of prosperity, among other factors, the total sum of money spent by candidates on vote buying can sometimes be quite high. One congressional candidate in the Southern Luzon region of the Philippines admitted to doling out 4 million pesos (US$160,000) to voters on the eve of the 1992 election (Tirol 1992). Some candidates running for office in Brazil's state assemblies reportedly hand out up to US$1 million each (see Chapter 7). Prosecutors at the Taiwanese Ministry of Justice reckon that a typical legislative candidate in an urban area might easily distribute up to NT$100 million (US$3 million).[1] The Nakhon Ratchsima Rajabhat Institute, which monitors poll fraud in Thailand, estimates that candidates gave out a total of 20 billion baht (US$460 million) to voters in the 2001 legislative elections (*Newsweek* 2001).

However old, widespread, and in some cases intense, there is much about vote buying that we do not understand: What exactly is it? Why does it appear in some places at some times but not others? What are its underlying causes? What is the comparative advantage of vote buying for candidates relative to other electoral strategies? What is its impact—on electoral outcomes, the quality of democracy, politics beyond the ballot box, or the economy? Is it possible to legislate or educate it away? These are the central questions that motivate this book.

The Twin Nature of Vote Buying

Insofar as vote buying represents a strategy to capture votes, it is a tool of electoral mobilization. Insofar as it represents a strategy to distort the expression of voter preferences, vote buying is a tool of electoral manipulation. The twin nature of vote buying, its Janus face as a mobilizational as well as a manipulative strategy, explains the double membership it holds in both electoral studies and democratization research. When conducting research on vote buying, we study democratic routines (electoral campaigns and voting behavior) at the same time that we inquire into antidemocratic practices (the colonization of individual autonomy by money).

Electoral Mobilization

Parties and candidates may mobilize voters on the basis of moral appeals that have no tangible implications for their material welfare. Issues like abortion, animal protection, and the content of history textbooks may touch voters to the heart, but they are, for most people, far removed from the pocketbook. As many authors have observed, however, electoral campaigns do normally appeal to citizens' economic self-interests. In "programmatic" campaigns, parties and candidates package material benefits into policy programs that are available to everyone, supporters and opponents alike. In "clientelist" campaigns (including those that rely on vote buying), parties and candidates promise or deliver material benefits selectively to their supporters alone (Kitschelt 2000).

The distinction between "programmatic" and "clientelist" strategies of electoral mobilization may be overly broad, however, to help us determine whether there is anything distinctive about vote buying. Toward that end, it may be more fruitful to conceptualize the dichotomy as a continuum of distributional strategies that candidates or elected officials may use to sway voters. From this perspective, vote buying occupies the far end of the continuum:

- *Allocational policies:* Enacting policies that distribute material rewards to entire, geographically dispersed classes of voters (unemployment insurance, middle-class tax cuts, healthcare benefits for the elderly, etc.).
- *Pork-barrel spending:* Channeling material benefits (often in the form of contracts, grants, or public works projects) to the local districts of elected officials.
- *Patronage:* Providing material support, at any time during the electoral cycle, to individuals, families, or communities within the context of enduring asymmetric, but reciprocal, relationships.
- *Vote buying:* Offering particularistic material rewards to individuals or families at election time.

There are several distinguishing characteristics of vote buying with regard to scope, timing, and legality. As shown in Table 1.1, these three features, taken together, distinguish vote buying from the other distributional strategies of electoral mobilization:

- *Scope:* Vote buying, like patronage, is particularistic. Material benefits accrue to individual voters or families—though in many instances patronage (say, in the form of wells or sewage pipes) can also be distributed to whole neighborhoods or villages as well (Salem 1992; Auyero 1999, 305–306). Given the particularistic targeting of vote buying (as well as some forms of patronage), politicians and their agents have a high degree of control over who receives the rewards. The benefits of pork, to the extent that they are public goods like dams or roadways, can typically be funneled only into larger collectivities, or perhaps (in the case of contracts) into businesses in a particular locale.
- *Timing:* Vote buying is a last-minute effort to influence electoral outcomes, typically taking place days or hours before an election, or on election day itself. The benefits derived from patronage, in contrast, tend to be

less episodic and election-centered, since they are distributed within the context of enduring relationships between patrons and their clients, while the delivery of pork and the benefits of allocational policies, because of the vicissitudes of budgetary politics, are difficult to time precisely.

• *Legality:* Vote buying often runs counter to legal norms. While pork and allocational policies are the stuff of lawful democratic politics, and patronage has nebulous legal status, vote buying is almost always illegal. Consequently, vote buying decisions—about how much to pay out and to whom—are almost everywhere reached in great secrecy by political parties, candidates, and their agents, whereas patronage decisions might be made either privately or publicly. Decisions about the distribution of pork or the enactment of allocational policies, in contrast, must typically adhere to public, governmental procedure.

Among distributional strategies of electoral mobilization then, vote buying is the most particularistic; it occurs closest to the time of voting, and it alone is unambiguously illegal.

Electoral Manipulation

Democratic observers tend to evaluate vote buying more negatively than other distributional strategies of electoral mobilization. While they may be critical of allocational policies, skeptical of pork-barrel politics, and cynical

Table 1.1   Comparing Distributional Strategies of Electoral Mobilization

Distributional Strategy of Electoral Mobilization	Scope (How widely are material benefits distributed?)	Timing (When are material benefits distributed?)	Legality (Is the distribution of material benefits legal?)
Allocational policies	Whole classes of voters (elderly, unemployed, etc.)	Hard to time exactly; can occur at any time during the electoral cycle	Legal
Pork-barrel spending	Local districts	Hard to time exactly; can occur at any time during the electoral cycle	Legal
Patronage	Neighborhoods, villages, families, individuals	Ongoing throughout the electoral cycle	Gray legal status
Vote buying	Families, individuals	Days or hours before election day, or on election day itself	Illegal

about patronage, they tend to condemn vote buying as an infraction of democratic norms. This is so because vote buying is more than just another strategy of electoral mobilization; it also constitutes a strategy of electoral manipulation.

There are a variety of ways in which elections can be manipulated and norms of democracy violated. The exclusion of opposition forces can restrict the range of democratic choice. Repression and unfair access to the media can place limits on the ability of electorates to formulate their preferences. Formal and informal disfranchisement can restrict who gets to choose. Fraudulent vote tallying can compromise the integrity of how preferences are aggregated. And of course, coercion—and vote buying—can block the free expression of citizen preferences. Table 1.2 shows more pre-

Table 1.2 Comparing Strategies of Electoral Manipulation

Strategy of Electoral Manipulation	Goal of Electoral Manipulation	Democratic Norm That Is Violated
Denying legal status to opposition forces Disqualifying candidates or parties from participating in elections	Restricting access of opposition forces to the electoral arena	Freedom of choice (citizens must be free to form, join, and support competing parties and candidates)
Limiting broadcast airtime allotted to opposition parties Restricting what opposition candidates can say Shutting down opposition newspapers Denying permits for opposition parties to hold rallies	Restricting the freedom of speech of opposition candidates and parties	Freedom to formulate preferences (citizens must be free to learn about available choices from alternative sources of information)
Putting in place discriminatory registration or voting devices (such as literacy tests, restrictive identification requirements, limited poll hours, cumbersome registration procedures) Tampering with voter registry	Disfranchising full members of the political community or enfranchising those who are ineligible to participate	Equal opportunity to express preferences (democracy assigns equal rights of participation to all full members of the political community)
Vote buying Voter intimidation	Unduly influencing the electoral choices made by voters	Freedom to express preferences (citizens must be free to express their electoral preferences)
Ballot box stuffing Padding or shaving vote tallies	Manipulating the vote count	Equal weighing of preferences (the democratic ideal of equality—one person, one vote—demands counting votes accurately)

Source: Adapted from Schedler 2002a, 39.

cisely where vote buying falls relative to other strategies of manipulation in terms of the goal each is intended to achieve and the way in which each violates norms of democracy.

What distinguishes vote buying from other strategies of manipulation? First, as shown in Table 1.2, vote buying, as with voter intimidation, is distinct insofar as it is intended to influence directly the electoral choices made by voters, and thus it directly compromises the freedom of voters to express their preferences. In addition, like voter intimidation, literacy tests, and double voting, vote buying is what we might call a "retail" strategy. It alters the outcome of an election one vote at a time. Vote padding, denying legal status to opposition forces, and imposing media restrictions, in contrast, are "wholesale" forms of manipulation that affect the choices or votes of a large number of citizens at the same time. However, unlike other retail strategies of manipulation—such as voter intimidation and discriminatory identification requirements—vote buying alone requires the willing complicity of voters. Whereas intimidated voters are the victims of unilateral coercion, and disfranchised voters are the unwilling objects of discriminatory intervention, vote sellers often engage in voluntary exchange.[2]

These differences are likely to be consequential. If so, the comparative study of discrete manipulative strategies such as vote buying should allow us to investigate, both empirically and theoretically, the ways in which each strategy transgresses the norms of democracy, its comparative advantages and disadvantages, its root causes, and what might be done to limit it. Too often we lump various kinds of democratic transgression together, and end up with fuzzy but encompassing categories like "illiberal" or "deficient" democracy. When this happens, differences that matter become obscured. The broad vision captures the forest, but not the trees.

The study of "diminished subtypes" of democracy (Collier and Levitsky 1997) might thus be enriched by disaggregated comparative studies of, say, unfair media access, informal disfranchisement, voter coercion, wholesale vote rigging, as well as vote buying. Seeing how various strategies of transgression work internally, and how they fit into a menu of mobilizational or manipulative options, should give us a better grasp of the precise ways in which the actual operation of democratic institutions fall short of our normative expectations. This book is a first step in such an effort.

The Impact of Vote Buying

Both as a strategy of mobilization and as a strategy of manipulation, vote buying has a range of consequences for politics and society. As a strategy of mobilization, vote buying (and other forms of clientelism) makes legislative politics less policy oriented, and increases the dependence of legislators on the executive (see Chapter 7).

Vote buying, as a mobilization strategy, can also be quite effective at getting people to the polls, even when they do not vote as instructed (Schaffer 2006). The high turnout of people who accept material rewards can be explained by a combination of factors. For sure, some people may feel compelled to vote for the candidate who pays them. But not all payment-accepting voters go to the polls simply to uphold their end of a vote buying contract. For instance, 45 percent of people given money in the Taiwanese township studied by Chin-Shou Wang and Charles Kurzman in Chapter 5 cast their ballots for candidates other than the one on whose behalf they were paid. For these voters, going to the polls may have provided cover. If they had stayed home, vote buyers would have known for sure that they had not voted for the designated candidate. By going to the polls, the recipients, at a minimum, kept vote buyers guessing, since vote secrecy is by and large respected in Taiwan. Face-to-face invitations probably mattered as well (as they did in the "get out the vote" field experiments conducted by Alan Gerber and Donald Green in the United States).[3] In Taiwan, as in many parts of the world, offers of money are made personally by village or neighborhood vote brokers. Material offers, in other words, are not simply monetary incentives; their individualized disbursement also constitutes a form of personal, face-to-face canvassing. From the perspective of mobilization, then, vote buying might be seen as an effective tool to get out the vote, and thus benign in its impact on democracy.

Nevertheless, we must recognize that vote buying is, at the same time, a strategy of manipulation that damages democracy in a variety of ways. Most obviously, vote trading violates the democratic norm of equality, since it allows well-endowed candidates to buy off shares of democratic influence from less-endowed voters, as Susan Stokes argues in Chapter 6 of this volume. It also subverts the meaning of elections as instruments of collective decisionmaking, since it tends to replace deliberation over public issues with narrow calculations of individual interest. Vote buying thus debilitates the egalitarian spirit of democracy and empties democratic elections of their policy content. We may deplore these violations of normative principles on their own. Few of us wish to see democratic politics fueled by private money, rather than public interests and ideas. But vote trading does more than violate broad democratic principles. It damages the quality of democracy in more specific ways:

• *Illegitimate outcomes:* Insofar as vote buying represents a strategy of electoral manipulation, it delegitimates electoral outcomes. If bought votes are fraudulent votes, bought electoral victories are fraudulent victories. With respect to vote buying, as with respect to most other strategies of electoral manipulation, it is difficult to gauge its effect on final vote tallies. Yet if electoral losers have "good reason" to believe that they owe their defeat to vote buying, they may refuse to consider the victory of their opponents legitimate. During the 2000 presidential campaign in Mexico, opposition candidates feared that massive vote buying by the ruling Institutional Revolutionary Party (PRI) could determine the outcome of the election. A close PRI victory, conservative candidate Vincente Fox declared, would be illegitimate, and left-wing candidate Cuauhtémoc Cárdenas even called for a postponement of the election and civic insurgency in case of a result attributable to vote buying (Schedler 2000, 14).

• *Bad selection:* The purchase of votes can lead to the selection of bad leaders. Politicians who get elected on the basis of purchased votes may not be the politicians best qualified to run a democratic government. A political class that owes its positions to the weight of money looks different from a political class that owes its position to policy competence. Constitutional reform in Thailand was animated by the belief that vote buying is a major source of political cronyism and incompetence. Similarly, a motivating idea of the anti–vote buying reform movement in the Philippines is that vote buying recycles corrupt or depraved politicians. In one extreme case, a congressman spent lavishly and won reelection even after having been convicted and jailed for child rape.

• *Wrong incentives:* If politicians get elected on the basis of short-term contracts—money for votes—they have little reason to care about the formulation of policies, the construction of programmatic parties, and practices of accountability. In the best cases, vote buying establishes a continuous obligation to provide clientelist services to constituencies. In the worst cases, it cuts the nexus of representation between voters and politicians. Once votes are paid for, politicians may feel free of any debt to their voters. In this case, purchased delegation is unconstrained delegation.

• *Skewed representation:* In many parts of the world, the poor are more likely to have their votes bought than those who are more wealthy. Being poor in Argentina dramatically increases one's chances of being a target of vote buying (see Chapter 6). In the Philippines, survey research indicates that many more poor voters than middle- or upper-class voters were offered money in the 2001 elections (see Chapter 10). Residents of the poor Brazilian state of Piauí are far more likely to have money offered to them in exchange for their votes than are people who live in the rich federal district of Brasília (see Chapter 7). This pattern of distribution is troubling, for it means that vote buying is particularly harmful to the quality of representation enjoyed by those who are already the most powerless.

• *Criminalization of politics:* The need to fund vote buying may provide perverse incentives for criminality and the criminalization of politics. In Argentina, rogue members of the police force raised money for the Peronist political machine through kidnapping-for-ransom (Rohter 2003). In Taiwan and the Philippines, vote buying candidates are often backed financially by drug syndicates, gambling lords, and strong-arm godfathers who are happy to provide funds in exchange for protection and influence (Chao 1997; Patiño 1998; Romero and Crisostomo 2003). The same was true in Thailand before the military took control of the government in 2006 (Ockey 2000). Vote buying can thus contribute to higher levels of lawlessness outside the political arena, and expand the influence of criminals within the political arena.

Of course, vote buying takes different forms in different places, and is more intense in some places than others. The degree to which democracy is afflicted by these ills, and the particular kinds of damage inflicted, thus vary. Vote buying, it should also be noted, has consequences that extend beyond the political realm. As Jean-Marie Baland and James Robinson demonstrate in Chapter 8, certain kinds of vote buying affect the economy by driving up land prices and concentrating landownership—developments that of course may have long-term political implications as well.

Book Overview

The chapters of this book are organized around four main questions. The introduction (Chapters 1 and 2) discusses concepts: What is the significance and nature of vote buying? Part 1 studies causes and logistics: When and how do politicians buy votes? Part 2 traces consequences: How does vote buying shape political and economic outcomes? Part 3 evaluates remedies: Is it possible to control vote buying through institutional reforms or civic education?

However important these questions, vote buying is difficult to study, because it is an illegal practice that is hard to observe directly or measure reliably. Still, different methods of empirical research can shed light on discrete aspects of vote buying. Participant observation, where possible, permits the direct inspection of how vote buyers operate. Qualitative interviews with politicians and citizens reveal the normative claims and empirical beliefs in which practices of vote buying are embedded. The study of election districts and geographical voting patterns allows us to draw inferences on spatial correlates of vote buying. Mass surveys provide rough estimates of how widespread money or goods are distributed. The spirit of this book is methodological pluralism. The authors bring diverse sets of tools to the study of vote buying that illuminate different facets of the practice.

Chapter 2, by myself and Andreas Schedler, asks whether vote buying is really a simple economic exchange, as our everyday language would suggest. By comparing the purchase of votes to purchases made in "normal" commercial markets embedded in networks of legal safeguards, Schedler and I find that vote buying is dogged by problems of compliance that most other commercial exchanges escape. Where vote secrecy prevails, as it does in many contemporary settings, little stops voters from taking the money, and voting as they wish. In response, vote buyers adopt a host of extramarket normative and coercive strategies to make sure voters uphold their end of the bargain. Depending on the set of strategies chosen, the act of vote buying can thus take on a host of appearances—from gift giving to threat making to signaling virtue—which helps explain why ethnographers have found that vote buying carries such a range of meaning in different cultural contexts. Schedler and I conclude that, in order to assess empirical claims as well as normative judgments about vote buying, we need to be aware of the gap between our idealized, commercial model of vote buying and the way it actually works in the world.

Part 1 discusses the contexts and calculations that motivate parties and candidates to buy votes. In Chapter 3, Fabrice Lehoucq offers an analytic synthesis of the literature on the historical origins of vote buying. The purchase of votes, he argues, is a demanding enterprise. Markets for votes tend to emerge only under two restrictive conditions. First, vote buying must appear as a cost-effective strategy, in particular when compared to blunter strategies of electoral manipulation, such as voter coercion and electoral fraud. Second, Lehoucq argues, politicians tend to engage in vote buying most heavily when they can ensure voter compliance. The purchase of votes seems to constitute a first-preference strategy of electoral mobilization only if voting takes place in public, or if politicians find effective ways to circumvent the secrecy of the franchise.

The subsequent chapters of Part 1 focus, more narrowly, on the institutional incentives and organizational demands that may encourage or inhibit vote buying. Chief among institutional incentives, according to Allen Hicken in Chapter 4, are candidate-centered electoral rules. His argument proceeds in two steps. First, he discusses the implications of candidate-centered electoral systems. Undermining party identities and programmatic appeals, such systems force politicians to cultivate a "personal vote." Second, Hicken examines the logic of personalistic electoral strategies. To build personal networks of support, candidates may rely on a broad menu of strategies, including the exploitation of personal fame, the threat of violence, and the distribution of pork. Buying votes becomes comparatively advantageous only when certain cultural, socioeconomic, and institutional conditions prevail, such as poverty, traditions of gift giving, and easy access to government largesse.

In Chapter 5, on the organizational challenges of vote buying, Chin-Shou Wang and Charles Kurzman report findings from the direct observation of, and interviews with, local Kuomintang (Nationalist Party) campaign workers in Taiwan. The unparalleled access gained by Wang provides a rare glimpse into the inner workings of a vote buying operation at a level of detail never before seen. As the authors explain, candidates who bet on the massive purchase of votes have to engage in a demanding exercise of organization building. Setting up multilayered networks of intermediaries—the human infrastructure of vote buying—involves complex organizational challenges. Politicians must seek insurance against the embezzlement of funds by brokers and voters, while at the same time guarding against the risk of detection and prosecution. To accomplish these goals, they rely on classic organizational devices, like surveillance, regulation, and the design of incentive schemes. Yet more than anything else, they strive to reduce leakage and risk by carefully choosing their intermediaries. To resolve their multiple, multilayered problems of enforcement, they recruit agents who possess intimate knowledge of local constituencies (local knowledge), who are embedded in these communities (social capital), and who enjoy a reputation for loyalty and integrity (personal trust). As a consequence, forging each link in the formidable organizational chain of vote buying involves a massive "mobilization of social relations." From these observations, the authors deduce several organizational requirements that any effective vote buying operation must meet: substantial funding, networks of trust, judicial protection, managers with in-depth local knowledge, and a system to avoid the duplication of efforts.

Part 2 explores the political and economic consequences of vote buying. In Chapter 6, Susan Stokes systematically examines how vote buying distorts democratic policymaking. Parties and candidates, she postulates, may choose to persuade poor voters by either offering selective incentives (vote buying) or public goods and policy programs (programmatic mobilization). Their relative cost effectiveness, and thus the mix of campaign strategies that parties implement, depends on a variety of factors, like the organizational requirements of vote buying, the communication costs of programmatic mobilization, constituency and population size, and the relative secrecy of the vote. Still, under conditions of socioeconomic inequality, all else being equal, parties and candidates are more likely to offer selective incentives to poor voters, and public goods to more affluent ones. "The more unequal the distribution of income, the more prevalent the vote buying," says Stokes. Everybody's vote is still counted and weighted equally, but the votes bought from the poor are empty vessels. They are void of any information about their sellers' policy preferences and demands for public goods. Vote buying thus violates the democratic principle of "equal consideration of interests" in policymaking. As a consequence, "because of their material poverty, a subset of the citizenry is deprived of effective participation in collective decisions." They fall out of the circle of democratic accountability.

It is important, too, to examine empirically the effects of vote buying on the actual operation of democratic institutions. Toward this end, Scott Desposato, in Chapter 7, examines the impact of vote buying on legislative politics. He contrasts two types of electoral markets. In vote buying markets, voters demand private goods; in programmatic markets, they demand public ones. The two types of electoral markets place contrasting demands on parties, politicians, and legislatures. In private-goods markets, politicians face the primary challenge of delivery: they have to distribute tangible material benefits to their constituencies. In public-goods markets, politicians face the primary challenge of credit claiming: they have to convince their constituencies that they have made reasonable efforts to translate their policy programs into reality. These divergent political challenges bear deep implications for legislative politics. As the author documents with evidence from a paired comparison of legislative behavior in two Brazilian federal states, private-goods markets weaken legislative parties as well as legislative accountability, while public-goods markets strengthen legislative parties as well as legislative accountability.

In Chapter 8, Jean-Marie Baland and James Robinson examine the impact of vote buying on the economy. In developing their analysis, they introduce the concept of "indirect" vote buying, which takes place when politicians purchase (indirectly) the votes of employees by purchasing (directly) the votes of their employers. Indirect vote buying works on the assumption that employers control the electoral behavior of their employees. According to the model developed by Baland and Robinson, employers are able to extract "electoral taxes" (votes) from their subordinates by granting them higher wages and benefits than they would have received otherwise. The authors argue, furthermore, that the "political profits from selling workers' votes" provide employers with incentives to hire more workers than they actually need. This increased demand for labor in agrarian economies drives up the demand for land, resulting in higher land prices and more concentrated landownership. Baland and Robinson support their argument through an empirical analysis of electoral reform in mid-twentieth-century Chile. By introducing the secret ballot, the Chilean 1958 reform led to the abrupt end of vote trading. As the authors show, together with a plummeting conservative vote, the number of dependent agricultural laborers fell, as did land prices and land concentration. Vote buying, as the authors document, bore real economic consequences, distorting labor markets, land prices, and the allocation of resources. Baland and Robinson conclude their chapter by presenting a simple formal model that supports the argument that vote buying, in addition to distorting the economy, distorts public policy making. As the authors infer, echoing Susan Stokes's line of reasoning, politicians tend to discount the utilities of those whose votes are sold.

Part 3 assesses possible remedies for the ills of vote buying. Broadly speaking, these remedies come in two kinds. "Supply-side" remedies seek to dissuade candidates from adopting vote buying as an electoral strategy, usually by altering the institutional incentives to engage in it. "Demand-side" remedies, in contrast, seek to modify the behavior of voters, and typically take the form of civic education. In Chapter 9, Allen Hicken inquires into the effectiveness of supply-side institutional reforms. His catalog of institutional strategies that may reduce the incidence of vote buying includes electoral rules that strengthen political parties and programmatic campaigning, larger constituencies, and the effective enforcement of legal prohibitions (by augmenting the probability of detection and punishment as well as the severity of sanctions). To assess the effectiveness of such institutional strategies, the author studies one of the most comprehensive and purposeful attempts at controlling vote buying through institutional engineering: the 1997 constitutional reform in Thailand. The new constitution was designed "chiefly to combat vote buying and reduce money politics." Still, as Hicken argues, its results were mixed at best. The constitution left the underlying socioeconomic structures untouched; not entirely consistent, it contained some provisions that actually encouraged vote buying; and last but not least, politicians displayed an "impressive flexibility . . . adapting their vote buying to the new institutional environment." Institutional redesign is important, it seems, but it cannot single-handedly carry the whole weight of anti–vote buying campaigns.

In Chapter 10, on the effectiveness of demand-side reforms that aim to alter the attitudinal foundations of vote buying, I cite scattered empirical evidence pointing to the ineffectiveness of civic education campaigns. This conclusion is confirmed by in-depth interviews that I conducted with poor voters in the Philippines, where (unlike in many other countries) civic education is the main vehicle of reform. I find that public campaigns in the Philippines are counterproductive, since they are based on misguided assumptions about the subjective meaning of vote buying to poor voters. The middle- and upper-class activists who typically design voter education campaigns tend to conceive vote buying as a simple commercial transaction in which corrupt politicians exploit voters' poverty. Poor citizens themselves are often offended by this assumption. They reject the market model and its (at least implicit) portrayal of voters as easy objects of manipulation who, destitute and amoral, are happy to commodify their political rights for a fistful of pesos. Many poor voters tend to read material offers not as purchase offers, I argue, but as signs of respect and care. They see politicians who distribute material benefits not as corrupt salesmen, but as respectful allies. The disjuncture of worldviews and assumptions between the designers and the objects of voter education programs seems to reflect a larger, and deeper, class gap. When middle- and upper-class reformers—in the Philippines and beyond—try to "clean up" politics by teaching moral lessons to lower-class voters who are struggling for dignity and recognition, they end up reinforcing the very mentalities that sustain this class divide.

Finally, Part 4 presents a brief conclusion to the volume. In Chapter 11, I review some of the main lessons learned, and find that vote buying is not as effective as one might suspect given the heavy financial and organizational investments that candidates and parties are willing to make. This inefficiency helps explain why vote buying tends to appear only when "hard" or "wholesale" strategies of manipulation no longer suffice or become unfeasible, or when the use of less costly strategies of "issue" mobilization is made difficult by particular social conditions or institutional configurations. Even if it is an electoral strategy of limited utility, vote buying (where widespread) can shape politics and society in profound and mostly deleterious ways. Still, however harmful vote buying is, efforts to thwart it through institutional redesign have had only mixed results, while efforts to prevent it through education have met with little success. Perhaps most heartening to me is the fact that at least one country—Taiwan—has been able to combat it effectively by vigorously prosecuting lawbreakers.

Vote buying is still very much a black box of comparative politics. We have little systematic knowledge, and even less comparative knowledge, about its presence across time and space, its forms and meanings, its causes and consequences. This volume is not, of course, an attempt to answer all questions about vote buying. But it lays out key questions and presents original theoretical and empirical research that sheds light on crucial aspects of this sometimes ordinary, sometimes alarming trade.

Notes

I would like to thank Andreas Schedler for his substantial contribution to the writing of this chapter.

1. Interview at the Department of Prosecutorial Affairs, Ministry of Justice, August 12, 2003.

2. The modifier "often" is necessary because sometimes the distinction between intimidation and buying becomes blurred. After all, at times vote buying can also be coercive, when for instance the prospective voter is told to "accept this money, or else!"

3. In one experiment, Alan Gerber and Donald Green (2000) conveyed nonpartisan "get out the vote" messages to some 30,000 randomly selected registered voters in New Haven, Connecticut, through personal canvassing, direct mail, and telephone calls. Their findings: door-to-door canvassing increased voter turnout by almost 10 percentage points, direct mail by less than 1 percentage point, and telephone calls had no effect on turnout at all.

2

What Is Vote Buying?

Frederic Charles Schaffer
& Andreas Schedler

Vote buying, in its literal sense, is a simple economic exchange. Candidates "buy" and citizens "sell" votes, as they buy and sell apples, shoes, or television sets. The act of vote buying by this view is a contract, or perhaps an auction, in which voters sell their votes to the highest bidder. This market model finds expression in our everyday language, as in the English *vote buying,* the Spanish *compra de votos,* the French *achat de voix,* or the German *Stimmenkauf.* It figures prominently in scholarly treatments of the phenomenon as well.[1]

Yet the simple market model of vote buying needs to be tempered. Parties and candidates who offer particularistic material benefits to voters may generally aspire to purchase political support at the ballot box in accordance with the idea of market exchange. Their commercial aspirations, however, may run into objective as well as intersubjective barriers. On the objective side, seller compliance is uncertain, as vote buying is an illicit business and as such does not take place within a "normal" market protected by social and legal norms. On the intersubjective side, empirical accounts of participant perspectives reveal that those electoral practices we describe as "vote buying" may carry different meanings in different cultural contexts.

Vote Buying as Market Exchange

In principle, the core notion of trading (buying and selling) seems unproblematic. It refers to a commercial transaction, the exchange of goods and services for money (or other forms of payment)—a routine operation that competent inhabitants of the modern capitalist world understand without difficulty. The commodity that changes hands in acts of vote trading carries a well-defined institutional meaning too. Votes are formalized expressions of

17

preference by individual members of decisionmaking bodies. Broadly speaking, vote trading propositions may target either electoral choices or electoral participation. They may be intended to persuade individuals to vote in certain ways, or to vote or not vote in the first place. Strategies to alter turnout may focus on demobilizing active opponents or on mobilizing passive supporters. As the former is often described as "negative" vote buying or "abstention buying," we may think of the latter as "participation buying."

Although instances of "vote buying" have been identified in contexts as dissimilar as national legislatures (such as the Brazilian) and the UN Security Council, this chapter (in line with the intent of this book) deals only with popular elections to public office. Overall, then, if we embrace a literal understanding of the term as anchored in the world of economic exchange, we may define the purchase of votes in the electoral arena as a market transaction in which parties, candidates, or intermediaries pay (in cash or kind) for "electoral services" delivered by individual citizens—a favorable vote or a favorable abstention.

The logic of trade demands that (1) the actors involved (buyers and sellers) engage in effective exchanges of money for goods or services. In the absence of mutual exchange, if buyers don't pay or sellers don't deliver, we do not speak of acts of trade but of instances of fraud or robbery. The logic of commercial transactions further demands that (2) buyers and sellers understand what they are doing: that they enter a reciprocal relationship of exchange. Trade involves a quid pro quo, objectively as well as intersubjectively.[2]

Buying something means acquiring some valued, scarce good or service the buyer would not get otherwise. It makes little sense (to the practical linguistic knowledge of average customers in modern market economies) to say someone "buys" something if that person pays for products or services she or he would get anyway (without the expense of money). Depending on the context, we may think of such an unsolicited payment as a donation, reward, mistake, or offense, but hardly as a purchase. In an analogous way, if candidates distribute material benefits to individual voters, they must get something in return for their electoral investment. Otherwise we would not recognize their campaign spending as part of a trade relationship. If voters accept the money, but vote as they had planned to do anyway, they do not take part in an act of exchange. They are not selling their votes, but earning unilateral gains.

In addition, if buyers and sellers in a monetary economy buy and sell goods and services, they are assumed to understand the nature of the transaction in which they are taking part. They are assumed to understand the social meaning of trade, to know, for example, that buying a thing is different from stealing it or receiving it as a gift. If participants lack such a common understanding, they will have difficulties completing their transaction without friction. Analogously, if politicians hand out cash or goods to voters, their offer represents the opening act of an exchange relationship only if both sides understand it as such. If either one fails to conceive it as an offer whose acceptance commits the recipient to an either explicit or implicit quid pro quo, it is not a commercial transaction we observe but "something else," like the exchange of gifts or a simple misunderstanding (in case givers and receivers adopt incongruent interpretations).

In sum, a literal understanding of vote buying as a market exchange imposes restrictive conditions on the use of the term. If we talk about vote buying and *mean* vote buying—in its narrow sense grounded in the world of commercial transactions—we put forward two related empirical claims, be it explicitly or tacitly. First, we claim that both sides actually trade something valuable—electoral services that would have been unavailable to the buyer in the absence of payment. Only if politicians buy something with their money, rather than squandering it without consequences, do we witness instances of commercial exchange (the objective side of vote buying). Second, be it explicitly or tacitly, we also claim that both politicians and citizens read their relationship as a relation of exchange (the intersubjective side of vote buying).

Both aspects are problematic, however. On the objective side, voters may fail to deliver their votes at election time. On the intersubjective side, voters may fail to read the overtures made to them as commercial offers.

Uncertain Compliance

Prospective vote buyers typically have no guarantees that voters who accept their material offers shall dutifully reciprocate on election day. This uncertainty is due to the fact that vote buying, even when akin to a commercial transaction, takes place in a nonlicensed "black" market of illicit exchange, rather than in a "normal" consumer market embedded in a network of legal safeguards. Securing the compliance of voters thus tends to be problematic for four reasons that are inherent to most vote trading arrangements, but absent in most consumer market transactions:

• *Problematic enforcement:* The enforcement of "contractual" vote trading obligations is inherently problematic. Vote buying typically creates the commitment problems that come along with the deferred delivery of goods and services. As vote buyers and sellers do not engage in instant exchanges of merchandise and money, the former face the challenging task of making the latter honor their future obligations, and they have to accomplish it without recourse to legal action. While licit consumer markets are institutionalized spheres of exchange created and protected by the law, markets for votes are neither regulated nor sanctioned by formal rules. If voters just grab the money, vote their conscience, and run, parties and candidates have no legal sanctions at their disposal to punish them.

• *Problematic monitoring:* From the perspective of buyers, the business of vote trading involves problems of surveillance as deep and troubling as the problems of enforcement. Most consumer markets are transparent insofar as contract compliance is relatively easy to verify. One needs only to determine whether a trading partner has delivered goods and services of the specified amount and quality. Markets for votes, in contrast, are opaque. Under the veil of secret voting, voter behavior is shielded from direct inspection. Vote buyers may have great difficulty knowing whether presumptive vote sellers actually honor their commitments on election day.

• *Countervailing norms:* Consumer markets, for the most part, are morally legitimate spheres of action that license the free exchange of commodities. In many contemporary settings, however, votes do not belong to the universe of legitimate commodities. The explicit purchase of votes runs counter to prevalent norms of democratic liberty and equality. Consequently, the social conventions and other "noncontractual" bases of contractual relations described by Emile Durkheim (1984 [1893]) that are so important to deterring opportunism and cheating in consumer markets, are often weak or absent when it comes to vote trading.

• *Countervailing laws:* Consumer markets are legal markets. Vote buying, even when consonant with local norms, is still illegal. Where laws against vote buying are enforced, and especially where hefty rewards are given to citizens who reveal the identities of vote buyers to police, givers need to worry that buyers will not only defect, but turn them in.

In short, what may look like a simple economic exchange is never quite so simple, since vote buyers cannot rely on social norms of fair exchange and the threat of legal sanctions that typically sustain licit market transactions. To be successful, vote buyers have to resolve intricate problems of monitoring and enforcement, and they may have to surmount, too, the obstacle of countervailing democratic norms as well as the risk of prosecution. Given the systematic uncertainties of compliance they face, they may be reluctant to bet their financial and political fortunes on the fragile resource of personal trust. If they wish to ensure the effective delivery of the electoral services they demand, they must turn to a range of supplementary strategies that effectively transform the incentive and information structures of vote trading. They must transform vote buying from an uncertain investment contaminated by high risks of voter defection into a profitable business that offers reasonable chances of contract compliance. Four common strategies designed to bolster voter compliance are personalized normative inducements, informal sanctions, electoral surveillance, and contingency payments.

Personalized Normative Inducements

To compensate for the weakness of generalized norms of fair economic exchange, vote buyers may invoke personalized social norms to make recipients honor their contracts in the voting booth. More specifically, they may seek to activate norms of personal obligation, and reinforce the weight of those obligations through the personal delivery of rewards.

Personal obligation. Clientelist exchanges of material rewards against political support are generally fed by expectations of reciprocity. When clientelism takes the form of patronage,[3] patrons help their clients, grant them favors, and give them presents, and expect to be paid back later with the currency of political support. The ongoing dispensation of help, favors, and gifts creates moral debts.[4] In the more ephemeral and election-centered exchanges that distinguish vote trading, buyers may also strive to create moral obligations of reciprocity to be honored at the polling booth. They may accomplish this by casting the (election-time) distribution of material rewards not as contractual payments but as gifts or favors freely and generously bestowed. Locales where episodic, election-related gift giving or favor rendering is common include Benin, Taiwan, Japan, northern Portugal, and the slums of Metro Manila.[5]

Moral debts can be created in more oblique manners as well. Vote seekers may try, for instance, to create social obligations of reciprocity by paying the recipient wages for rendering some nominal service for the candidate (poll watching, distributing ballots, hanging posters, delivering messages, playing music), the goal of which is to generate gratitude toward the candidate or cognitive dissonance were the recipient to vote for another candidate. As one Filipino observer noted:

> Once a candidate has sworn in a registered voter as a partisan poll watcher, he or she can expect that the latter will vote for him or her. Our Filipino trait of *utang na loob* [debt of gratitude] is evident on [*sic*] this case. Once a person has granted us something, a favor, we would do everything to pay that favor back to him or her, sometimes even at the expense of ourselves. We tend to view persons who did us some good things as benefactors, and we view ourselves as beneficiaries who can please them by doing the same for them. (Bava 1998)

This practice, sometimes called "indirect" vote buying (as it rests upon payoffs that are not directly and explicitly tied to reciprocity in the polling booth), was also known in nineteenth-century England and early-twentieth-century France, and is common today in the Philippines and in the squatter settlements of Quito in Ecuador (Seymour 1915, 181; Knaub 1970, 33; Burgwal 1995, 116).

Personal delivery of rewards. Parties and candidates may try to reinforce norms of reciprocal obligation by managing the purchase of votes
through established social networks and personal relations, rather than
organizing anonymous, impersonal exchanges as they take place in large
consumer markets. By personalizing the trade relationship, they may instill
in recipients a sense of personal obligation whose motivational force sur-
passes the seductive pull of material rewards as well as the faint calling of
generic social norms. Accordingly, candidates often recruit intermediaries
who are respected members of their communities, or others to whom recipients feel bonds of personal accountability. In Taiwan, vote brokers typically
approach only relatives, friends, and neighbors (see Chapter 5). A similar
tactic was commonly employed in Thailand prior to the 2006 coup. In the
1992 election, for instance, campaign workers for one candidate sought in
each village "to recruit the person best placed to deliver support, generally
someone with significant social status in the village. Other qualifications
include being respectable, well-known, a local leader (either official or unof-
ficial), the candidate's relative or close friend, or some other characteristics
that would make people honour their vote promises" (Callahan 2000, 25).

Informal Sanctions

To make up for the unavailability of legal sanctions, parties, candidates, and
their agents may seek to impose informal sanctions on voters who refuse
material offers, or who do not vote as instructed. Wayward voters expose
themselves, among other things, to the risk of ostracism. In the Philippines,
as one vote seller explained, "refusing an offer like that might be construed
to be an act in defiance of the candidate's goodwill. It would also identify
you as a voter against the candidate. You would also be seen as going
against the flow." Or as another Filipino vote seller put it more pithily, "it's
about keeping good relations" (Schaffer 2002a). Defiant voters also become
vulnerable to more concrete forms of retribution. Vote brokers in both Peru
and Mexico, for instance, made it clear to voters in past elections that
behaving incorrectly would cause them to lose their access to social programs (Pfeiffer 2004, 77).

Electoral Surveillance

The imposition of informal sanctions is dependent on the prior ability to
discern instances of noncompliance. Surveillance and punishment, to use
the vocabulary introduced by Michel Foucault (1979) in his history of modern prison systems, are mutually constitutive core elements of the exercise
of power. Surveillance provides the epistemic conditions to dispense punishment. Sanctions rest upon knowledge about misbehavior. Thus, to gener-

ate or reinforce compliance, givers often strive to monitor electoral behavior by lifting (discreetly) the veil of electoral secrecy. In doing so, they may target either individuals or communities.

Givers may monitor how *individuals* vote as either a condition for postvoting payment, or as a prelude to postvoting retribution if the recipient does not do as instructed. Sometimes election officials can be counted on to observe how voters fill out their ballots, as they commonly did in early-twentieth-century Adams County in Ohio (Gist 1961, 63). Even when direct observation is not possible, there are a number of ways to monitor how individual ballots are cast. Where voters write in names on the ballot, they might be given carbon paper to record how they voted, as in the Philippines. Or they might be instructed to fold the ballot in a distinctive way, or to put a pinhole in one corner of the ballot, as happens in Corsica.[6] Another way is to give a voter a fake or stolen filled-in ballot before he or she enters the polling station. The voter casts the filled-in ballot, and gives the blank official ballot he or she received in the polling station to another voter waiting outside, who then fills out the official ballot to the buyer's satisfaction, goes into the polling place, and repeats the process. The practice, called "the caterpillar" in Russia, and "the shuttle" *(lanzadera)* in the Philippines, was also common in nineteenth-century Australia and United States, where it was known as the "Tasmanian dodge" (Borisova 2000; Schaffer 2002b). In a more modern twist, vote buyers in Italy send voters into the polling booth with cell-phone videocameras, which the voters use to send back images of the properly filled out ballot (*BBC News* 2003). In locales where there are dense social networks, as in some urban areas of Argentina, it is also often possible for givers to make "reliable inferences" about those who accepted their offers without openly violating the secret vote (Brusco, Nazareno, and Stokes 2004, 84).

A further strategy to ease problems of monitoring is to pay voters for abstaining from voting altogether, thereby preventing them from casting ballots for one's opponent. *Turnout* is much easier to watch than voting. "Negative" vote buying proliferated in late-nineteenth-century Maryland and rural New York (Argersinger 1987, 234; Cox and Kousser 1981). It has also been used in Guyana, where agents campaigning for the ruling party in the 1997 election bought voter identification cards belonging to the opposition's supporters. In western Australia, poor indigenous voters are lured away from the polls by free-flowing liquor (Orr 2003, 134). In the Philippines, party workers hire buses to take voters on out-of-town excursions on election day, or pay registered voters to disqualify themselves from voting by dipping their index fingers in indelible ink, as voters are required to do after casting their ballots (Schaffer 2002b). Similar practices have been reported in Mexico and Venezuela (Cornelius 2004, 53; Kornblith 2002).

Givers can also monitor the *aggregate* election results for villages or neighborhoods. This strategy is especially relevant in places where candidates and their agents distribute material incentives widely within entire villages or neighborhoods, as happened in parts of England after the introduction of the secret ballot in 1872, and in Taiwan in the late 1980s, among other places (Seymour 1915, 438; Rigger 1994, 13). Collective monitoring is made easier when votes are counted at the precinct level, as in India, Senegal, and Thailand prior to the 1997 reforms (Schaffer 2002b, 78–79; Schaffer 1998, 136; Callahan 2002, 7).[7]

Contingency Payments

In the purchase of votes, instrumental motives alone are rarely sufficient. Even if recipients change their electoral behavior in exchange for tangible benefits, economic rewards are almost always accompanied and reinforced by noneconomic inducements. However, vote buyers may indeed achieve something close to purely instrumental compliance when they overcome the problem of deferred delivery. They may do so by postponing payment and dispensing it conditionally upon the right candidate winning. Rather than offering advance payments and suffering the tortuous uncertainties of deferred delivery, vote buyers may thus offer contingency payments that make the provision of rewards to individual voters dependent on aggregate election results.[8]

In early-twentieth-century France, givers sometimes distributed half a banknote prior to the election, and provided the other half only if their candidate won (Knaub 1970, 33). The same strategy has been carried out in other places with pairs of shoes. In a more sophisticated variant, Kuomintang (National Party) officials in the 2000 Taiwan election used a gambling scheme to provide monetary incentives for voters to turn out in favor of the party's presidential candidate. As one journalist explained:

> Organizers for the ruling National Party and local gangsters are offering heavily loaded odds to lure votes to Lien Chan, the party's candidate. Although opinion polls indicate that support is evenly divided in the three-way race, they are promising to pay the equivalent of Pounds 10 for every Pounds 1 bet on a win for Mr. Lien. The odds being offered for the other two candidates are just 80 pence for every Pounds 1 bet. (*Times of London* 2000)

A similar tactic was used in Thailand, where operatives sold election lottery tickets (Callahan and McCargo 1996, 387).

*   *   *

To improve the odds of voter compliance, then, buyers may pursue a host of supplementary strategies. They may strive to compensate for the lack of formal sanctions by mobilizing personalized norms and informal sanctions; they may try to solve their information deficits by breaking into the secrecy of the vote; or they may aim to overcome the risks of deferred delivery by making their payments contingent on electoral outcomes. Yet the structural uncertainties of vote trading are not limited to its objective side (the presumption of effective exchange), but also extend to its intersubjective side (the presumption of shared meaning).

Multiple Meanings

As an illicit activity, vote buying is largely hidden from public inspection. Most of the steps it involves are not readily observable. Often, it is only the opening tender we can actually see. The rest remains shut off from observation by outsiders—be it electoral authorities, competing parties, fellow citizens, the press, or academic writers. If voter compliance is uncertain to the extent that it is withdrawn from the public eye, the same is true for the social meaning voters attach to the material offers they receive. Indeed, money interpreted by external observers as constituting a binding payment may be understood by voters themselves in manifold ways. They may view it, for instance, as a nonbinding gift, a show of virtue, a veiled threat, or a sign of corruption, to name just a few possibilities. This potential disjuncture between what is observed and what is experienced makes it important to explore the range of meanings an offer may hold for recipients. A catalog of such meanings would have to include the following:

• *An advance payment:* Citizens who place themselves within the parameters of the classical market model may perceive material offers as advance payments for electoral services. Such payments are part of a commercial relationship. If voters accept the material offer, they know they are expected to deliver their part of the deal at the polling station. As one voter in rural Mexico expressed the straightforward logic of commercial exchange: "Here, if you give someone a chicken, he will vote for the chicken" (Schedler 2004, 84).

• *A wage:* Citizens may understand material campaign offers not as initiating an exchange relationship but as concluding one. In such circumstances, payments usually come in the form of wages earned for performing nominal concrete services during the campaign or on election day, such as poster hanging or poll watching.

• *A gift:* Gifts (as well as small favors) are unilateral transfers that do not create an explicit obligation to reciprocate at the ballot box. For example, Shelley Rigger (1994, 219) explains how Taiwanese vote brokers bear "gifts" when they visit people's homes to make pitches for their candidates.

Interpreting material offers as advance payment, wage, and gift places such offers within the realm of mutual exchange. But offers can also carry a range of more symbolic or implicit meanings to recipients, including the following:

- *A reparation:* An offer might be understood as amends for wrongs suffered in the past. In Benin, for instance, offers are seen by many voters as opportunities to get back money that politicians have stolen (Banégas 1998, 78–79). Villagers in the Philippines see offers as "practically their only opportunity to get anything from people in government" (Kerkvliet 1991, 231). Accepting an offer, in other words, is a way for poor Filipinos to stake a rightful claim to the resources of those higher up. It is a momentary opportunity for the ordinary citizen to transform unequal, sometimes coercive relationships into something more equal and just. It is an arrangement that allows the voter not only to gain materially, but also to achieve a measure of dignity (Ibana 1996, 130–131).

- *An affront:* An offer may cause offense. To accept the offer would damage one's self-respect. Many poor voters in rural Mexico "perceive the sale of political rights as an attack on personal dignity" (Schedler 2004, 88). Some poor urban Filipinos similarly see accepting payment as "surrendering one's right to vote" or "selling one's principles" (Schaffer 2002a).

- *A threat:* Some offers cannot be refused safely. Declining them generates fear of retaliation from candidates or operatives. In Metro Manila, for instance, money offered as a gesture of goodwill comes with implicit pressure to accept it, lest the recipient be branded as someone defiant (Schaffer 2002a). What is presented like a generous gesture carries the mark of extortion.

- *A sign of virtue:* Not all payments are part of a quid pro quo. Citizens may understand material offers less in instrumental than in expressive terms. The practical utility of goods and services is less important than their *informational value.* Citizens may take them as pieces of information that reveal the positive personal qualities of the giver, such as generosity, politeness, responsiveness, and respect. In Taiwan, for instance, "gift-giving demonstrates respect for the recipient; to give someone a gift is to give that person face" (Rigger 1994, 219). The dispensation of gifts may thus lead citizens to believe that the candidate is good or worthy (see Chapter 10).

- *A sign of vice:* If voters, by contrast, dislike the gesture of giving out cash and goodies, they may take electoral largesse as a sign not of virtue but of personal defect on the part of the giver, such as arrogance and disrespect. The offer (which may or may not have been accepted) may send a signal to voters that the candidate is morally wrong, politically dumb, and the like. For example, in rural Mexico, citizens described efforts to buy their votes as deceptive, manipulative, and exploitative (Schedler 2004, 81, 85).

• *A sign of strength:* An offer can signal that the candidate is confident of winning. The public display of wealth creates expectations of electoral success. In Nigeria, "citizens who wish to support a winner will view the payment as evidence that the candidate is very powerful or has the support of powerful forces" (van de Walle 2002, 16). Such information is of great value to voters insofar as backing a loser might result in a loss of access to state resources. The effect is circular, as in many games of expectation: candidates win because voters expect them to win.

To individual voters, then, receiving and responding to an offer may hold a variety of social meanings. They may understand their interaction with the respective party, candidate, or intermediary in manifold ways. Participants may view themselves as engaging in a simple economic exchange, in accordance with the market model, or they may situate themselves outside the logic of commercial exchange and conceive themselves as (among other things) securing amends, receiving a gift, recognizing power, or acknowledging goodwill. Thus in accepting or rejecting offers, or in changing or not changing their electoral behavior, citizens may be moved by a variety of motives. They may act out of material self-interest, or they may act instead out of fear, duty, gratitude, indignation, and the like.[9]

Some of these intersubjective meanings likely develop in response to the objective uncertainties involved in vote buying. To bolster compliance outside the framework of a normal market, as we have seen, vote buyers adopt a range of enforcement strategies that may generate, be it intentionally or counterintentionally, the particular meanings citizens attach to vote buying. For instance, the need for personalized normative strategies (to compensate for weak norms of fair exchange) can transform payments into gifts, while the need for informal sanctions (to make up for the absence of legal sanctions) can turn them into extortionary threats.

Whatever their origins, we may expect such intersubjective differences in the meaning of material rewards to be consequential for the objective success of vote trading. All things being equal, we might conjecture, for instance, that a voter who views an offer as an expression of caring or benevolence will be more prone to vote for the designated candidate than a voter who views the same offer as amends for previous wrongs, or a voter who sees it as an attack on her or his dignity. In addition, differences in social meaning are likely to have implications for the relationship between citizens and their representatives. In general, we may expect vote trading to diminish the programmatic accountability of parties and politicians. Still, different conceptions of vote buying may lead voters to embrace somewhat different conceptions of political accountability. Attitudes toward elected officeholders are likely to diverge, for instance, between citizens who literally sell their votes for a drink and those who reward what they perceive to be the personal benevolence of a candidate. In the former case, accountability may extend no further than the demand for the intermittent electoral payoff. In the latter case, the politician may be subject to ongoing demands for help. In the slums of Buenos Aires, where material offers often take the form of favor doing, residents see politicians as an essential part of their everyday "problem-solving network." Before as well as after elections, local politicians face a daily stream of requests for food, medicine, clothing, emergency home repairs, and more (Auyero 1999). In short, how voters understand the offers they receive at election time may have far-reaching implications for their political expectations and behavior between elections.

Conclusion

The distributive activities we conventionally describe as "vote buying"—vote seekers handing out fistfuls of cash to individual citizens—at first blush look like simple market transactions. Voters, it seems, driven by a simple calculus of economic gain, sell their electoral services to the highest bidder. Yet what seems to be a straightforward commodification of voting rights is often anything but. Vote trading, understood literally, is a demanding business whose objective and intersubjective requirements are difficult to meet. On the objective side, the purchase of votes demands that citizens effectively change their voting behavior in response to and in accordance with the particularistic material offers they receive. Unless voters accept and reciprocate the offers they receive, the commercial transaction remains truncated. On the intersubjective side, vote trading demands that both business partners comprehend their interaction as a commercial relationship. While it presupposes that recipients vote in accordance with the electoral preferences of givers, it demands furthermore that they understand their electoral choice as a payment delivered in exchange for money or other personal benefits they have received (or have been promised to receive) from a party, a candidate, or their intermediaries. More often than not, the empirical realities of "vote buying" diverge from one of these two core assumptions of the market model.

To vote buyers, the lack of formal sanctions, the opacity of the voting act, the weight of countervailing norms, and the illegal nature of vote buying render the enforcement of voter compliance a much trickier endeavor than it would be under "normal" market conditions. The remedial strategies that vote buyers may devise—invoking social norms of reciprocity, violating the secret vote, monitoring turnout, devising informal sanctions, or introducing contingency payments—tend to ameliorate the problem of voter defection, although they almost invariably fall short of *guaranteeing* the compliance of voters.

To vote sellers, the exchange of money for votes can carry a host of meanings, many of which extend beyond the realm of market trade. We know little about the empirical distribution of popular attitudes toward vote buying in the new democracies of the developing world. Yet it may well be the case that the simple idea of selling off hard-won suffrage rights to the highest bidder is alien to most citizens targeted by aspiring vote buyers. In terms of intersubjective understandings, the marketization of votes may well be a rare and rather exceptional phenomenon.

The further away politicians and voters move from a simple commercial transaction, a "normal" act of trade, the less plausible (and the less exact) it is to describe their relationship on the basis of the market model, and to speak of the "purchase" of votes, "vote buying," a "market" for votes, and the like. The market transaction may provide an idealized model of what transpires between giver and recipient, and a convenient set of categories to use. Yet it too easily causes us to overlook what we cannot readily observe: the degree of compliance on behalf of voters as well as the range of meanings they attach to the offers they receive.

This is not to argue that the market model has no analytic utility. On the contrary, it allows us to identify the specific ways in which concrete vote buying practices really do approximate straightforward market transactions, and to identify the range of consequences that should ensue as a result. Among other benefits, the model enables us to apply various tools of economic theory, as some of the authors do, carefully and fruitfully, in this volume.

Still, to assess empirical claims as well as normative judgments about vote buying, we need to be aware of the gap that so often appears between the entailments of the market model and the way vote buying really works, and is judged, around the world. To answer key questions about the causes and consequences of vote buying, we need to gather more systematic factual knowledge about the manifold strategies of electoral mobilization and manipulation which political and academic observers are often too quick to describe as "vote buying." In particular, if we wish to know whether the instances of vote buying we observe are straightforward commercial transactions or something else, we need to dig beneath the surface of facile appearances. We need richer and deeper understandings of their institutional and cultural contexts. We need, that is, to generate robust empirical accounts of both their objective and intersubjective foundations.

Notes

1. Among others, see Cox and Thies 2000; Orr 2003; Brusco, Nazareno, and Stokes 2004; Cornelius 2004; and Pfeiffer 2004.

2. Here we sidestep the issue of whether vote buying has to be an individual transaction or whether it can also be "collective." Both are consistent with a market model. I can buy something from you, or my association can buy something from you. For the sake of simplicity, we limit our attention to individual transactions (as all other chapters in this volume do, except Chapter 8). This allows us to bracket the whole range of principal-agent problems that arise when political entrepreneurs step into the market for votes by negotiating "package deals" with parties and candidates that commit the votes of their followers.

3. On the distinction between patronage and vote buying, and how both fall within the category of clientelism, see Chapter 1.

4. On the "unequal reciprocity" involved in clientelist exchanges, see Scott 1972b, 93–94; Eisenstadt and Roniger 1984, 250–263; Putnam 1993, 172; Mainwaring 1999, 178.

5. See Banégas 1998; Bosco 1994, 39–41; Rigger 1994, 219; Cox and Thies 2000, 39; Silva 1994, 39. See also Chapter 10.

6. Interview conducted by Frederic Schaffer with the president of the Tribunal Administratif de Bastia, January 1999.

7. Note that monitoring individual votes is but one strategy available to candidates and their operatives to increase the likelihood that voters will cast their ballots in the desired way. Some scholars argue that effective vote buying requires an ability to observe how individual recipients vote (Rusk 1974, 1041–1042; Gerber 1994, 136; Heckelman 1995). This assessment is in need of serious qualification. Even where an individual is able to vote secretly, givers may still have a smorgasbord of options available to them, depending on the cultural, social, and institutional circumstances they find themselves in. Only under certain circumstances will the disruption of individual vote monitoring lead to the abandonment of vote buying.

8. For some brief observations on contingency payments in the legal profession and the insurance business, within a larger conceptual discussion of political contingency, see Schedler forthcoming.

9. Naturally, there can be significant diversity in how members who live or work in a community view the same actions of a giver. We see significant variation, not only across different locales, but also within a single community (Auyero 1999, 305–306; Schaffer 2002a).

Part 1

When and How Do Politicians Buy Votes?

3

When Does a Market for Votes Emerge?

Fabrice Lehoucq

> There are not in the enormous majority of country towns any working men
> who have much opinion about politics or sufficient self-respect to abstain
> from selling their vote.
>
> —Walter Bagehot, *The English Constitution,* 1867

> Many people sold their vote
> For to buy an overcoat
> Or to buy a sack of flour,
> Thinking it a prosperous hour.
>
> —*Literary Digest,* 1911

When do parties buy votes? We do not have very good answers to this question. Like other topics in the understudied field of electoral fraud (Lehoucq
2003), only a handful of papers exist on vote buying. While vote buying in a
former Soviet or even in a Latin American republic does not surprise us,
purchasing votes in the United States or England does—even though both
have been among the most electorally corrupt places in modern times. US
president Lyndon Johnson's rise to power is replete with references of how
he and other politicians won office in Texas during the 1940s and 1950s
with the right connections, government contracts, and, of course, enough
bought votes (Caro 1990). And it was in 1999 that Democrats and
Republicans literally auctioned for absentee ballots in Dodge County,
Georgia, and no less than in the county courthouse (Hasen 2000, 1328).
Aside from these and numerous other anecdotes, however, little is known
about the politics of trading money for votes.

Buying a vote is trading something of value—usually, but not only,
cash—for someone's choice on election day (see Chapters 1 and 2). As several studies point out, vote buying is remarkably similar to vote trading.
"I'll vote for a school in your district, if you vote for latrines in mine," is a
common enough refrain in legislatures, one that is often sealed in omnibus

bills so that congressional majorities back them. Buying a vote also sounds a lot like the sort of conditional promises that politicians make: "I'll cut your taxes if you vote for me." What a US legal scholar calls "wholesale" vote buying (Karlan 1994) is perfectly legal and helps to underwrite accountability—the glue that makes for legitimate democratic politics. On reflection, both logrolling and wholesale vote buying sound illicit because they involve trades and thereby inject the supposedly noble human activity of politics with an air of baseness.

I follow precedent and define vote buying narrowly. What distinguishes vote buying from other vote trades is that sellers of votes receive private benefits. Logrolling does not involve trading support for a measure for a bribe that only benefits a particular legislator. Vote buying, however, is raw. It involves trading a vote for cash. This is why vote buying is also referred to as electoral corruption; like other forms of corruption, it involves trading a public good—the right to vote—for a fee. This is why corruption is objectionable to so many. Indeed, our common and reviled image of vote buying—that of the local potentate buying votes from the poor to ensure that elected officials do not threaten his or her authority—stems from the belief that such exchanges lead to governments that serve the interests of the few precisely because they have taken advantage of the poor.

In this chapter, I review research on more than half a dozen countries over the past 150 years to identify two conditions that lead to the emergence of a market for votes. Most of the articles and books I examine do not permit rigorously testing more fine-grained theories of vote buying, because, with a handful of exceptions, these works do not quantitatively measure the variables of theoretical interest. Nonetheless, the patterns I find in Europe (England, Germany, Ireland, and Spain), the Americas (Costa Rica, Mexico, and the United States), and Asia (Taiwan and Thailand) all point in the same direction. My reading of this literature suggests that, first, parties will consider buying votes if they can solve the principal-agent problem of trading money for votes. Though all investments in electoral campaigns can fail to elicit support, buying votes is an inherently risky proposition because of "slippage"—the possibility that voters will take the money and run. Public ballots turn out to be a key way that patrons or parties solve their principal-agent problem. Second, my reading of this research indicates that parties will only bid for voters if there are no other cost-efficient ways of influencing voters or rigging election results.

The Political Economy of Vote Buying

In nineteenth-century England—a place where electoral corruption was commonplace, as the opening quotation from Bagehot's *The English*

Constitution (1867) reveals—vote buying involved the outright purchase of votes. In the borough of Stafford, for example, parties spent more than 5,000 pounds on 850 voters in 1832, virtually every registered voter in this constituency of 1,000 voters—an extremely expensive case, even for nineteenth-century England. In many boroughs, the price of a vote was low for the first voters (often those with surnames starting at the beginning of the alphabet) and increased if the election remained close during voting day. If a candidate clearly became a front-runner, however, the price of votes fell as buyers stopped purchasing votes. In many boroughs, parties showered money on favored charities—like public hospitals—to obtain electoral support. In others, they provided "head-money" to voters, monetary donations to citizens who had just voted in lieu of the election dinners that were so common in other boroughs. In still other boroughs, "the simplest means of indirect bribery was the hiring of electors to serve on sinecure committees and the payment of extravagant wages to voters for services which entailed but little time and effort" (Seymour 1915, 181).

The political geography of voting in nineteenth-century England shows that electoral corruption emerges only when parties can monitor the behavior of voters. According to Charles Seymour's classic study of electoral reform, it was "*in the larger boroughs* where there was something like an independent electorate, that independence was regarded merely as an opportunity for selling the vote to the highest bidder." It was not in the counties—the rural constituencies—where the market for votes flourished. "The use of money was not general before 1832 since it was unnecessary; the power of the patron was so complete that *the few votes cast* could be secured without bribery (1915, 166, emphasis added)." After passage of the first reform act, in 1832, and the concomitant expansion of suffrage rights, the electorate increased by 49 percent between 1831 and 1833, 43 percent of whom resided in the boroughs (1915, 533). Furthermore, both in rural counties and urbanizing boroughs, the 1832 act redistributed voters among these districts and eliminated some of the worst "rotten boroughs"—the constituencies that comprised only a handful of voters. The chief result of equalization was to fuel bribery on election day. "Where [the patrons] had before commanded," Seymour wrote, "now they must buy. A numerous electorate, composed often of persons whose circumstances laid them open to temptation," led to a political system where "the corrupt were thus increased to hundreds and thousands" (1915, 170).

Nineteenth-century politics in Ireland also saw a market for votes develop in urban areas—places where parties could observe the behavior of "their" candidates and where no cost-efficient alternatives existed for stuffing the ballot box. In his comprehensive study, K. Theodore Hoppen noted that vote buying was widespread in the boroughs, but uncommon in the counties. "Whether the towns of Ireland were ever the bright centers of radical consciousness, they were certainly the home of the outstretched hand, the bulging pocket, and the floating voter adrift on seas of whiskey, beer and stout." Over half of the petitions that parties sent parliament between 1832 and 1883 denounced vote buying in boroughs even though less than a third of the electorate resided in these urban constituencies. A market for votes never really emerged in the counties, "not for reasons of superior morality," but because "the coercive power of landlords short-circuited the electric attractions of cash" (1984, 74–75). Even after the establishment of the secret ballot in 1872, coercion, influence, and corruption only declined gradually, because many constituencies remained small and, Hoppen averred, because the pressures of community and the inertia of tradition kept voters before the gaze of their superiors and peers.

That boroughs—and not rural counties—were the places that spawned vote buying seemingly contradicts the claim that district size characteristics—including the absolute size of the electorate as well as its relative size (e.g., vote-to-seat ratios)—and bribery are inversely related (see Chapters 4 and 6, which draw on Cox 1987, 57). My finding suggests that, as a general proposition, there is no linear relationship between district size characteristics and vote buying because other things are not equal (a point also made in Chapters 4 and 6). While monitoring a smaller number of voters is easier, all else being equal, the relationship between district size characteristics and vote buying hinges on whether the ballot is public or secret, on the electoral formula (e.g., majoritarian or proportional), and on whether government officials aggressively prosecute vote buyers and sellers. Even large districts can experience vote buying if they consist of a large number of precincts that are each populated by communities with dense social networks. And if seats are allocated to the plurality winner, then solving the vote buying principal-agent problem in a handful of districts in a close race may be sufficient to throw national-level election results. Only when the absolute and relative number of voters in each district became substantially large (more than a couple thousand)—and after the secret ballot came into effect (1872) and government officials began to enforce antibribery legislation—did the linear relationship between district size characteristics and vote buying emerge in England. In 1831, before the first reform act (1832), there were an average of 1,307 electors per district, most of which were two-member constituencies (a number that conceals a high level of malapportionment). In 1886, after the third reform act (1884–1885), there were an average of 8,082 voters per district, the overwhelming number of which became single-member constituencies.[1] The key variable of interest, therefore, is how parties can reduce uncertainty about the behavior of voters; solving the principal-agent problem requires discovering how a panoply of institutional, partisan, and sociological factors interact to create a market for votes.

Electoral historians of Spain also find that a market for votes only emerged when parties could monitor the behavior of voters and when they could not resort to intimidating citizens, manipulating the electoral registry, or manipulating the tally of the vote. According to Carlos Dardé (1996), Javier Tusell (1991), José Varela-Ortega (2001a, 2001b), there were two Spains until well into the 1930s. The first Spain was rural. Depending on the region, the central government, local *caciques* (chieftains), or some combination of both controlled these constituencies. Before election day, they cooked the electoral rolls so that only citizens beholden to the government could vote publicly for candidates the government selected for single-member, plurality districts—known as the *encasillados* (pigeonholed candidates). If these tactics failed, the government and the *caciques* relied on public employees, economic dependence, or the fraudulent tally of the votes to ensure the complacency of the countryside. Even after the establishment in 1890 of suffrage rights for all men aged twenty-five and older, and of secret ballots, most rural districts returned uncontested candidates to the Cortes (parliament) in Madrid, because parties continued to supply voters with ballots. In the second, largely urban Spain, all manner of fraudulent practices took place, because the electorate was not easily controlled. Manipulation of the public payroll and eviction of opposition voters and poll watchers from precincts also flourished as tactics in Madrid. And it was here that a market for votes emerged, even if Spanish historians debate how decisive purchased votes were for final electoral outcomes (Tusell 1969, 93–124).

In imperial Germany, a market for votes did not emerge, because landlords and capitalists, very much like their rural English and Irish counterparts, could use cost-efficient alternatives to win elections. Between 1867 and 1912, when all men aged twenty-five and older possessed suffrage rights, Germans did not complain about bribery (or, for that matter, physical force or the falsification of results on election day). Most election "scrutinies"—the complaints that parties filed with the Reichstag—condemned the Catholic hierarchy, landlords, and factory owners for using "influence" on voters. This influence ranged from priests cajoling parishioners to vote for Catholic parties, to landlords threatening to evict retainers. In industrial areas, capitalists threatened to fire employees if they did not vote for probusiness candidates (Anderson 2000; Fairbairn 1997). Charges and countercharges of electoral misconduct revolved around procedural violations of electoral laws, since the Reichstag considered employer pressure to be a private matter until 1912—eleven years after an electoral reform replaced party-supplied ballots with the Australian ballot, that is, the use of a single, government-supplied ballot containing the names of registered candidates and parties.

Qualitative research on nineteenth-century US politics also concludes that the abundance of information about electoral preferences did lead to vote buying, among other things. Despite the existence of a secret ballot, there was no Australian ballot until late in the century. Because parties supplied voters with ballots, and could undertake legally recognized poll watching, they were able to ascertain voting behavior. Based on his study of appeals that losers filed with the US House of Representatives between 1850 and 1870, Richard Bensel (2004) shows that parties did reward voters with whiskey, meals, and even lodging in exchange for their votes and help on election day. Parties also found other ways to win elections. According to Bensel's study, the most common allegations of fraud involved intimidation and use of violence against undecided or opposition voters. Voting was a boisterous and often violent affair in the United States in the nineteenth century, because so much information about the preferences of voters was available and because crowds typically gathered in the buildings that housed polling stations. In urban areas, citizens cast party-supplied ballots in precincts that their party and ethnic group controlled; voting in the wrong place, Bensel points out, could lead to a confrontation with the rival gangs whom local parties deployed around their polling stations. In rural communities that had only one polling station, peer pressure could replace blunter forms of intimidation to ensure results.

Even though most US states adopted the Australian ballot by the 1910s, thus effectively guaranteeing the privacy rights of voters, parties circumvented the balloting law well into the twentieth century to keep tabs on voters. For example, the relative smallness of late-nineteenth-century Adams County, Ohio, made it possible for vote buyers to ensure that farmers would vote in agreed-upon ways (Gist 1961). For voters whose allegiances were fickle or unknown—"floaters"—party chairmen would request that they mark their ballots in specified ways in order to ascertain, during the tally of the vote at the end of the day, whether such ballots existed. Another way to monitor voters consisted of enlisting polling station officials "to sort of shake open" the ballot boxes to see if particular voters had voted in accordance with their "contracts." Finally, poll watchers would look over citizens' shoulders as they marked their ballots. For both partisan diehards and floaters, the 1910 price of a vote oscillated between a drink of whisky and US$25, with the average price being US$8 per vote (Gist 1961, 62–63). In his much acclaimed biography of President Lyndon Johnson, Robert Caro (1990) showed how Johnson, like many other Texan politicians, purchased votes from Mexican American farm workers and had local sheriffs spy on voters to ensure that they complied with their end of the bargain.

Instead of paying voters to go to the polls, parties can also solve their principal-agent problems by bribing rival voters to stay at home on election day (see Chapter 2). In a study begging to be replicated elsewhere, Gary Cox and J. Morgan Kousser (1981) combed more than forty-eight New York newspapers over the ten election periods between 1879 and 1908 for reports of vote buying. After comparing 108 reports before and 173 reports after the establishment of the secret franchise in 1890, they concluded that the dramatic increase after 1890 was unlikely to have occurred randomly. Buying off the opposition (paying voters US$10–$25 to stay at home), whose members party canvassers identified in the weeks before election day, worked in a world of stable communities—places where party activists knew every citizen and therefore could reasonably predict the inclinations of voters.

Social networks can be so dense, in fact, that parties can buy votes even when voters expect their choices to be private. In both contemporary Taiwan and Thailand, markets for votes emerged by the 1980s because parties found ways to penetrate the veil of secrecy that is essential for modern politics. First, increasingly competitive elections encouraged parties to use a variety of techniques to win legislative office. Second, candidates circumvented the secret ballot by working with local brokers, who, in the context of small and tightly knit rural communities, could reasonably predict the behavior of voters (Callahan 2000, 17–44; Callahan and McCargo 1996; Chapter 5, this volume). Moreover, that each voter in pre-1997 Thailand had a number of votes equal to the number of seats in his constituency created a "surplus" of votes that encouraged rural Thais to sell their additional votes to the highest bidder. Interestingly, in both cases, traditional norms of filial piety and gift giving cemented the bonds of reciprocity, which both candidates and rural voters find beneficial. In both cases, a well-organized political machine of brokers must use abundant amounts of cash to ply enough voters to sell their votes. As Allen Hicken argues in Chapter 9, the dismantling of the multiple voter system in Thailand in 1997 did not eliminate the market for votes, in part because rural social networks still facilitated vote trades between candidates and citizens.

Cost-efficiency explains why electoral corruption does not proliferate, even when the public ballot allows parties to keep tabs on voters. Systematic research on Costa Rica reveals that, when citizens in this country could vote publicly (before 1925), only a small number of accusations of electoral misconduct involved vote buying. Between 1901 and 1923, only 0.01 percent of fraud accusations (or 10 out of 584 individual complaints) that parties filed with Congress—the body that is constitutionally authorized to evaluate such claims—referred to vote buying (Lehoucq and Molina 2002, 49–50, 97–98), even though observers at the time claimed that electoral corruption was commonplace (Munro 1918, 153).

Two reasons explain why parties in Costa Rica's public-voting electoral system did not bribe voters. First, parties could use a host of techniques to pad voting totals in their favor when voting occurred in public, all of which did not require going to the expense of bribing voters. Approximately 50 percent of the accusations against polling stations (58.6 of all the charges) that Congress received between 1901 and 1923 consisted of allegations that parties violated formal requirements governing the opening and operation of polling stations. During the heyday of the public ballot (and when men aged twenty-one and older who met a vaguely stated and inconsequential property requirement could vote), parties tried to shape electoral outcomes either by denouncing procedural violations of electoral law or by committing such violations. Second, vote buying was expensive in Costa Rica, especially given the range of actions parties could take to change electoral results. Though data are hard to obtain, estimates from the early 1940s (when the secret and the Australian ballots were in effect) suggest that parties could buy voter identification cards, which in 1943 cost 2–20 colones, or the equivalent of two to five days of work on a coffee farm (Lehoucq and Molina 2002, 169). In 1942, buying 20,000 votes, about 14 percent of the electorate, cost 40,000–400,000 colones. Assuming that running a presidential campaign cost 2 million colones in the mid-1940s, a purchase of 20,000 votes potentially required 20 percent of a well-oiled candidate's funds (Lehoucq and Molina 2002, 159), not to mention the costs of monitoring the behavior of voters in an electorally competitive system. This finding is consistent with Chin-Shou Wang and Charles Kurzman's finding in Chapter 5 that the expected utility of vote buying is not high: it requires a "significant budget" and does not guarantee that citizens who accept bribes will uphold their end of the bargain.

Time series data on Costa Rica provide a natural experiment to gauge the effects of cost-efficient ways of rigging elections while curtailing the ability of parties to monitor the behavior of voters. In the mid-1920s, the Costa Rican Congress dismantled the public ballot. Between 1925 and 1927, Congress approved the president's request to establish a secret Australian ballot, because he made his support for more and better guarantees of transparent elections contingent on enactment of a truly secret franchise. Despite these institutional changes, allegations of vote buying increased to 13.7 percent of all complaints filed with Congress between 1925 and 1938 (from less than 1.0 percent in the previous two and a half decades), though such allegations completely disappeared in subsequent decades.

It was uncertainty that drove parties to experiment with vote buying in Costa Rica. Testimonies from the period reveal that the reforms of the mid-1920s really did put voters beyond the gaze of poll watchers (Lehoucq and Molina 2002, 158–159). In a context of competitive elections and during the presidencies of several men who did not take sides in electoral combat, parties were left with little option but to stuff the ballot box or to try to ply voters with money and favors. But charges of voter corruption disappeared by the 1940s because parties realized that it was too expensive to buy votes and that the secret Australian ballot made it impossible for them to determine whether voters had honored their end of a vote trade.

In Mexico, research on electoral fraud during the waning decades of the

Institutional Revolutionary Party (PRI) dictatorship also shows why the existence of both cost-efficient alternatives and the secret ballot undercut the development of a market for votes. According to Civic Alliance of Mexico, a nongovernmental organization, observers saw money or objects exchanged for votes in only 2.6 percent of polling stations in the 1994 federal elections, in a sample of 1,870 precincts, even though they reported that the secrecy of the vote was violated in 38.6 percent. Polling station officials, electoral observers, and *caciques* pressured voters in 25.0 percent of the voting precincts (Calderón-Alzati and Cazés 1996; Cazés et al. 1996, 179–181). Wayne Cornelius (2002; see also Aparicio 2002), using a postelection survey of a panel of Mexicans, found that 26.1 percent of respondents received gifts from parties or candidates in the 2000 elections. His statistical models also showed that PRI operatives were much less successful than either of the main opposition parties in procuring votes using preelection rewards—exchanges more accurately classified as gifts than bribes.

The findings on Mexico should not be surprising. Even when electoral competition began to intensify in the 1980s, a market for votes did not develop because the first condition—that of solving principal-agent problems—was no longer present. Even though secret and Australian ballots have existed in Mexico since 1911, voters could still ask someone to help them vote, either if they were illiterate or if they wanted to vote for a candidate not listed on the ballot (the latter provision was on the books between 1943 and 1989). Voting with a "friend" (and no doubt a PRI member) was one of the ways Mexico's hegemonic party kept control over a society who did not become more than three-fourths literate until 1970 (INEGHI 1994, 118). And even if literate Mexicans had been ostensibly voting in secret since the second decade of the twentieth century, the PRI's control of the vote tally (Molinar 1991) and of Congress—where, in line with classical constitutional theory, legislators certified elections (Lehoucq 2002)—ensured that it did not have to go to the expense of bribing individual voters in order to win elections. By the second half of the 1990s, with the construction of an independent electoral commission to organize, hold, and certify elections (Becerra, Salazar, and Woldenberg 2000; Eisenstadt 2003), however, a genuinely secret franchise and impartial vote counts empowered citizens to take the PRI's money and run.

In England, though impartial vote counts preceded the reforms that robbed parties of their ability to monitor the behavior of voters, much the same story can be told about the more gradual decline of the market for votes. With the establishment of the secret ballot in 1872, partisan canvassing—the partisan mobilization and monitoring of voters—rapidly fell in importance, as the privatization of voting severely limited the amount of information available on election day about citizen preferences. Two other, previously enacted reforms also helped to reduce electoral corruption: the transferal of the power to rule on petitions for electoral nullification from the House of Commons to the courts in 1868, and the campaign finance reform that began with an anticorruption act in 1854 and continued until the end of the century. Subject to stricter reporting requirements and facing an impartial judiciary, parties had an increasingly harder time spending money to purchase votes, a set of transactions that the secret ballot had made impossible to monitor. As a result, the infamous market for votes in England was dead by the turn of the century (O'Leary 1962).

Vote buying therefore disappears from politics because parties can no longer solve an important principal-agent problem. Once parties cannot figure out whether vote trades are being honored, they gravitate to other ways of fixing electoral returns, as political developments in Costa Rica and Mexico demonstrate. Yet cost-efficient ways of rigging election returns proved to have relatively short lifespans in these two cases, because electoral reforms ended up depriving parties of the ability to manipulate election results. In England, the sequencing was reversed, but the outcome was identical: the establishment of a genuinely secret ballot and the elimination of other ways of rigging election results gradually put an end to vote buying and electoral fraud.

Conclusion

Parties, politicians, and political machines use a large array of tactics to win public office. Many of these—including making speeches, distributing leaflets, and promising to build infrastructure—remain perfectly legal. Buying votes, however, though practiced, is an unacceptable way of winning an election.

I find that two conditions must exist for vote buying to proliferate. First, parties must be able to monitor the behavior of their agents. Electoral laws that place poll watchers in the voting precinct and that allow parties to supply voters with ballots are among the tools that allow parties to solve the principal-agent problems inherent in vote buying. Alternatively, to the extent that the secret ballot is not enforced or circumvented, party representatives acquire the knowledge necessary to ensure that bargains are kept. The market for votes will decline, however, as the secrecy of the ballot becomes complete.

Parties can use other tactics to ensure the allegiance of voters, even if they can solve their principal-agent problems. Parties, landlords, and capitalists can threaten to punish voters who refuse to vote in specified ways. Tightly knit communities—typically found in rural and "traditional" areas—can provide the webs of social relations that permit insiders to detect and punish defectors. Failure to vote in accordance with machine preferences can lead to the denial of access to community resources like irrigated water, forests, and other valued goods. To the extent that parties can activate these tactics, they will prefer not to buy votes. The second condition, therefore, for the emergence of a market for votes seems to be cost-efficiency: parties buy votes as the efficacy of other ways of influencing voters and rigging election results declines.

Figure 3.1 groups these cases accordingly. Along the vertical axis, I place cases according to whether parties solved their principal-agent problems. The public ballot is the single most important way that parties can determine voter behavior. However, parties can partially solve this problem even when the secret ballot exists. Tightly knit, stable, and small communities in which everyone knows one another can generate good information about voter preferences.

Along the horizontal axis in Figure 3.1, I place cases according to whether there are other cost-efficient ways of rigging election results. Situations in which this condition is met include monopolization of candidate registration rules, manipulation of the registry to exclude opposition voters, intimidation of voters, and, most important, control over the certification of electoral results. When the ability of parties to monitor the behavior of voters is low and they cannot easily fabricate votes, they will end up competing for votes in an open electoral market.

The findings of this chapter raise three implications for the study of vote buying. First, the conditions for the development of a market for votes are not commonplace. Account after account suggests that a market for votes does not emerge when voters are under the thumbs of landlords, capitalists, or *caciques.* Under the public ballot, coercion and kinship ties generate block-voting behavior in favor of candidates controlled by the local elite. Single-party dominance will also deprive citizens of their suffrage rights, either because the secret ballot is violated (as it apparently was in

Figure 3.1   When Does a Market for Votes Emerge?

High	*Vote Buying*
	English boroughs, pre-1872
	Irish boroughs, pre-1872
	Rural New York, 1879–1990
	Spanish (urban) multimember
	    districts, 1868–1930s
	Rural Ohio, circa 1900
	Rural Taiwan, 1980s–1990s
	Rural Thailand, 1980s–1990s
		Coercion and Deference
		English counties, pre-1872
		Germany, 1867–1912
		Irish counties, pre-1872
		Spanish (rural) single-member
		    districts, 1868–1930s

Ability of Parties to Solve Principal-Agent Problems		
	Competitive Elections Costa Rica, post-1950s England, post-1890s Mexico, post-1990s	*Election Rigging* Mexico, pre-1990s Costa Rica, 1927–1948
Low		

Low ◄——— Availability of Other Cost-Efficient ———► High
Ways of Rigging Election Results

much of rural Mexico for much of the twentieth century) or because any-thing but support for a candidate is a pointless exercise in political dissent. While the powerful might buy a round of drinks for their retainers on elec-tion day, it is fairly clear that economic dependence allows the powerful to use more cost-efficient ways of stuffing the ballot box. The market for votes requires that voters be independent enough to sell their votes, a political sit-uation in which coercion of citizens is not viable, and a legal and social sit-uation that generates significant information about the actual choices made by voters on election day.

Second, vote buying is more complex than the conventional condemna-tions suggest. Cases from nineteenth-century England to contemporary Thailand show that voters can benefit from the existence of a market for votes. That they cannot be coerced into voting for a particular candidate empowers them to extract compensation from their social and political superiors for the seemingly eternal privileges of class. Money, dinner, and a drink of whiskey at a local potentate's expense are in many imperfectly democratic places still part of the electoral repertoire. Indeed, as the proba-bility of defeating the powerful declines, it makes sense for each voter to exact a payment from one or more parties for his vote. The collective out-come of such behavior helps to explain why perfectly rational voters sup-port candidates, parties, and political systems that legislate rents to narrow social interests.

Finally, this chapter provides some insight into why bans on buying and selling votes are much more widespread than bans on campaign contribu-tions. Parties, I suggest, agree to make the market for votes illegal because they find it too expensive to bribe voters, especially if legal reforms make it increasingly difficult to confirm whether sellers follow through on their end of the bargain. What tipped the balance in favor of reform in England, for example, was the growing expense of electioneering. Even with the promul-gation of the secret ballot in 1872, the average reported cost of a vote in the 1880 general elections in districts where parties impugned results was more than £3 (and more than £2 in remaining districts). And in boroughs investi-gated by government commissions, 8–53 percent of voters were accused of having accepted a bribe (O'Leary 1962, 155–156). Three years later, in 1883, Whigs passed the Corrupt and Illegal Practices Act, which, among other things, put a severe limit on campaign expenditures. So, even when parties help create a market for votes, they face powerful incentives to coor-dinate their actions to ban the market for votes. This is why, I believe, there is much more legislation against vote buying than against campaign contri-butions; while a market for votes increases expenditures for parties, cam-paign contributions increase their revenues. And once parties collectively agree to respect the secrecy of the franchise, they gradually consolidate electoral competition that is free of fraud and of vote buying.

Notes

An earlier version of this chapter was presented at the conference "Trading Political Rights: The Comparative Politics of Vote Buying," Massachusetts Institute of Technology, August 26–28, 2002. I thank Frederic Schaffer and Andreas Schedler (conference chairs) for detailed comments, as well as other participants for their observations, on that earlier version.

    1. I use two sources to establish these calculations: Seymour 1915, 533, provides estimates of the size of the electorate before and after major reform acts. Caramani 2004, 53, provides the number of constituencies.

4

How Do Rules and Institutions Encourage Vote Buying?

Allen D. Hicken

As this volume demonstrates, vote buying is a complex phenomenon, in terms of both its causes and its consequences. Chapter 3 discusses a variety of conditions that lead to a market for votes, including the availability of cost-efficient alternatives to vote buying. In this chapter, I explore a few of the political and institutional factors that can make vote buying a more or less attractive strategy for parties and candidates vis-à-vis some of these alternatives. In doing so, I discuss only briefly various structural and cultural explanations of vote buying, such as level of economic development, cultural norms, and the prevalence of patron-client networks. Each of these certainly plays a part in shaping the mix of electoral strategies that parties and candidates choose to employ. However, in this chapter I focus on the ways in which various rules and institutions can affect the incentive and capacity to buy votes.[1] I do not discuss here the logistics of vote buying—how candidates and parties organize vote brokers, avoid detection, and minimize slippage. These issues are dealt with at length in Chapters 3 and 5.

Why focus on institutions if they are only part of a chain of variables that can motivate or discourage vote buying? First, certain institutions have independent, predictable, and discernible effects on vote buying incentives. While they are only one piece of the puzzle, they are an important piece. Second, although institutional reform is by no means easy, institutions such as electoral rules and campaign finance regulations are arguably more malleable than cultural norms or levels of development in the short to medium term. As a result, institutional reform is often an important part of anti–vote buying campaigns (see Chapter 9).

I consider here the factors that motivate candidates to adopt personal electoral strategies, including vote buying. These include candidate-centered electoral systems, access to government resources, and decentralized party nomination and funding procedures. Each candidate for elected office must select an electoral strategy (or mix of strategies) by determining when partisan appeals will be successful and when candidate-centered campaigns will be more effective.

Given strong incentives to adopt a personal campaign strategy, what sort of personal appeals do candidates choose to make? A variety of personal strategies are available to candidates, including relying on name and fame, voter intimidation, delivering (or promising) pork or patronage, or directly exchanging cash or goods for votes.[2] Again, a mix of socioeconomic, cultural, and institutional factors influences the combination of personal strategies that candidates employ. In short, I argue that incentives to cultivate a personal vote interact with other variables to affect the probability that a candidate will choose to pursue vote buying.[3] I do not contend that candidates and parties will never buy votes in the absence of such personal vote incentives; indeed, in the absence of those incentives they may still attempt to affect the outcome of an election via massive vote buying. Rather, I simply contend that vote buying is more likely (given certain conditions) where those incentives exist.

Political and Institutional Incentives for Pursuing Personal Strategies

There is no single root cause of vote buying. Socioeconomic factors such as income levels, education, and urbanization can shape the market for votes, as can societal patterns and norms (e.g., the pervasiveness of patron-client links). Vote buying is also located within a larger political order. For example, in Thailand and the Philippines, vote buying is fueled by the chronic neglect of poor and rural areas (see Chapter 9; see also Nelson 1998b; Sombat 1993, 1997; Anek 1997; Ammar n.d.). Likewise, the rules and institutions under which candidates must operate can also influence their incentives to purchase electoral support. Certain sets of institutions encourage candidates to focus their efforts on building personal networks of electoral support, with vote buying potentially playing a large role in those efforts.

Recently the literature on comparative parties and elections has begun to focus on the extent to which the electoral and party rules generate a party vote and party-centered campaigns versus a personal vote and candidate-centered campaigns (e.g., Katz 1986; Cain, Ferejohn, and Fiorina 1987; Ames 1995; Carey and Shugart 1995; Samuels 1999; Golden and Chang 2001; Hicken 2002; Golden 2003).[4] In some democratic systems, candidates for public office distinguish themselves from competitors on the basis of partisan differences.[5] In electoral contests, the party's label and reputation constitute the key currency for candidates. In other systems, personal reputation and candidate-focused appeals supplant partisan appeals as the medium of exchange.

Candidate-Centered Electoral Rules

Certain features of the electoral system strongly influence candidates' choice of strategy. At the most basic level, whether or not voters cast a vote for a party or party list or for an individual candidate affects candidate incentives. All else being equal, where electoral systems limit voters to a single choice among parties, as in closed-list proportional representation systems, candidates are more likely to rely on party-centered strategies. Conversely, where voters can cast votes for individual candidates or can cast multiple votes, the incentives to cultivate a personal vote tend to be stronger (Carey and Shugart 1995; Hicken 2002). However, the feature that has received the most attention in terms of personal vote and candidate-centered campaigning is intraparty competition (Shugart and Carey 1992; Katz 1986; Reed 1994; Lijphart 1994; Carey and Shugart 1995).

Intraparty competition occurs when members of the same party (copartisans) must campaign against each other within the same district. In many systems, a candidate's party affiliation is a useful tool for both candidates and voters (Downs 1957; Popkin 1991). Voters can rely on partisan affiliation to help determine where a candidate stands on issues of importance to the voters, while candidates can use the party label to distinguish themselves from competitors. In electoral systems with intraparty competition, however, the party label is not a tool voters or candidates can use to separate one candidate from another, since there are multiple candidates from the same party in the race. In other words, an appeal to party policies and principles may not be sufficient when a candidate is directly competing against a copartisan. Voters must be given a reason to select a particular candidate over candidates from other parties *and* over (or at least before) candidates from within the same party. Thus, candidates competing in an environment with intraparty competition face strong incentives to cultivate a personal vote.

Intraparty competition arises in a diverse set of electoral systems. All electoral systems that (1) give each voter "the option of casting one or more votes directly for candidates" (Samuels 1999, 490), (2) allow for more than one candidate from the same party to run in a given district, and (3) award seats to candidates on the basis of their individual vote totals, have the potential to produce intraparty competition (Samuels 1999, 490).[6] Probably the best-known examples of systems with intraparty competition are single nontransferable vote and open-list proportional representation. In the former, voters cast a single vote for a candidate in multiseat districts, and seats are awarded to candidates on the basis of the plurality rule. The single nontransferable vote system has been used in pre-1994 Japan, Taiwan, and post-1997 Thailand (for Senate elections) (Hicken and Kasuya 2003). In open-list proportional representation systems, voters have the option of casting a vote for a party list, or voting/indicating a preference for a specific candidate, or both. The number of seats a party receives reflects its vote share, but the distribution of preference votes among that party's candidates determines who will fill those seats. Open-list proportional representation systems have been used in Brazil, pre-1994 Italy, Poland, and Chile.

Besides these two well-studied electoral systems, other candidate-centered electoral systems can produce intraparty competition. These include single transferable vote systems (e.g., Ireland, Malta, Australian Senate),[7] block-vote systems (e.g., Thailand, Mauritius, Philippine Senate), and single-member district plurality systems, which use primary elections (e.g., the United States) or which allow multiple candidates from the same party to run in a district (e.g., the Philippines).

A variety of electoral systems present strong incentives to candidates to emphasize person over party. Given these incentives, how do candidates go about setting themselves apart from their copartisans? How do they cultivate a personal vote? One option is relying on name and fame to win the support of voters. Obviously, not all candidates can use this strategy, but it is often employed in candidate-centered electoral systems by the likes of entertainment and sports celebrities, well-known activists, or members of powerful families. Likewise, violence and voter intimidation can also be used to create personal support networks.

Another means of cultivating a personal vote is to emphasize policy or factional differences within the party (Cox and Thies 1998; Samuels 1999) (in fact, intraparty competition is often associated with the rise of institutionalized party factions).[8] This is a common strategy in US primary campaigns, in which candidates often go to great lengths to paint their copartisans as too far to the left or right to be trusted by the party's voters. In the 2004 Democratic presidential primary campaign, one candidate argued that he represented the Democratic (read: liberal) wing of the Democratic Party, while another countered that he represented the electable (read: moderate) wing of the party (*Newsweek Online* 2003). The temptation for candidates to play up intraparty policy and factional differences presents party leaders with a dilemma. Leaders recognize the need for party members to cultivate a personal vote, but "would prefer that candidates not fight publicly over policy because this might make it less clear what the party stands for, perhaps reducing the number of voters choosing the party in the first place" (Cox and Thies 1998, 272). In short, fighting between copartisans risks undermining party cohesion and diluting the value of the party label.

One way out of this dilemma is for party leaders to allow or encourage candidates to cultivate a personal support network by directing (or promising to direct) pork and other particularistic forms of government largesse to a candidate's constituents. This is a form of personal strategy common to virtually every democracy, but especially those with candidate-centered electoral systems. Particularistic benefits can come in several forms. These include public goods targeted to specific geographic constituencies,[9] constituency service (e.g., cutting red tape and other interventions with the bureaucracy), public sector jobs, and access to rents (via government contracts, licenses, etc.). Indeed, candidates typically use a mix of particularistic benefits to create and maintain personal networks of support (Ferejohn 1974; Cain, Ferejohn, and Fiorina 1987; Golden 2003).

Finally, candidates can cultivate a personal vote through vote buying. As this volume demonstrates, there are a wide variety of activities that can fall under the general category of vote buying. However, I wish to distinguish vote buying from pork or other forms of partcularism, in terms of the nature of the exchange. Vote buying involves the *individual, immediate,* and *private* exchange of goods, services, or cash for electoral support, usually in violation of legal norms (see Chapter 1 for more detail on this distinction).

In summary, candidate-centered electoral systems, particularly those with intraparty competition, generate strong incentives for candidates to eschew party-oriented campaign strategies in favor of cultivating a personal vote. The effects of these incentives are apparent in the electoral, party, and public policy arenas. Electorally, intraparty competition produces more expensive campaigns (Cox and Thies 1998; Golden and Chang 2001). On the party front, candidate-centered electoral systems tend to undermine party cohesion and party discipline (Reed 1994; Hicken 2002). Finally, governments in candidate-centered electoral systems tend to be more corrupt (Geddes and Neto 1992; Golden and Chang 2001; Golden 2003),[10] tend to be more bureaucratically inefficient (Golden 2003), and tend to oversupply particularistic goods and services while undersupplying needed national public goods (Cox and McCubbins 2001; Hicken 2002; Golden 2003).

Electoral systems carry with them certain incentives for parties and candidates. However, even within a candidate-centered electoral system, a variety of other factors can mitigate the incentives to cultivate a personal vote, including party-specific characteristics and whether or not a party has access to government resources.

Party Rules and Organization

The way in which party leaders organize and manage the party has a lot to do with what sort of strategy candidates find attractive. For example, where a centralized party leadership controls nominations or access to the party label, members of that party are more likely to toe the party line and adopt a party-centered strategy (e.g., Carey and Shugart 1995).[11] Conversely, if nomination control is decentralized or out of the party's hands altogether (as is the case with open primaries), then candidates have much weaker incentives to privilege party strategies. These party features can vary independently of the type of electoral system (i.e., parties within the same electoral system may differ in terms of their organization and hence in the types of strategies their candidates pursue).

A similar logic holds for control of campaign finance and access to pork. Where party members are dependent on a centralized party leadership for campaign funds or access to the pork barrel, they will be attuned to the preferences and priorities of party leaders seeking to promote and protect the value of the party label. Candidates who must generate their own campaign funds or who can easily and directly access resources for pork are better able to pursue personal strategies without the fear of reprisals from party leaders (Carey and Shugart 1995; Mainwaring and Scully 1995; Samuels 1999). For example, in pre-1997 Thailand and post-1982 Brazil, legislators could obtain a significant amount of pork without the approval or input of party leaders (Hicken 2003; Ames 1995), while in pre-1973 Chile an extremely centralized party leadership controlled access to the pork barrel (Valenzuela 1977; Samuels 1999). All three of these countries used candidate-centered electoral systems, but the incentives to cultivate a personal vote were much stronger in Thailand and Brazil compared to Chile.

Access to Government Resources

In many candidate-centered electoral systems there exists a party (or parties) that is an exception to the norm of personalized parties—a party that is highly cohesive and actively promotes its ideological and policy distinctiveness. Often, these are parties that have been largely shut out of government. Without the resources of government, candidate-centered strategies that rely on these resources as the currency of campaigning are less viable. As an alternative, these parties may opt for party-centered strategies that emphasize the promotion and protection of the party's label.[12]

Italy, Brazil, and Japan each contain examples of programmatic parties in the midst of candidate-centered electoral systems. All of these parties were consistently in the opposition. Miriam Golden and Eric Chang argue that Italy's Communist Party, without access to the national government, overcame "the incentives to personalism" to create a "well-disciplined and centralized organization" (2001, 604). Brazil's Workers Party did the same. "Because the [party] was not linked to government, was not formed from within the Congress, did not have an established team of well-known politicians, and generally lacked financial resources, it could not compete on the same turf as other parties by using similar tactics" (Samuels 1999, 512). Instead, the party opted to cultivate a strong and distinct party label. Finally, Japan's Socialist Party, out of power for the entire single nontransferable vote period and unable to compete with the Liberal Democratic Party in the market for personal votes, "settled for the second-best solution of policy-based campaigns" (Cox and Thies 1998, 280).[13]

Competitiveness

The degree of electoral competition candidates face can also affect their incentives to cultivate a personal vote. However, the strength of this effect depends on the nature of the competition. Increased competition from copartisans is positively correlated with candidate-centered campaigning. The more intense the degree of intraparty competition, the more candidates will seek to cultivate a personal vote, all else being equal (Cox and Thies 1998; Golden and Chang 2001). Evidence of the effect of interparty competition, however, is mixed. Gary Cox and Michael Thies find that candidates do respond to tougher competition from other-party candidates, but also find that reaction to tougher intraparty competition is much stronger (1998, 287).[14] In contrast, Golden and Chang find no significant relationship between the level of interparty competition and their proxy for candidate-centered campaigning (2001, 594).[15]

To summarize, the types of strategies candidates adopt in their effort to win office vary depending on the surrounding institutional and political environment. Candidate-centered electoral systems, especially those with intraparty competition, generate strong incentives for candidates to cultivate a personal vote. The nature of party organization, candidate access to government resources, and the level of competition can also affect a candidate's incentive to adopt personal rather party-centered strategies.

Vote Buying vs. Alternative Personal Strategies

The fact that candidates must adopt personal strategies does not necessarily imply that vote buying will be the preferred vehicle for pursuing those strategies. Indeed, as discussed previously, a variety of means and methods can be employed by candidates in an effort to create personal support networks. Along with vote buying, these can include:

- targeting governmental pork and patronage to a candidate's constituents
- relying on name and fame to cultivate a personal vote
- using patron-client relationships to engender loyalty and support
- emphasizing intraparty policy differences
- violence and intimidation (directed toward voters and other candidates)

This list is certainly not exhaustive, but each of these is a common method of cultivating a personal vote in candidate-centered electoral systems. It should also be clear that these strategies are not mutually exclusive. Patron-client networks can be mobilized in support of vote buying efforts, or voter intimidation might be used to pressure voters into accepting money and voting as instructed. The question for the remainder of this chapter is: Under what conditions is vote buying one of the preferred methods for candidates? Careful research is needed to completely answer the question, but I discuss here some of the factors that shape whether vote buying will be a major part of a candidate's arsenal. First, I argue that most candidates cannot rely solely on violence and intimidation, fame, and personal patronage—there are natural limits and risks associated with the use of these strategies. Second, concerning the question of vote buying versus pork or intraparty policy differentiation, I argue that a mix of socioeconomic, cultural, and institutional factors influences the expected utility of vote buying vis-à-vis other personal strategies. While a thorough test of the arguments is not possible here, part of the purpose of this volume is to help chart a research agenda for the future. In that spirit, I lay out several arguments about vote buying incentives— hypotheses that can be tested as the necessary data become available.

One way for candidates to cultivate personal support networks is by relying on name and fame and using personal resources to build patron-client relationships with potential voters. However, there are natural limits to the use of personal patronage or personal and family fame as a campaign strategy. Few candidates can rely on fame alone. Likewise, only a small fraction of the candidates in any given election have the means and influence necessary to act as a traditional patron. Cultivating client loyalty via the use of personal patronage takes consistent generosity over time, and most candidates lack the resources necessary for such a sustained investment. Even among those with the means to become traditional patrons, personal patronage is usually mixed with other strategies, such as vote buying (McVey 2000b; Arghiros 2000).[16]

Violence and intimidation, while not uncommon in the run-up to elections in many countries, is not a primary strategy for most candidates in most elections. Violence and intimidation on a scale large enough to achieve electoral success are costly. Most candidates lack the sufficient resources (money, men, and connections) to use violence as their primary electoral strategy. In addition, the use of violence and intimidation generally carries greater risks than other personal strategies such as vote buying. Violence against political rivals runs the risk of reprisal, and if caught, the penalty for violence and intimidation is usually greater than the penalty for vote buying. In short, the cost and risk of violence place some limits on their use and make other strategies, such as vote buying, relatively more attractive.

The Expected Utility of Vote Buying

Given the limits on violence, personal wealth, and fame as exclusive electoral strategies, let us consider why candidates may choose to buy votes instead of or in addition to other strategies—for example, relying on government pork and patronage or emphasizing intraparty policy differences. The latter two strategies are evident in virtually all candidate-centered electoral systems, while vote buying is relatively less common (although by no means rare). To return to the questions posed earlier: How can we explain the prevalence of vote buying in some candidate-centered systems and not others? What factors affect the relative cost and benefits—the expected utility or opportunity cost—of vote buying vis-à-vis other strategies?

Structural, cultural, and socioeconomic factors can certainly shape the market for votes. For example, cultural norms of gift giving and the pervasiveness of patron-client links can create a social atmosphere conducive to vote buying.[17] Socioeconomic factors such as the level of development/ income and urbanization can also have a bearing on the incentives to buy votes.

Many scholars and policymakers draw a connection between the level of economic development and the prevalence of vote buying. They argue that the demand for and susceptibility to vote buying and other forms of clientelism are fueled by poverty (see, e.g., Anand 2001; Brusco, Nazareno, and Stokes 2002). As incomes rise, the cost of vote buying will rise while the benefits decline, all else being equal, thus making other strategies more appealing. Specifically, as incomes rise, the marginal benefit to a voter of a given sum of money from a candidate decreases.[18] To maintain a given level of support via vote buying, candidates must increase the amount of money they distribute. In light of this, candidates may find it more appealing to curtail vote buying and switch to alternative personal vote strategies that produce a better return.[19]

However, there are reasons to be cautious about drawing too strong a link between economic underdevelopment and vote buying. On theoretical grounds, one might question the assumption implicit in arguments about the decreasing marginal utility of vote buying—namely that a candidate's vote buying funds remain fixed or at least rise more slowly than average incomes. Alternatively, one might assume that a candidate's capacity to buy votes increases commensurate with increases in average incomes. Development, in other words, means more resources for both voters *and* candidates. If this is the case, then development may have no effect on the prevalence of vote buying. Ultimately the relationship between development and vote buying is a matter for testing. Preliminary evidence from surveys in the Philippines and Brazil suggests that the link between income and vote buying is not as straightforward as some have supposed, but more empirical work is needed (Schaffer 2004; Speck and Abramo 2001).

Urbanization also has a negative impact on a candidate's propensity to buy votes. If the development hypothesis holds, part of the reason for this will be the relatively higher incomes found in urban areas.[20] However, urbanization has an impact on candidate strategy independent of the income effects described above (Ramseyer and Rosenbluth 1993; Shugart and Nielson 1999; Bloom, Craig, and Malaney 2001). First, the move to cities destroys the traditional patron-client networks through which candidate funds can be distributed, thus raising the cost of vote buying for candidates. Second, it is difficult to re-create patron-client relationships in urban areas. Due to the high price of land, urban voters are less likely to be homeowners and so move more frequently than do rural voters (Ramseyer and Rosenbluth 1993, 39). Thus, candidates will find it relatively difficult to develop and maintain a core group of supporters. Third, urban voters tend to have a higher demand for public goods than do rural voters. As the attention of urbanites turns to issues such as traffic congestion, crime, and garbage collection, they begin to support candidates who campaign on local public-goods issues (pork).

While cultural and socioeconomic factors can influence the choice of personal strategy, it is important to remember that vote buying is embedded within a larger political order. Thus a variety of political and institutional factors can affect the expected utility of vote buying relative to other strategies. These include features of the electoral system and the strength of anti–vote buying legal measures.

Just as features of the electoral system can influence the decision to cultivate a personal or party vote, electoral rules and the nature of electoral competition can have a similar effect on the mix of personal strategies that candidates choose to employ. For example, electoral systems differ in their propensity to produce a supply of surplus votes. Where voters can cast multiple votes, each vote may not hold the same value. Voters may reserve some votes for the "true" expression of their preferences for candidates or parties, but view the others as extra votes, available for sale to the highest bidder. (See Chapter 9 for a discussion of the market for surplus votes in Thailand.) Thus, all else being equal, vote buying will be more likely where voters have multiple votes and a potential supply of surplus votes exists, than where voters cast a single vote.

Another electoral variable that can affect the expected utility of vote buying is district population size. All else being equal, the larger the district, the larger the amount of money required to buy a winning number of votes and the weaker or less dense the social networks needed to distribute money and monitor compliance (see Chapter 5).[21] As vote buying becomes more costly and more difficult to carry out logistically, candidates face incentives to switch from individual-level vote buying to strategies aimed at larger numbers of constituents using government resources, such as pork barreling and patronage.[22] For example, Gary Cox traces the decline of vote buying (and certain other personal strategies) in nineteenth-century England to the growth of electoral districts. As districts grew, a fixed amount of money "would buy a smaller portion of the total votes . . . if the average price of votes was not less" (1987, 57). As a consequence, candidates reduced vote buying in favor of other vote getting strategies.

Note that there is some disagreement among scholars about the effects of increasing district size in Great Britain (see Chapter 3). It may be that there is a curvilinear relationship between district size and incentives to buy votes. In very small districts where patron-client networks and political hierarchies are entrenched, candidates may be able to command support from voters without resorting to vote buying. Increasing the size of these districts should undermine the ability of candidates to generate this "command vote" and increase the incentives to buy votes. As district size continues to increase, however, the incentives to buy votes should decrease as described above.

Perhaps the political factor that has the most direct impact on the expected utility of vote buying is the degree to which anti–vote buying rules and institutions exist and are enforced. Legislation prohibiting or at least strictly regulating vote buying is a first step, but this is clearly not enough. In Thailand, for example, vote buying has been illegal throughout the country's democratic history, yet has reportedly grown worse in each election. Anti–vote buying rules have little effect if the punishment for vote buying is light or if the chance of being detected is slim. To seriously deter candidates from buying votes, anti–vote buying measures must raise both the probability of being caught and the associated penalty. Penalties can run the gamut, from small fines to lifetime bans from politics. Generally speaking, penalties that put vote buyers in jail or ban them from public office for a significant period are more costly to ambitious politicians than monetary penalties alone.[23] There are also a variety of ways to raise the probability of detecting, reporting, and punishing vote buying, including strict campaign finance regulation and reporting requirements. Another common strategy is moving responsibility for administering elections out of the hands of elected politicians and into an autonomous or semiautonomous body (e.g., the Federal Elections Commission in the United States and the recently created Election Commission of Thailand). Once created, anti–vote buying efforts hinge on the funding, staffing, and powers that these bodies are given to monitor elections, investigate vote buying allegations, and administer penalties. Finally, one election is not enough to change candidate and party expectations about the risks and rewards of vote buying, as the case of Thailand demonstrates (see Chapter 9). In order to reduce the expected utility of vote buying, monitoring and enforcement must be consistent from election to election.

Conclusion

This chapter has explored the roots of vote buying with special attention to political and institutional variables. In exploring the conditions under which candidates have incentives to employ programmatic, ideological, or partisan appeals, and the conditions under which they have incentives to cultivate a personal vote, I find that candidate-centered electoral systems, weak parties, and access to government resources can motivate candidates to adopt personal electoral strategies, including vote buying. In considering the question of when vote buying will be included in a candidate's arsenal as she or he seeks to cultivate a personal vote, I find that the expected utility of vote buying relative to other personal strategies, particularly pork barreling, is a function of a mix of socioeconomic, cultural, and institutional factors. While the effects of development are ambiguous, urbanization tends to undermine the incentives of candidates to buy votes. On the institutional side, surplus votes, small districts, and weak anti–vote buying laws contribute to a market for votes.

Notes

1. My focus is mainly on electoral and party rules (e.g., the rules of competition). However, it is important to note that rules of electoral governance (e.g., secret ballot, voting procedures, legal restrictions on vote buying) might also affect the propensity to buy votes. (See Mozaffar and Schedler 2002 for more on the distinction between these two types of rules.) For the most part, I leave the discussion of electoral governance to others.

2. I use Gary Cox and Mathew McCubbins's definition of pork (2001). They divide pork into public goods that are directed or allocated on the basis of political rather than economic calculations (morsels), and rents that are extracted from the government.

3. For convenience I will generally refer to the candidate as the vote buyer. In some cases, however, it may be others buying votes on behalf of the candidate (e.g., supporters, factions, or political parties).

4. There is lively debate in the literature on the link between electoral systems and corruption (see Persson, Tabellini, and Trebbi 2003; Kunicova and Rose-Ackerman 2005; Chang and Golden forthcoming; Birch 2005). While there is some overlap in the logic that underlies the link between electoral institutions and corruption or vote buying, I will restrict my focus to the latter.

5. There may also be important differences between candidates and parties within a given system, as discussed in more detail later. See also Cox and Thies 1998; Samuels 1999; and Golden and Chang 2001.

6. Candidates may be elected solely on the basis of their individual vote totals, or party vote totals might determine a party's seat allocation while candidate vote totals are used to fill those seats (or order the party's list).

7. Under the single transferable vote, voters rank as many candidates as they wish, both within parties and across different parties. Any candidates who reach a certain quota of first-choice votes are deemed elected. The surplus votes (votes above the quota) of elected candidates are then transferred to the second-choice candidates as marked on the ballots. Once the vote transfers are complete, candidates who have reached the quota are declared winners. If seats still remain, the candidate with fewest votes is eliminated and his or her votes are transferred in a similar manner. This process continues until all the seats are filled.

8. On Japanese factions, see, for example, Reed 1994; Cox and Rosenbluth 1993, 1996. On Italian factions, see, for example, Golden and Chang 2001. On Thai factions, see, for example, Hicken 2002.

9. See Ferejohn 1974 for some well-known examples from US politics.

10. For an opposing view, see Persson, Tabellini, and Trebbi 2001 and 2003.

11. Of course, the party's strategy might be to allow candidates to differentiate themselves via the use of personal strategies—à la the LDP in Japan.

12. The need to pursue this alternative strategy may motivate these parties to centralize power and rigorously enforce discipline, as described in the previous section. However, other strategies, apart from relying on a centralized, programmatic partisan strategy, are also possible, including the use of personal strategies that do not depend on government resources.

13. Not only do these parties differ from their counterparts in terms of organization and electoral strategy, but they also differ in terms of the types of candidates they attract. Programmatic parties tend to attract more ideological, policy-oriented candidates than do their candidate-centered competitors.

14. Consistent with its more programmatic nature, Cox and Thies (1998) find that this relationship does not hold for Japan's Socialist Party.

15. Another dimension of competitiveness, quite apart from its effect on the incentives to cultivate a personal vote, is the closeness of the contest. Where electoral contests are close, hinging on the support of a small number of swing voters, the incentives to buy votes should be stronger, all else being equal. Here the electoral system should also play a role. Single-seat district, first-past-the-post systems, in which changes in a few swing votes can lead to a dramatically different outcome in a close race, should generate stronger vote buying incentives than do multiseat proportional representation systems.

16. Ruth McVey (2000b) and Daniel Arghiros (2000) note a decline in Thailand in the use of personal patronage over time in favor of a greater reliance on vote buying.

17. For an interesting example of this argument from the Election Commission of Thailand, see http://www.ect.go.th/english/national/senate/nat7-13.html. Relying on patron-client relationships to explain vote buying, however, is not as straightforward as some have assumed. First, it is not clear that the "patron-client relationship" is an accurate description of the relationship between vote buyers (candidates) and vote sellers (voters) (see Nelson 1998a for an interesting discussion on this point). Second, even if one grants that patron-client relationships lie at the heart of vote buying networks, this still does not explain why patron-client links are primarily used to buy votes, as opposed to some other election-related purpose (e.g., intimidating voters or mobilizing supporters using nonmonetary means). In other words, why does vote buying dominate the exchange between voters and candidates rather than some other form of exchange (e.g., votes in exchange for pork, patronage, or policy)?

18. This assumes that the amount of the money, not just the receipt of a gift, affects the voter's behavior.

19. Greater economic development can also undermine the value of personal strategies more generally. As incomes rise, so too does voter involvement in the broader national economy. Thus the impact of government policies on voters' economic well-being also increases. Things like tax rates, exchange rates, growth rates, interest rates, and wage rates become more important to voters as their incomes rise. Thus the opportunity cost of voting for politicians who rely on personal strategies increases relative to voting for candidates who campaign on the policy position of a particular party over a set of issues important to the voter. See Chapter 7 for more on

this point. See Chapter 6 for further discussion on the link between income and vote buying.

20. Note, though, that if the development hypothesis is correct, we should see strategies within urban areas varying according to differences in income levels. In fact, in his study of Thai elections, Sombat Chantornvong found just such a relationship. While noting that vote buying was not an effective strategy in most of Bangkok, he found that vote buying was a viable strategy in the poorer areas of the city (Sombat 1993).

21. District size can change due to the redrawing of district boundaries, population growth, or the enfranchisement of new voters. Large fluctuations in voter turnout also have the effect of increasing or decreasing the number of votes needed to win.

22. Population growth can eventually undermine even these personal strategies.

23. It is also possible to punish vote sellers, though examples of this are rare.

5

The Logistics: How to Buy Votes

Chin-Shou Wang & Charles Kurzman

Imagine that you are interested in buying votes. How do you go about it? Virtually everywhere in the world, vote buying is illegal, so you will need to be discreet. But it is difficult to reach large numbers of voters discreetly. To do so, you will need an extensive organization of brokers, each of whom will approach a small number of voters. This chapter discusses how one vote buying candidate running for county executive in Taiwan in 1993 found qualified brokers and kept them in line. This campaign faced certain challenges that were specific to the Taiwanese context, but the basic requirements of building a broker organization may be applicable to other places and times. It is hard to know just how representative this instance is, since the level of insider access gained by the first author of this chapter (Wang) has not been matched in other studies. Nonetheless, we offer the following hypotheses in the most general terms: that broker organization requires (1) campaign managers with tremendous local knowledge, (2) a significant budget, (3) networks of trust to claim broker loyalty, (4) a system to avoid duplication of effort, and (5) judicial protection. The campaign described here met these requirements, and won its election by a margin of votes lower than the number of votes bought. Despite this effectiveness, as discussed in a companion piece (Wang and Kurzman, forthcoming), the vote buying process was highly inefficient, with at least 45 percent of voters casting their ballots for a candidate other than the one who had paid for their vote.

Background

After retreating from the mainland of China to the island of Taiwan in 1949, the Kuomintang (Nationalist Party) faced a Taiwanese population with whom it had little previous connection. The intention of the Kuomintang in building an electoral institution was not to create a democratic system;

rather, national ruling elites viewed the establishment of electoral institutions as the only way to secure popular support and elicit cooperation from local elites (Wu 1987, 196–197). With few exceptions, elections were restricted to the local level for almost forty years. Citizens could elect local officeholders, from village executives to members of the provincial assembly, but the most important positions—president, members of the national congress, and governors—were unelected.

One of the Kuomintang's primary tools for electoral mobilization was vote buying.[1] "To mobilize voters," a Kuomintang campaign manager said in an interview, "is to build a vote-buying organization" (Interviewee 18). Even in the early years of democratization, after 1987, opposition candidates complained that "money is the meat on the faction skeleton; without money, factions are worthless bones" (Bosco 1994, 40–41).[2] Academic discussion of vote buying in Taiwan dates back to Bernard Gallin's 1968 analysis, in which he argued that vote buying had been a common practice throughout the country since the 1950s, when candidates gave voters a few packages of cigarettes or some bath towels and soap in exchange for votes. Since that time, however, aside from brief mentions (e.g., Jacobs 1980; Bosco 1994), vote buying has scarcely been included in English-language discussions of Taiwan's electoral process, though many scholars assume it exists. "It is hard to say which is more difficult: finding someone in Taiwan who denies that vote-buying exists, or finding concrete evidence to prove that it does" (Rigger 1999b, 94). In Taiwanese scholarship, however, such evidence is well established. In the 1990s, surveys in various cities in Taiwan found that a quarter to a half of respondents admitted to selling their vote in the most recent election: 24 percent of 1,618 respondents nationwide in 1992 (Yang 1994); 27 percent of 1,168 respondents in 1999 in Taichung County and Taichung City, Taiwan's third largest metropolis (Cheng, Wang, and Chen 2000); 30 percent of 1,198 respondents nationwide in 1992 (Chu 1994); and 45 percent of 1,263 respondents in 1992 in Kaohsiung, Taiwan's second largest city (Ho 1995).

In 1993, Taiwan held elections for county executives around the country. The case under study is a largely rural, agricultural county with a population at that time of close to 1 million. The structure of local factions in this county was typical of faction organization throughout Taiwan. There were two county-level factions, which the Kuomintang had to ask to cooperate with each other to mobilize votes for Kuomintang candidates. At the same time that they were asked to cooperate, the electoral system, involving the single nontransferable vote and multimember districts, frequently forced local factions to compete with each other for Kuomintang nominations and political positions. As noted by Allen Hicken in Chapter 4, single nontransferable vote electoral systems may be more likely to experience vote buying than other systems. As it happens, though, the 1993 Taiwan case study involved a single seat, so single nontransferable vote dynamics were not particularly visible.

In this race, a non-Kuomintang official affiliated with the opposition Democratic Progressive Party (DPP) was the incumbent in the county executive race under investigation, having won the 1989 election. Prior to that time, he was a provincial assembly representative and was highly praised not only in his home county but also elsewhere in Taiwan. Before the 1993 election, most surveys showed that he would likely win. Because this candidate was so strong, the Kuomintang mobilized more political and economic resources and personnel for this race than for any other county executive elections in the country.

The study of vote buying, like the study of other illegal activities, is by nature fraught with difficulties. This is one reason why there has been so little empirical research on the mechanics of vote buying. "Simply put, no one who stuffs the ballot box wants to leave a trail of incriminating evidence" (Lehoucq 2003, 233). Other researchers have used newspapers (Cox and Kousser 1981), legal documents (Lehoucq and Molina 2002), and interviews (Callahan and McCargo 1996) to study electoral fraud.

Our study uses observation and interviews, through which we gained the trust of key personnel in a 1993 Taiwanese electoral campaign through two months of work in the campaign headquarters and at a branch office in "Township 20." The first author (Wang) was introduced to campaign officials by an important local figure, and was allowed to observe many of the goings-on in the campaign office and speak informally with campaign workers. Several campaign staff knew the research purpose of Wang's observations and conversations, and did not object. Interviews with sixteen Kuomintang campaign officials, two DPP campaign officials, and two knowledgeable local observers were conducted after the election and the fieldwork had finished. More than a hundred further interviews were conducted in the region in subsequent years. These campaign officials and the documents that they made available open an unprecedented window onto the process of vote buying.

Vote buying was central to the Kuomintang's campaign in this 1993 election. An official in the mobilization department of campaign headquarters said succinctly in an interview that the most important duty of his unit was "to arrange the organization for vote-buying" (Interviewee 18). Accordingly, the Kuomintang arranged for vote buying throughout the county. This was arranged through campaign branch offices, one in each township, called Campaign Committees for the Kuomintang Candidate. These offices were each led by a campaign manager who was familiar with the local situation and was responsible for building the broker organization.

The Importance of the Campaign Manager

Campaign managers are crucial in any electoral contest. But different skills are involved when the campaign involves or does not involve vote buying. In a local election in Taiwan in 2001, for example, six of the seven successful candidates bought votes. The seventh candidate, affiliated with the DPP, refused. His campaign hired a manager and staff who were young, highly educated, and relatively unconnected with the local population. With few local supporters and little understanding of local politics, they focused their energies on crafting an idealistic platform, getting their candidate into the news, and producing high-quality flyers and brochures, which were widely said to be the best in the election.

The vote buying campaigns, by contrast, hired local politicos who had detailed knowledge of the local populations: who knew whom, who trusted whom, and how these relationships could be used to influence staff and voters.[3] Ideological skills and media sophistication are useful as well, but vote buying campaigns do not rely exclusively on such impersonal connections with voters as brochures and media reports (for further analysis of different personal strategies, see Chapter 4). When the primary contact with voters is one-on-one, through the act of vote buying, the campaign manager has to be a walking encyclopedia of local knowledge.

The currents of local politics are complicated in many parts of Taiwan by the existence of multiple local factions that compete with one another for political advantage and are loath to cooperate. Yet Kuomintang candidates in the county under study, as elsewhere in Taiwan, could not afford to side with one faction and alienate the others. They had to be induced to work together—or at least to work in parallel. Towns without factions were an even greater challenge. At least the factions provided a ready-made source of brokers for vote buying. Where factions did not exist, campaign managers had to find brokers on their own.

It was not easy to find people with the political skills and local knowledge needed to fill the role of campaign manager. As a result, Kuomintang campaign offices went to great pains to get the best possible people for the most competitive races. For example, the president of the campaign committee in Township 20 spent much time searching for the proper person to hold the post of campaign manager, technically termed the "executive officer" of the campaign committee. The campaign manager who was eventually hired was highly qualified: he had never lost an election in his twenty-plus years of managing campaigns, and was widely praised as the best campaign manager in the township. People in town said that the Kuomintang candidate would not have won without him. This man was a Kuomintang member in 1993, but not a hard-core supporter. Indeed, he sympathized with the DPP's "clean government" platform and often voted for the DPP in national elections. In local elections, he had worked for several Kuomintang candidates, one DPP candidate, and one independent, following the widespread Taiwanese dictum, "In national elections, party first; in local ones, [candidate] first." To encourage the manager to join the campaign, the president of the campaign committee, a local dignitary, visited him several times as a show of respect. In addition, the campaign could draw on the manager's feelings of gratitude and debt toward a campaign committee official's father who had procured a job for him a long time previously.

Township 3 during the 1993 elections provides an example of the great difficulty of managing local mobilization. Faction A tended to be pro-Kuomintang, but the Kuomintang approached Faction B first, because Faction B had won the Farmers Association election and was considered the dominant faction. The leaders of Faction A then intended to support the DPP candidate, and in fact the DPP approached Faction A for support (Interviewee 13). The campaign headquarters of the Kuomintang candidate tried to dissuade Faction A from supporting the DPP candidate, using a variety of connections, but failed. Finally, the manager at the campaign headquarters—a wily and experienced campaigner known locally as "little deity"—went to talk with a local political figure who had two generations of connections with the family of the founder of Faction A. The manager asked this man to persuade Faction A to take a neutral stance, at the least, and perhaps even to support the Kuomintang candidate. The strategy worked, and Faction A joined the Kuomintang campaign. This sort of local knowledge and political skill was crucial for close races.

In nonfactional townships, campaign managers have the primary responsibility for locating and hiring a sufficient number of brokers, a process that requires intimate knowledge of local personalities and relationships. For example, in Township 20 in the 1993 election, a local political figure offered to support the Kuomintang campaign, but the campaign manager did not trust him, since he had campaigned for DPP candidates in national elections. Only when the campaign manager learned that another political figure in town, a trustworthy Kuomintang supporter, had vouched for the other man did the manager agree to bring him into the campaign organization.

Local knowledge is important in any campaign, whether or not it plans to buy votes. But when vote buying is involved, the importance is all the greater. Every botched personnel decision carries the risk that the vote buying scheme will be discovered. In Taiwan, one could not always count on party loyalty, as local political figures were known to switch affiliations. Even the undefeated campaign manager in Township 20, for example, went on to manage a DPP campaign for township executive the following year.

Budgeting for Vote Buying

Vote buying can be expensive. In Township 20 in 1993, the Kuomintang bought 14,090 votes for 300 Taiwanese dollars each (about US$10), equivalent to the cost of two meals in an inexpensive restaurant.[4] This price was set by the campaign and was nonnegotiable, though not arbitrary, as it had grown out of the party's experience with the market in vote buying in this county over the previous decades. Campaign officials must have calculated that a smaller amount might have been considered an insult to the voters, and a larger amount would not have been worth the extra loyalty that it might have delivered.

Yet even this modest price generated a significant cost. In Township 20, the campaign bought 67 percent of the eligible votes; if this rate is extrapolated to the entire county, then the campaign spent more than US$4 million on vote buying alone. This was an unusually high figure, and was due to the special attention given to this race. The Kuomintang had made this particular county executive campaign a national priority, because it wanted desperately to win back the office from the DPP. This was one of the few countywide offices held by the DPP anywhere in Taiwan at that time. Locals called the 1993 race "the battle of the century."

Presumably, the Kuomintang drew on its national coffers to finance the county campaign, but we have no information on this. This subject was too sensitive to be raised in interviews, and was not observed during fieldwork in 1993. During a later election in the same county, a low-level campaign official suggested that the national Kuomintang headquarters gave the candidate a sum that is comparable to the US$4 million figure we have estimated, but we cannot vouch for the reliability of this information.

Whatever its source, we can follow the money once it reached campaign headquarters. In consultation with local campaign officials, the campaign headquarters set target vote buying rates for each township in the county (Interviewee 18). For Township 20, for example, the campaign set a rate of 70–80 percent, and township campaign officials aimed to buy 75 percent of the vote (ending up with 67 percent). In areas where the campaign expected to encounter difficulties, the target rate might be higher, but the campaign worried that too high a rate would encourage brokers to feel that they could get away with embezzling the vote buying money, since the candidate would be sure to win a majority in the precinct (Interviewee 10).

The campaign then budgeted a 10 percent "commission" for local campaign operatives on top of the cost of buying votes. This commission has become conventional in almost all large-scale elections in this region of Taiwan, though it may be supplemented by cases of cigarettes or other gifts (Interviewees 8, 10). Campaign headquarters paid the commission to local campaign offices without stipulating how the money should be spent.

The vote buying money was delivered to the township campaign offices in three installments. The first two were small, intended mainly to cover office work, and were sent two months and one month before the election, respectively. The third and main installment was supposed to arrive about ten days before the election. If it came too late, as it had in the 1989 county executive election in Township 20, one of the local campaign leaders could pocket the money and brokers or other local leaders would not have enough time to report the embezzlement to campaign headquarters in order to receive new funds prior to the election (Interviewee 14). To prevent embezzlement, campaign headquarters had adopted a strategy of asking four or five witnesses, such as factions leaders or local party officials, to observe the transfer of funds (Interviewee 18). In the 1993 election, the vote buying money arrived one week before the polling day.

In Township 20, the local campaign office then distributed the money to the precinct campaign directors in two installments, one fifty days prior to the election, to induce the brokers to visit voters, and one a week prior to the election, in amounts based on the number of voters in each precinct, averaging about 15,000 Taiwanese dollars (US$500) per precinct. The first installment, called an "administration fee," was used to buy cigarettes, tea, and areca nut, which many Taiwanese chew socially. When brokers visited voters, they often gave each a cigarette and lit it, as a sign of respect. The second installment included an additional administration fee, twice the amount of the first installment; the brokers' commissions, which could be combined or replaced with the administration fee; and the money for buying votes.

The precinct campaign directors then distributed the money to the brokers. The amount per voter was fixed by headquarters, but the distribution of the commission was left to the discretion of the precinct directors. Each director handled the money differently. One threw luncheon parties for brokers (Interviewee 5), another bought cigarettes or gifts for brokers (Interviewees 6, 7), another bought them coupons to exchange for free gasoline (Interviewees 1, 7). The directors then passed along the remaining funds to the brokers in cash, sometimes proportional to the number of voters for whom a broker was responsible, and sometimes in equal amounts. The brokers in Township 20 generally received 500–2,000 Taiwanese dollars (US$17–67) in commissions, but some received nothing, because they had been assigned so few voters.

In the 1993 election under study, the Kuomintang campaign created a further, unusual incentive system for brokers (Interviewee 1). After the election, the campaign compared the number of votes in each precinct with the number received by the Kuomintang candidate in the previous county executive election. The precinct's campaign workers received a bonus of 30,000 Taiwanese dollars (US$1,000) if the number of votes increased by 50;

50,000 Taiwanese dollars (US$1,667) if it increased by 100; and 100,000 Taiwanese dollars (US$3,333) if it increased by 200. In Township 20, twelve of eighteen precincts qualified for these bonuses, the distribution of which was left to the precinct campaign directors. One director bought brokers a tourist trip, one bought brokers sportswear, and others donated to community welfare organizations, temples, or elder associations.

A few brokers asked for additional material rewards. One asked the campaign to promise that the government would finance a community project in his village, and a few asked for favors such as reassignment into a better government job. Yet the primary material rewards came in the form of expectations, sometimes explicit and often unspoken, that the successful candidate would reward followers after the election. Like "pork barrel" politics everywhere, campaign leaders stressed repeatedly that the candidate would do his best to bring government projects to constituents (Interviewee 2). In the month after he won the election, the Kuomintang candidate received hundreds of requests for jobs or financial support from campaign officials.

Nonetheless, material incentives alone were insufficient. The broker payments were not particularly large, even in a relatively poor county with an average annual income of approximately 225,000 Taiwanese dollars (US$7,500). In fact, in some elections, certain officials even paid to participate in the campaign (Interviewees 5, 7). Mau-Kuei Chang and Chun-Chue Chen (1986) have noted that campaign mobilization in Taiwan draws on a combination of social relationships and financial incentives. In Township 20 in 1993, the social relationships far outweighed the financial incentives.

Finding Trustworthy Brokers

In Taiwan, the act of vote buying is conducted by brokers, called *tiau-a-ka* (literally, "pillars"; for a discussion of this role, see Rigger 1994, chaps. 4–5; Rigger 1999b, 87–102). The Kuomintang hires a large number of brokers, each of whom approaches a small number of voters (in one precinct in 1993, this number ranged from six to fifty-six, with a mean of twenty-one, according to a campaign document). The broker offers money in exchange for support on election day, and delivers the money from the campaign office to the voters on the eve of the elections. Given the secrecy of the ballot, brokers must guess which voters can be counted on to deliver votes. As a result, the vote buying operation is only as good as its brokers.[5]

Township 20 in 1993, for example, had no factions, so the Kuomintang had to create a broker organization from scratch. For a county election with approximately 21,000 eligible voters, the Kuomintang hired 522 brokers, plus 99 assistant directors (called "superbrokers") and 26 directors, all of whom also served as brokers and bought votes. Three months before election day, Township 20's service station, the local branch of the Kuomintang party office, held a meeting for leading local supporters, during which the party office introduced the candidate and his platform to party members. One month later, the local party branch held another meeting, at which the president and vice presidents of the campaign committee were selected. The president then appointed a planning officer and other campaign officials. These officials and the vice presidents chose the directors, who then appointed assistant directors (Interviewee 11).

Personal connections were crucial in making these appointments. Of the 26 directors, 25 had social connections with top-level campaign officials: they were classmates in school, natives of the same small village, relatives, colleagues, or veterans of past Kuomintang mobilization networks. Where these ties were insufficient, the directors were mobilized by third parties who had close ties to the party leadership. With close associates making the request, few people refused to serve.

The directors and assistant directors then selected the brokers. Some used their institutional position. For example, one village chief used neighborhood chiefs as the primary source for brokers (Interviewee 19); the secretary-general of the local Farmers Association relied primarily on association staff members and activists (Interviewee 6). Others used personal ties, such as a director who asked his good friends to be brokers, including some who owed him favors (Interviewee 7). In addition, some people were selected simply because they were politically active and had an interest in the campaign, for one reason or another. Over time, experienced campaign officials get to know who these people are, since Taiwan holds elections almost every year. Brokers came from many social backgrounds, including farmers, fishermen, small business owners, governmental officials, and even teachers.

The campaign needed strong social ties to build a sufficient network of brokers for vote buying. The brokers had to be trustworthy enough that they would not divulge campaign secrets to the opposition or the authorities, or waste or embezzle the campaign's resources. The question of "honor among thieves" arises in any illegal collective action, and the Kuomintang used social ties and oversight mechanisms to try to address the constant fear that it would be cheated. There is an irony here: the efficient avoidance of external accountability required careful systems of internal accountability.

Even with strong social ties, trust was an ongoing concern. "Supporting the candidate is supporting me," one precinct director told his brokers (Interviewee 7). Other directors appealed to the prestige of the local campaign leader, a man who grew up in Township 20 and had remained active in local affairs, including the festivities in key temples. He was known to have used his connections in the government to obtain funds for infrastructure in the township. His friendship with the candidate was a major boon for the campaign.

From the campaign office, to the precinct directors, to brokers, to voters, each link in the vote buying chain involved the mobilization of social relations. The candidate did not establish a connection directly with voters, but only indirectly through a series of trusted intermediaries.

Managing the Brokers

The interests of the brokers and the interests of the campaign did not always match perfectly. Some brokers considered pocketing the money instead of passing it along to voters. Aside from outright embezzlement, some brokers wished to pad their own income by purchasing a large number of votes, though the campaign might not have trusted their ability to make good on their promise. Some brokers wanted to channel campaign money to their family or friends, even if these people had no intention of voting for the candidate. In addition, some brokers wished to repurchase votes of the same individuals, wasting campaign resources.

As a result, the campaign reserved the right to filter or add voters to the lists that the brokers drew up (Interviewee 1; Minute Books 3, 6).[6] One month before the 1993 election, the campaign manager in one district gathered all the brokers in a single meeting and reviewed the voter lists. The group discussed whether each voter was a hard-core DPP supporter, and therefore not worth approaching. If the voter was not, the campaign officials solicited brokers who thought they could successfully buy this particular vote. If more than one broker volunteered, the campaign officials asked them about the kind of relationship they had with the voter, and how strong this relationships was.

Residential location was the most important factor in deciding how to distribute brokers among voters, simply because brokers would not need much time to visit their voters. Social networks were often residentially based, and many neighbors had preexisting social relationships of friendship or kinship.[7] Therefore the campaign made an effort to select brokers who lived in each precinct in the electoral district. But sometimes a strong relationship might win out over residential proximity, for example if the broker and the voter were brothers. In one precinct, a voter who had recently arrived in the community had no strong relationship with the brokers who lived nearest to him, so a broker who lived farther away but who knew the voter from their common line of business, and had done the voter some favors, was assigned to him (Interviewee 20).

Frequently, brokers would be assigned to a household rather than an individual.[8] One broker (Interviewee 20) who was active and popular in local politics in Township 20, for example, was responsible for vote buying in ten households, in addition to his immediate family members. These households could be divided into three categories, according to their social relations with the broker: relatives, friends, and neighbors. In the case of this particular broker:

- *Relatives:* One voter was a nephew of the broker and helped the broker to buy votes in the families of the voter's brother and two daughters; another relative, a cousin, helped the broker deliver the vote buying money to the voter's neighbors.
- *Friends:* One voter not only accepted money from the broker, but also helped the broker distribute money to the voter's brothers.
- *Neighbors:* The broker bought votes from one neighboring household.

The last stage of the process was "vote calling," on election day. Brokers visited voters, secured their votes, responded to the voters' needs, and most importantly, amplified the effects of mobilization and vote buying as much as possible through their connections with the voters. They had to determine how many voters would be home, how many family members who were away would return to vote, and whether they would vote for the candidate whom the broker recommended. If a voter had not been persuaded by a particular broker, that broker would turn to another who might have closer ties to the voter. The link between brokers and voters was not simply a cash nexus; indeed, for vote buying to work, it had to be situated within a broader array of social relations between brokers and voters. From the campaign committee to the superbrokers, from the superbrokers to the brokers, and from the brokers to voters, the mobilization of social relations must extend in a smooth continuum for the system to be successful.

Judicial Protection

Vote buying has always been illegal in Taiwan. This was one reason to limit brokers' assignments to close social relations: doing so reduced the risk that a voter would report the practice to law enforcement authorities, in that such a report would be a breach of trust. Still, vote buying campaigns needed protection from judicial review if they were to operate successfully. In Thailand, and in the Philippines too, vote buying campaigns counted on the willingness of the local police to look the other way (Callahan and McCargo 1996, 390; Tordesillas 1998, 77). In Taiwan, Kuomintang campaign officials had little fear of being punished for vote buying, since they assumed that police and prosecutors would not take much of an interest

(Interviewees 1, 7). "Vote-buying is quite open," the campaign manager said in an interview. "Most candidates buy votes. People are rarely afraid of being caught" (Interviewee 1).

Prior to democratization, the Kuomintang rarely allowed the judiciary system to pursue vote buying allegations. One prosecutor investigated a vote buying case and caught five persons, but was blocked by his supervisor from further investigations, and never had the chance to question the Kuomintang candidate (Interviewee 116). Another prosecutor went straight to the county chair of the Kuomintang to report that he had received allegations of vote buying, essentially ratting out the whistleblower to the chief suspect (Huang 1997, 401–402). As late as 1995, the secretary of the Kuomintang's central committee, Shuei-De Shiu, bragged, "The courts are owned by the ruling party" (Yang 1995, 25).

In the mid-1990s, this was starting to change. With democratization, the DPP began to make vote buying, and corruption more generally, a campaign issue. In one local case in 1995, a young prosecutor's investigation managed to keep a powerful legislator from buying 50,000 votes; he only bought 30,000 votes, and was so shaken that he refused to run for reelection again (Interviewee 115). After the DPP won the 2000 presidential election and announced that it would investigate vote buying actively and seek jail time for brokers during the 2001 elections, some brokers panicked and abandoned vote buying campaigns (Interviewees 1, 51). Some campaign managers dared not hold broker meetings or discuss vote buying by telephone. They sought new ways to avoid suspicion, such as withdrawing cash from campaign bank accounts several months before election day so as not to create an obvious paper trail. They also tried not to generate incriminating documents, such as lists of brokers and their voters (Interviewee 1).

But in 1993, the Kuomintang campaign was more concerned about opposing candidates, rather than police or prosecutors, learning of its strategies. Meetings about vote buying were held in the basement of the campaign office, with no care taken to distance the campaign from the vote buying operation. Documents detailing the campaign's vote buying were kept in campaign offices, not destroyed. In past years, the local district attorney and several judges had been members of the Kuomintang campaign committee (we did not have access to the committee list for 1993).

One reason for discretion in vote buying was that if DPP supporters knew which broker was buying which votes, they might find someone with a strong social relationship with the broker or the voter and persuade them not to support the Kuomintang candidate. Indeed, several local DPP candidates also bought votes—in other elections, though not in 1993—and the Kuomintang campaign worried that their bought votes would be rebought by other campaigns. This was why Kuomintang brokers generally waited to deliver money to voters until the eve of election day, on the supposition that the campaign that paid last, paid best (Interviewees 1, 7).

The Kuomintang also used its cozy relationship with the judiciary to attack DPP candidates. In one instance, the Kuomintang requested that the Bureau of Investigation and a local prosecutor investigate a city park project that the party felt would implicate a DPP incumbent official. In another investigation, the district attorney told prosecutors to detain a DPP county official suspected of granting illegal favors to a golf club, hoping to embarrass the DPP during campaign season. Both of these attempts failed. The DPP candidate was not indicted in either case: the prosecutor in the golf case refused to detain the DPP official, and the parks investigation backfired when a Kuomintang legislator was discovered to be involved. The Kuomintang then had the Bureau of Investigation agents reassigned, but the prosecutor leaked the information to a newspaper and the agents were returned to the parks case. By 1993, democratization had already brought some limits to Kuomintang manipulation of the judicial system.

Conclusion

In the 1993 election, the Kuomintang candidate defeated the DPP candidate, a highly praised incumbent, winning 51.3 percent of the vote. Vote buying worked. This study has suggested that five elements were crucial to this success: an excellent campaign manager, a generous budget, a sufficient number of trustworthy brokers, and a system to supervise them and avoid duplication of effort, and protection from a compliant judicial system. How generalizable are these findings?

Several factors make the campaign under study distinctive. First, the Kuomintang party committed disproportionate energy to this campaign, hoping to dislodge an incumbent from the opposition party. Most races in Taiwan at the time did not attract this much attention or resources. Second, the political system in Taiwan was undergoing significant changes, becoming more democratic. As a result, the vote buying system in 1993 may not be representative of vote buying systems before or since (on the transformation of electoral clientelism in Taiwan, see Wang 2004). Third, the political system in Taiwan is hardly representative of political systems around the world. Alternatives can be found for almost every element of the Kuomintang vote buying operation.

How Many Brokers Does a Vote Buying Campaign Need?

In Taiwan in the case under study, a large number of brokers each purchased a small number of votes. As a result, the campaign manager had to recruit an extensive broker organization, which necessitated a detailed knowledge of the social and political personalities in the district. In some other countries, by contrast, a small number of brokers each purchase a large number of votes (Gay 1994, 1999, on Brazil; Landé 1965, 132, on the Philippines; Schmidt 1977, 305–306, on Colombia; Valenzuela 1977, 80–83, on Chile). In Brazil, for example, the leader of a poor *favela* (shantytown) neighborhood buys the entire community's votes, apparently without intermediaries (Gay 1994, 102).

Does the Vote Buying Campaign Rely on Preexisting Social Networks?

According to Fabrice Lehoucq (Chapter 3) and Susan Stokes (2005), dense social networks can be used by parties and politicians to overcome informational barriers to vote buying by finding out which voters would be amenable to selling their votes, and likely to follow through. In Taiwan in 1993, the Kuomintang organized its campaign wherever possible through preexisting "factions," but where these were not available, it built its own broker organization from scratch. In some other countries, it seems, campaigns rely exclusively on preexisting family networks as "gatekeepers" of the community, piggybacking on existing patronage structures within the community (Auyero 2000; Caciagli and Belloni 1981, 40–41; Knoke 1990, 144–146; Powell 1970, 413; Silverman 1977). Where this is the case, the campaign need only mobilize relationships of trust at the top of the hierarchy, leaving the lower-level brokers to be mobilized by patronage leaders.

Are Brokers Local Residents?

In Taiwan, yes. In Thailand, yes (Callahan and McCargo 1996, 383). In Mexico, not necessarily. In the latter country, in addition to brokers who are local residents, the longtime ruling party organizes brigades of *mapaches,* young people brought in from outside the community to visit voters' homes, offer money or construction materials in exchange for votes, transport voters to the polls on election day, and on occasion engage in ballot box fraud or coercion (Hernández Carrochano 2003, 1–2). Presumably these brigades' enthusiasm and party ambition outweigh their lack of local knowledge. Their relationship with voters involves a cash/barter nexus rather than neighborly or family trust.

Can Vote Buying Be Coercive?

As noted by Frederic Schaffer and Andreas Schedler in Chapter 2, vote buying is often accompanied by coercion. However, in Taiwan in 1993, coercion played a very limited role in the Kuomintang campaign, though the Kuomintang would sometimes purge local factions by legal means (Wu 1987, 324–327). In some other countries, however, coercion is either common or commonly feared. A comparison of broker organizations in Taiwan and Mexico, for example, found that the use of coercion and other negative sanctions was far more frequent in the latter (Rigger 1999a). Indeed, scholars speak of a "fear vote" in Mexico that involves reprisals by the ruling party for supporting the opposition (Fox and Hernández 1995, 30; see also Cornelius 2004). In these situations, trust may be less important than fear.

Is Vote Buying Expensive?

In Taiwan in 1993, the amount paid per vote was low, compared with voters' annual income, but the campaign bought so many votes that the budget had to be considerable. Elsewhere, even lesser amounts may be paid to voters. In the Philippines in 1998, for example, the going rate was 100 Philippine pesos (less than US$3) (Tordesillas 1998, 77; for further information, see Chapter 1 of this volume). In addition, some campaigns may keep costs down by targeting their vote buying efforts at swing voters, rather than wasting resources on ideologically or otherwise committed voters.

Are Brokers Independent Agents?

In Taiwan in 1993, relatively few brokers were staff employees of the Kuomintang, and many worked on occasion for non-Kuomintang candidates. In some other countries, this level of autonomy would be unthinkable: brokers are party employees, and disloyalty to the party is frowned upon, even punished. In a comparison of brokers in Mexico and Venezuela, for example, Michael Coppedge (1993) found that single-party dominance in Mexico (in the early 1990s) forced local political agents to ally with the ruling party, while the failure of single-party dominance in Venezuela allowed choice among multiple clientelistic hierarchies.

Are Opposition Parties Allowed to Compete?

As noted by Allen Hicken in Chapter 4, the degree of electoral competitiveness may affect candidates' incentives to mobilize personal strategies, including vote buying. In Taiwan in 1993, the Kuomintang tried to disrupt DPP campaigns in shady ways, such as opening Bureau of Investigation cases, but did not often cross the line into systematic repression of the opposition. Moreover, the Kuomintang allowed votes to be counted fairly: its vote buying efforts were not combined with other forms of fraud, such as ballot stuffing, stealing, or miscounting. In some other countries, ruling parties are not so restrained. Those in power have resorted to a host of strategies for electoral manipulation, including reserving positions, reserving domains, excluding opposition forces, fragmenting opposition forces, repression, unfairness, formal and informal disfranchisement, coercion, corruption, electoral fraud, institutional bias, tutelage, and reversal of electoral results (Schedler 2002a).

Are Votes Anonymous?

Campaigns that cannot monitor the behavior of voters are less likely to buy votes, since they cannot ensure that their money will be well spent, as Lehoucq notes in Chapter 3. In Taiwan in 1993, voters could count on their votes being anonymous, at least at the individual level (as elsewhere, precinct-level results were publicly available). Therefore the brokers used social relations to overcome the uncertainty over whether voters would deliver the votes they had sold. The system was imperfect—a considerable portion of the electorate failed to vote for the Kuomintang after selling their votes to the party (Wang and Kurzman, forthcoming)—but the vote buying effort anticipated this and planned accordingly. Over the course of the twentieth century, almost all countries adopted the Australian ballot, which lists multiple candidates on a single card and therefore allows for a discreet selection, as opposed to earlier systems that required the voter to select one party's card (Fredman 1968; Markoff 1999, 674–677). With secret ballots, the price of a vote plummeted in some countries, since the purchasers could no longer be certain that they were receiving the services they paid for (Schaffer 2002b, 79).

Even with the Australian ballot, however, voters in some countries are not always certain that their individual vote will be secret if election personnel are ruling-party members (on ruling-party management of elections, see Lehoucq 2002). Indeed, election observers in Mexico found that 39 percent of polling stations in 1994 violated the secrecy of the ballot in one way or another (Lehoucq 2003, 248). Or the ruling party may be endowed with near-magical powers of surveillance that make individual votes known, as in Chiapas, Mexico, during the 2000 elections, when voters worried that the ruling party had a satellite watching the ballot box or that ballots could be linked to them by fingerprints (Hernández Carrochano 2003, 7).[9]

*   *   *

This list of exceptions suggests that the Taiwanese experience is not the only form that vote buying can take. Still, we propose that our basic findings may be applicable even to quite different vote buying systems. As compared with non–vote buying campaigns, vote buying involves more one-on-

one contact with voters. Regardless of whether this contact is made by a large or small number of brokers, from within or outside the party, and with or without coercion, vote buying campaigns need to build or tap into a system for reaching voters discreetly. They need skilled leaders who possess tremendous local knowledge, sufficient resources to make the vote buying worthwhile, and sufficient trust to minimize mishaps. They need protection from judicial systems. Vote buying campaigns, in short, may not be so different from other criminal enterprises: they make up for their legal vulnerabilities by ensconcing themselves in local networks of protection, and they administer resources to motivate these networks to protect them. This picture suggests that vote buying parties, even ruling parties, may not be so powerful as commonly perceived. If the legal apparatus of the state is on guard to prevent and prosecute vote buying, then even a ruling party such as the Kuomintang in Taiwan may have to work hard to avoid public scrutiny. As research continues on the subject of vote buying, insider information from a variety of contexts will corroborate or disconfirm these hypotheses.

Notes

1. Kuomintang candidates were not the only ones who bought votes; many other candidates did so as well, though usually on a smaller scale.
2. Factions are local sociopolitical organizations that the Kuomintang allied itself with to mobilize voters, beginning in the 1950s (Bosco 1992, 1994). The party rewarded local factions with various privileges, such as regional charters for banking, credit, and transport; advantage in government loans, procurement, contracts, and zoning; and protection of illegal business activities (Chen and Chu 1992; Chu 1989, 148–152). In return, local factions helped the party rule areas that it found difficult to penetrate. From 1954 to 1994, 61.9 percent of the party's nominees for Taiwan's provincial assembly had a local faction background, and 92.6 percent of those candidates were elected (Lin 1998, 164). In addition, the party controlled local factions through a variety of coercive, though almost always nonviolent, mechanisms (Wu 1987).
3. On the role of campaign managers in vote buying in other contexts, see Tordesillas 1998 on the Philippines, and Callahan and McCargo 1996 on Thailand.
4. In Township 17, two local dignitaries donated their own money to increase the payment to 500 Taiwanese dollars per vote (Interviewee 17).
5. For a similar point about vote buying brokers in Thailand, see Callahan and McCargo 1996, 382–383, 386.
6. The minutes are internal documents of the campaign committee in Township 20.
7. In Thailand, one interviewee in William Callahan's study (2002, 11) said that canvassers used "a more subtle direct sales method to buy votes from relatives and close friends who were unlikely to turn them into the ECT (Election Commission of Thailand)."
8. This tactic is also used in the Philippines (Tirol 1992).
9. Voting-booth secrecy can also be exploited for vote buying purposes. In the Philippines, for example, voters who had been bought would take a completed ballot

into the booth and turn it in as their own, and then take the blank ballot that they had been issued back out with them to give to the broker to fill in for the next voter (Hofileña 2001, 19; Tordesillas 1998, 77). Kuwaiti election officials countered this strategy with ballot booths that concealed voters' hands but not their arms and body, so as to make switching ballots visible (Tétreault 2000, 124–125).

Part 2

How Does Vote Buying Shape Politics and the Economy?

6

Is Vote Buying Undemocratic?

Susan C. Stokes

Most of us have a gut instinct that vote buying is undemocratic. Whether he is an early-nineteenth-century English gentleman-candidate "feasting" local constituents, or a late-twentieth-century Institutional Revolutionary Party operative in Mexico regaling voters with everything from tortillas to washing machines, the figure of the politician trying to buy the support of individual voters strikes us as violating democracy in profound and harmful ways. Yet, surprisingly, few have attempted to explain why.[1] We lack a full explanation of why this is many people's intuition, and more crucially, whether the intuition holds up on deeper reflection. This chapter is too brief to do more than suggest answers to these questions. Furthermore, whether vote buying is undemocratic depends on one's empirical model of vote buying: one's account of why it can be a useful strategy for politicians, and why voters acquiesce to sell their votes. We are far from a consensus on an empirical model. Instead I briefly sketch one empirical model of vote buying, and then explain why, if this is a good model, vote buying is indeed undemocratic.[2] The answer concerns the introduction of social and economic inequalities into the realm of politics. Vote buying allows politicians and governments to ignore the interests of poor people, and it can undermine the autonomy of vote sellers.

A Model of Vote Buying

I take it as axiomatic that the value people derive from consuming something depends (among other things) on how wealthy they are. A poor person who finds a dollar on the street will be made happier by finding it than will a wealthy person; we experience diminishing marginal utility of income. Consider a society in which people's incomes are unequal, and imagine that we can locate everyone in that society on a dimension of income, from the

81

poorest to the richest. Assume that a political party can secure a person's vote by giving her something that she values sufficiently highly. It follows that the same outlay of resources by the party will buy more votes among poor than among wealthy voters.[3] A party that wants to win enough votes to get elected at the lowest possible cost would start by giving the poorest person something, then the next poorest, and so on until the party has purchased just enough votes to win. Vote buying starts at the bottom, not the top, of the income distribution (see Dixit and Londregan 1996). And as the party moves up the income distribution, each next voter's support has to be purchased at a higher price.[4]

Now let's assume that if our party started with the poorest voter and bought votes one by one until its money gave out, it would run out of money before it got to the voter whose support would put it over the top. There is another strategy that will allow it to add the votes of some wealthier voters: programmatic mobilization. Programmatic mobilization means promising (and, once in office, delivering) public goods (e.g., national security, clean air), or redistributive goods that go to all members of some abstractly defined category of citizens, regardless of their vote (e.g., all unemployed people get unemployment insurance, all elderly retirees get old-age pensions).

Both vote buying and programmatic mobilization have disadvantages from the perspective of parties thirsting for power. Vote buying, as we have seen, can become prohibitively expensive when extended to wealthier voters. But programmatic mobilization is not a sure thing. Because (by definition) the people who benefit from public goods get these goods whether or not they vote for the party providing them, beneficiaries have weaker incentives to cast their vote for the party. Therefore the parties that provide public goods (or promise them in campaigns) and hope they will generate electoral support are taking a leap of faith. If people made their voting decisions by a strict calculation of costs and benefits (which obviously most do not), programmatic mobilization would be a weak strategy, both for the often observed reason that a person's vote almost never makes a difference in the outcome of the election, and for the less often observed reason that a person reaps the benefits of the party's program whether or not he voted for it.

At first glance, vote buying appears to be an even shakier proposition. If the ballot is secret, and vote sellers therefore can take their payments and vote as they choose, why does vote buying work at all? My answer (Brusco, Nazareno, and Stokes 2004) is that certain kinds of parties—call them "clientelist" parties—can overcome the secret ballot and make fairly accurate inferences about whether people whom they "paid" actually voted for them. Clientelist parties have certain distinguishing structural features.[5] They are bottom-heavy and rely on an army of local-level organizers, people who live in the neighborhoods under their political responsibility, know everyone's name, know who went to the polls and who didn't, and know who was able to look them in the eye the day after the election. Clientelist parties use this fine-grained information—this "tremendous local knowledge" as Chin-Shou Wang and Charles Kurzman put it in Chapter 5 in reference to vote buying in Taiwan—to make inferences about how individuals voted, extending favors to voters for whom they believe these inducements really matter and punishing voters who they think have defected from the implicit clientelist bargain. When asked what happens to neighbors who have received her help but then didn't attend a party event, a Peronist organizer in a working-class neighborhood in Argentina gave the pregnant answer, "We take it into account." She continued, "You have to apply discipline *(poner correctivo),* because otherwise they'll do whatever they want." When asked what happens when she suspects that someone in her political orbit voted for another party, she responded, "He's dead. He died, forever."[6]

Hence we have an asymmetry: the people who exchange their votes for a personal "payment" only benefit from an ongoing flow of goods if they continue to vote for the benefactor-party, whereas everyone gets public goods, whether or not they voted for the party providing them. This asymmetry suggests that, all else being equal, vote buying can be a more powerful inducement to return the favor with a vote than is programmatic mobilization. In the language of probabilities, direct "payment" for a vote increases the probability of compliance with the exchange more than do diffuse "payments" of public and programmatic goods. Faced with a party that gives a voter goods conditional on his (inferred) support and a party that offers programmatic benefits, the voter might well vote for the former. If the latter's program were sufficiently appealing, he would vote for the former and hope that the latter wins.

To draw attention to the contrast between vote buying and mobilization with programmatic goods, I adopt a "probabilistic selective incentives" approach to clientelism or vote buying (Brusco, Nazareno, and Stokes 2004). Mancur Olson (1965) defined selective incentives as goods that could be extended to people who contributed to the provision of a public good and denied to people who didn't contribute. Individualized payments for votes are *probabilistic* selective incentives because, as long as individuals' votes are not fully observable, politicians will inevitably make some mistakes of inference, and sometimes punish people who actually supported them and reward those who didn't.[7] In contrast to Olson's selective incentives, which encourage people to contribute to the provision of public goods, payments for votes as probabilistic selective incentives have the opposite effect, of reducing the incentives for politicians and governments to provide public goods.

Both vote buying and programmatic mobilization entail exchanges; in both, parties can be thought of as paying a price per vote. The basic advantage of vote buying is its more fine-grained targeting of benefits to likely supporters. The basic advantage of programmatic mobilization is its ability to reach large swaths of the electorate. Vote buying thus has advantages of precision and leverage; programmatic mobilization has advantages of scope.

In many political systems, one observes a mix of vote buying and programmatic appeals, not to mention the many other methods of political mobilization (ideological, charismatic, identity-based, etc.). Even individual parties use a mix of strategies. What determines the mix of vote buying and programmatic strategies? To answer this question we must consider the advantages and disadvantages, the costs of benefits, of each, and how these vary as a function of other factors.

The main costs of vote buying are in maintaining a network of party organizers who can help detect who has stuck with the bargain and who may have defected, and the costs of the items actually used to purchase the vote—the cash, the food and drink, the building materials, the articles of clothing, and so on (see Chapter 5). The costs of the programmatic strategy are those of communicating programmatic appeals to voters: maintaining a party press, advertising, and the like. Programmatic parties have to communicate when they are in the opposition and want to win office, as well as when they are incumbents and want to retain office. In the first case they must announce to voters what programs they will provide if elected; in the second, they must give their "spin" on the programs and achievements of their tenure.[8] Programmatic strategies also impose costs on parties of generating or acquiring the knowledge to devise programs. As for the costs of public programs themselves, in some political systems we can assume that these are borne by the public at large. In others, however, where politicians are prone to pocket money from the treasury, expenditures on public goods and programs can cut into the politicians' personal wealth. There may be more subtle political costs, such as the loss of support from some constituents who oppose programs aimed at others; a party that emphasizes old-age pensions may have to pay more or work harder for the votes of young people.

That parties will try to buy the votes of the poor, assuming declining marginal utility of income, suggests that the degree of inequality is central to determining the relative effectiveness of vote buying versus programmatic appeals. All else being equal, we expect that the more unequal the distribution of income, the more prevalent the vote buying. Let's assume that the amount of resources parties and governments have at their disposal with which to buy votes is a direct function of the country's per capita (average) income. In a country with high income inequality, where the gap between those below and those above the average is large, the party will have to pay relatively little to win many (relatively) poor people's votes. In a country where the gap between those below and those above the average is small, the party will have to pay more to win the same number of votes.[9] Generally speaking, the poorer the country, the more unequal its income distribution (Deininger and Squire 1996); because of this, it follows that the poorer the country, the more widespread the vote buying.

Another factor that influences the relative advantages of vote buying and programmatic strategies is party organization. An important dimension of party organization in this regard is the degree of centralization. Allen Hicken, in Chapter 4, notes that decentralized parties promote personalized candidacies, which he links to clientelist appeals. Decentralized, machine-like party organizations also have a greater capacity to efficiently deliver goods in exchange for votes (Dixit and Londregan 1996). Highly decentralized party organizations are crucial for vote buying because organization is what allows parties to monitor voters and punish defectors (see Stokes 2005; see also Chapter 5 of this volume). My guess is that these organizational costs are higher in wealthy countries than in poor ones, relative to the resources that parties command, and that this is one reason why vote buying today is mainly a phenomenon of the developing world. The party operatives and ward heelers who make vote buying work are relatively skilled, savvy people who, as a country develops, find more remunerative outlets for their skills.

These organizational costs are operational or ongoing costs. But there are substantial setup or "sunk" costs as well. Once a party has ingratiated itself into local social networks—indeed, helped create these local networks—there is a certain stability to its presence in a community. A party that is not already involved in local networks would have to make this investment de novo if it were to pursue vote buying. Hence the price of "buying" a vote with personalized handouts will be higher for the party that has not already made such investments. The history of Argentina's Peronist party is instructive in how parties may acquire the capacity to monitor as a by-product of earlier charismatic or class appeals. From the 1940s through the 1970s, the Peronist party derived support from the charisma of Juan and Eva Perón, from its strong backing by labor unions, and from its ideological appeal to the poor and *descamisados,* or "shirtless ones." Early Peronism's working-class orientation helped it create strong loyalties and strong networks in working-class communities. After the death of its charismatic leaders and after its 1990s programmatic reorientation toward neoliberalism, the party stanched a potential outflow of working-class support by shifting toward clientelism (Levitsky 2003). In doing so it relied heavily on social networks inherited from the earlier era. Without this inheritance, the cost of a shift to vote buying would have been much more substantial.

We have seen that mass communications are a major cost for programmatic parties. The lower the costs of broadcasting one's program and accomplishments, all else being equal, the more attractive the programmatic versus the vote buying strategy. The costs of mass communications fall as countries modernize: one has only to think of the Anatolian Chief in Daniel Lerner's parable of modernization (1958), forced to bring one product of modernity, a radio, into his home. Higher education tends to become more widespread as countries develop, hence reducing the knowledge-costs associated with programmatic mobilization.

I have suggested that there are economies of scale in the provision of public goods. A government that invests in reducing air pollution may have to spend a lot, materially and politically, to provide this good, but the number of beneficiaries is vast, and the cost small, on a per-head basis (this is the flip side of the disadvantage, mentioned earlier, that a party or government can't exclude nonsupporters from access to public goods). In contrast, the amount that a party must spend on buying votes increases as the number of constituents increases (assuming, as I am, that there are no economies of scale so that the average price of the vote does not fall). Hence (as usual, all else being equal), vote buying will decline, and programmatic mobilization will increase, as constituency size grows.[10] Constituencies can grow with population growth, or with extensions of the franchise, or with changes in districting.

Gary Cox has made just this point regarding nineteenth-century Britain, where subsequent reform bills eliminated small rotten boroughs and folded their constituents into larger districts, and where the expansion of the franchise enlarged many constituencies. These changes led members of parliament to shift from "bribery and influence" to a focus on national issues. Cox writes: "The reason for the lesser reliance on bribery and influence in the larger boroughs seems to be that these electoral strategies were simply less effective there—at least relative to the strategy of taking stands on matters of national policy. Certainly a fixed amount of money would buy a smaller proportion of the total votes in larger towns if the average price of votes was not less" (1987, 57).

As an "all else being equal" proposition, the idea that vote buying decreases as constituency size grows is sound. Yet we know from many studies that parties try to buy votes even when the constituency is enormous, as in presidential elections. To explain why vote buying is not just a phenomenon of local elections in small towns, or of elections of representatives to national bodies from small constituencies (e.g., the member of parliament from the tiny rotten borough), one must bear in mind the greater potential for a party to nail down a vote, as it were, with a payoff (a selective incentive) than with a program (a public good). Assuming some secrecy of the vote (an inappropriate assumption in Britain, as Cox notes, until after 1872), what parties buy is not votes but *expected* votes. Because of uncertainty that either strategy will work, it takes greater outlays to buy one expected vote than it would to buy a vote if there were no uncertainty. If the money spent on a programmatic benefit would buy fewer expected votes than would vote buying, the party will favor the latter strategy. In effect, uncertainty of results can raise the average price per vote of programmatic mobilization.

The effect of *constituency* size on the relative costs and effectiveness of vote buying and programmatic mobilization should not be confused with the effect of the *population* size of the community in which the voter lives. In general, parties can monitor votes more easily in small communities than in large ones, whether they are trying to monitor votes for the national president or for the local dogcatcher. This is because social relations in small communities are multifaceted: one's dentist is also one's brother-in-law and fellow church member and neighbor. Multifaceted social relations make it easier for party operatives to keep track of who went to the polls and who didn't, in the company of whom, and to use disaggregated election returns to sort out likely cooperators from likely defectors. In Argentina, whether a voter is wealthy or poor, sympathizes with Peronists, with Radicals, or with some other party or with no party, whether male or female, young or old, my research turns up robust evidence that the smaller the population size of the municipality in which the voter lives, the more likely she is to accept minor handouts during election campaigns and to acknowledge that these handouts influenced her vote (Brusco, Nazareno, and Stokes 2004).

My frequent use of the "all else being equal" formula in this discussion is meant to underscore that, in order to understand the mix of strategies that parties deploy in any given setting, one would have to bring all relevant factors simultaneously into play. To illustrate, in the United States today, an incumbent president may spend US$200 million trying to get himself reelected. Even if vote buying were not illegal in the United States, it's hard to imagine him deploying these resources principally toward vote buying. Subtracting the costs of maintaining the kind of organization that would be required to monitor voters, if he were to divide the remainder into cash payments for the 60 million or so voters whose support he needs, the amounts would be tiny and probably few voters would be swayed. Deploying a large portion of these funds to air major-market television advertisements is much more effective. Here we have four factors converging to make vote buying unlikely: the wealth of the population, its large size, the large size of the constituency, and the ready availability of technologies of mass communication.

No discussion of the relative costs and effectiveness of vote buying versus programmatic mobilization would be complete without mention of electoral technologies, which shape *how* people cast votes. All technological features that affect the transparency of the vote affect the effectiveness of vote buying. One can think of secrecy as a continuum, from voice voting, where a person's vote is perfectly transparent,[11] to voting in a big anonymous city with a voting machine. There are many gradations in between:

people can have the ballot but be forced to cast it at an open table, within the range of vision of party operatives; ballots can be distinguishable by color or by the weight of the paper; and numeric codes can allow a ballot to be traced to the individuals who cast it. Countries can have the secret ballot but not the Australian ballot: one produced by public authorities at public expense, distributed through carefully controlled channels on or soon before election day, and in which all candidates for a given office are listed simultaneously. Instead they may use party-issued ballots. In three Latin American countries today, Argentina, Panama, and Uruguay, people still vote with ballots that are issued by political parties. In Colombia until 1991, one could *only* vote with ballots issued and distributed by political parties. In Argentina, one can acquire a ballot from a party operative in the weeks leading up to the election, or one can acquire it inside the voting booth. The poorer an Argentine voter, the more likely she is to vote with a ballot given to her by a party operative. And whatever her income, a person who votes with a party-distributed ballot is more likely to have received some other handout during the campaign, and more likely than people who received handouts but not ballots to say that the handout influenced her vote. My explanation is that when clientelist parties distribute ballots and handouts simultaneously, they send the message that if people expect handouts in the future, they had better vote for the party (Brusco, Nazareno, and Stokes 2004).

If the parties' strategists have studied economics, they deploy their resources toward each strategy to the point where an additional dollar (or peso, yen, etc.) buys it the same (expected) number of votes as that same additional dollar would buy using the other strategy. If their studies are in the realm of applied politics, they are more likely to use rules-of-thumb that roughly approximate this calculation.[12]

I have sketched a model in which parties buy votes as part of an overall strategy to win elections. They pay for poor people's votes before attempting to buy the votes of wealthier people; they can pay poor voters a relatively modest price, whereas they would have to pay wealthier voters more. The proportions of the electorate whose votes parties attempt to buy with personal payments, or to solicit with programs, depend on levels of economic development and inequality, on organizational capacities to monitor the vote, on the availability of mass communications, on constituency size and population size, and on the technologies of voting.

The probabilistic selective incentives model is not the only conceivable one of vote buying. Another model involves a "norms of reciprocity" approach (Brusco, Nazareno, and Stokes 2004). The fundamental difference between this approach and the probabilistic selective incentives approach is that under norms of reciprocity, in the absence of enforceable contracts, vote buying parties rely on people's feelings of obligation to return the favor with their vote, rather than, as in the probabilistic selective incentives approach, relying on people's fears that, were they to defect, the party operative would withhold valuable payments in the future (see also Chapters 2 and 5). In settings where norms of reciprocity generate compliance with the clientelist bargain, we would expect organization to be somewhat less important for parties that buy votes. They still need organizations through which to channel gifts, but they don't need them to monitor voters' choices; the norm of reciprocity makes their compliance spontaneous. In another way, the probabilistic selective incentives and norms of reciprocity models are quite similar. Presumably, the power of the gift to induce the recipient to reciprocate with her vote is greater the more the recipient values the gift, and by the logic of diminishing marginal utility of income, gifts have more force among the poor. Hence the norms of reciprocity model, like probabilistic selective incentives, predicts that parties will buy the votes of the poor before trying to buy those of the wealthy.

A more distinctive model involves the "high discount rate" approach. It relies centrally on two ideas. The first is that vote buying is effective among voters who discount programmatic promises at an especially high rate. They may heavily discount programmatic promises if their circumstances lead them to prefer a less valuable reward now over a more valuable reward later. Even if a person would be willing to wait for a valuable reward, she will still prefer the lesser but certain immediate payoff if skeptical that the future reward will actually materialize. The second central idea is that poor people are most likely both to employ high discount rates and to be uncertain about future promised benefits (see Scott 1969; Kitschelt 2000).

Social scientists are only beginning to build causal models of vote buying and clientelism, let alone test these models against one another empirically. In my research in Argentina, the probabilistic selective incentives model better explained survey data than did either the norms of reciprocity model or the high discount rate model (Brusco, Nazareno, and Stokes 2004; Stokes 2005).

The Implications of Models of Vote Buying for Democracy

To begin to understand the essential conflict between vote buying and democracy, we must focus on the centrality of equality to democracy, both in theory and in practice. This is not to say that democratic theorists generally believe that, for a political system to be a democracy, its members must be on an equal economic footing. No contemporary treatment of democracy that I know of insists that democracy does not exist, in a definitional sense, if people within it have unequal incomes or assets or even opportunities (although some would say that economic inequalities can have *consequences* that are harmful to democracy; indeed, that is the direction in which this chapter is headed). Democratic theorists, instead, insist that citizens in a democracy have, or ought to have, political rights and political opportunities in common and in equal proportion. Robert Dahl (1971, 1987) contends that in democracies, nearly all citizens ought to have the right to vote and to have their votes counted equally, independent of who casts them. This right flows from what he calls the "Principle of Equal Consideration of Interests": "during processes of collective decision-making, the interests of every person who is subject to the decision must (within the limits of feasibility) be accurately interpreted and made known" (1987, 86).

Under vote buying under the probabilistic selective incentives approach, the right to vote is equally shared, and no one's vote is given more weight than anyone else's in deciding which candidate or party wins. But in a crucial sense, vote buying violates Dahl's equal consideration principle.

Vote sellers' votes carry little information about their interests. Hence their interests are not made known and cannot be accurately interpreted. How big should the state be? What are the appropriate dimensions of income transfers, and how should they be carried out? Should abortion be legal? Should we go to war? Did the current incumbent do a good job? The votes of vote sellers contain no information about their views on these matters. Their interests and preferences do not help shape policy mandates. Nor are their views included in collective assessments of how an incumbent has performed. A person whose vote is purchased for an individualized payment is, for all practical purposes, lost to the process of collective deliberation, mandate making, and retrospective evaluations of governments.

The violation of democratic equality is exacerbated by the fact that it is not people at random whose voices will not be heard by politicians on matters of collective concern. Not random members of the polity but *poor* members of the polity will tend to have their voices muted. The essence of the violation of democracy represented by vote buying can hence be summarized thus: because of their material poverty, a subset of the citizenry is deprived of effective participation in collective decisions to which they will be subject. In what follows, I show that the violation holds whether one thinks of elections as prospective affairs that generate mandates for policies, or as retrospective affairs that generate collective judgments of incumbents' performance. Whether elections create mandates or offer retrospective judgments (or some mix of the two), vote buying under the probabilistic selective incentives approach reduces the power of elections to induce responsiveness in politicians.

Vote Buying and Mandate Making

One way to think about elections is that candidates in campaigns make policy pronouncements, people vote for the candidate whose policy pronouncements they like best, and the candidate with the most popular policy pronouncements wins. The winner then carries out the promised policies. This mandate interpretation of elections is in the tradition of Anthony Downs (1957). Downs showed that, under certain conditions, the policy that the winner pursues is the one preferred by the median voter. These conditions turned out to be very restrictive indeed.[13] Yet unless one believes that policymaking is chaotic, it is fair to say that generations of revisions to Downs leave more or less intact the insight that policymakers will often feel a strong tug toward the middle of the distribution of what voters prefer.

With the spatial model in mind, a highly stylized example gives a sense of the distorting effect of vote buying. Assume that people's preferred level of public services, and hence of taxation, depends on their incomes. Poor people prefer higher taxes and more services, wealthy people prefer lower taxes and fewer services. The preferred tax level of the median voter is, say, 30 percent of the gross domestic product (GDP). But vote buying effectively lops off a large bottom portion of the income distribution in the electorate. The preferred tax level of the median voter among the remaining voters, those who vote for the party with the best tax policy, is, say, 15 percent. A vote buying party that wins by handing out goodies to the poor and appealing to the others with a popular tax policy wins with a mandate to set taxes at 15 percent of GDP.

Someone might object that mandates are, for several reasons, elusive. Voters often don't know the policy positions that candidates adopt, in part because candidates are often deliberately vague (but see Alvarez 1997). There are too many dimensions to politics to know what a person's vote means—did he vote for the candidate because he wanted lower taxes, or because he favored gun control, or because he's a Catholic? And if politics is multidimensional, then even if the public's mood on each issue could be discerned from its vote, politicians can make policies cycle and remain basically unconstrained by the preferences of the median voter on any dimension (McKelvey 1976).

I have laid out elsewhere why I believe that mandates are meaningful in democracies, despite these objections (Stokes 2001). But even if mandates are weak, hard to define, and prone to being subverted by issue cycling, it's not hard to see that muffling the voice of a segment of the electorate by buying their votes just makes mandates weaker. For example, one could contend with some justification that the lower the voter turnout, the less clear the mandate that an election produces: the new leadership has effectively heard from only a portion of the electorate. Something very similar is true when vote buying (under the probabilistic selective incentives approach) is widespread: although turnout may be very high, the significance of the policy message the new leadership receives is reduced by the failure of vote sellers to contribute with their votes to this message.

Vote Buying and Retrospective Judgments

Another way of looking at elections is that they give voters an opportunity
to make a consequential statement about the performance of incumbents. In
this interpretation, a government is elected and serves its term. Voters set a
threshold of performance and, at the end of the term, if the government has
reached this threshold, they vote to reelect; if not, they vote for the opposition. A long line of democratic theorists, normative and empirical, from
James Madison (Madison, Hamilton, and Jay 2000 [1788]) to David
Mayhew (1974) to Morris Fiorina (1981) to Bernard Manin (1997), contend
that these retrospective judgments do more than satisfy an urge to get back
at politicians, and in fact make governments function better. Politicians'
"anticipation of the future retrospective judgment of voters," in Manin's
phrase, induces them to perform responsively during their term.

The retrospective or accountability interpretation of elections is not
without difficulties. Given the many dimensions on which people can judge
an incumbent's performance, it is also subject to a cycling problem, and
John Ferejohn (1986) shows that voters need to adopt a common yardstick
for their evaluation (e.g., they should pay attention to the GDP growth rate
and not their own incomes). Term limits tend to interfere with people's
efforts to hold politicians accountable, especially in settings where political
parties are weak: if the incumbent can't run and his party won't punish him
for bad performance, voters can't hold him accountable (see Cleary 2003;
Carey 1996). Mandate and accountability mechanisms can interfere with
one another. A voter who uses both prospective (mandate) and retrospective
(accountability) mechanisms will sometimes find himself voting to reelect a
bad incumbent or voting for an unappealing opponent (see Fearon 1999).
Still, positive political theory, not to mention the intuition of most voters,
does not disconfirm the idea that past performance is one element that
explains how people vote, and that when voters can cast consequential retrospective judgments they are better able to induce their political leaders to
be responsive.

Because holding incumbents accountable is itself a public good, vote
buying vitiates elections as moments of retrospective judgment. People who
vote for a party because they believe they are in danger of losing particularistic benefits will not be inclined to use their ballots to cast retrospective
judgment on the government's performance. Hence one problem with vote
buying under the probabilistic selective incentives approach is that, with the
future choices of a subset of the electorate captured by minor inducements,
the instrument of accountability is wielded by fewer voters and is propor-
tionally weakened.

Vote buying violates Dahl's equal consideration principle in elections
in which people hold governments accountable, just as it does in elections

in which people give mandates. The assessed quality of a government's performance frequently depends on one's interests and preferences. Vote buying truncates the range of economic interests that shape the retrospective judgments of incumbents, quieting the voices of those judges among the citizenry who are poor.

Thus we have seen that, whether we think of elections as sending mandates or as holding politicians accountable, vote buying deprives a subset of the citizenry of having their interests "accurately interpreted and made known." We have also seen that vote buying reduces the effectiveness of elections as an instrument of responsiveness.

Vote Buying and Efficiency

One might be tempted to think that the disadvantage of depriving people of having their interests interpreted and made known is balanced by some efficiency gains. Vote buying is indeed efficient for politicians. It allows them to more efficiently allocate their resources as they compete for office. There may be good reasons to want to reduce the amount of money and other resources politicians expend gaining office, but when one considers the inefficiencies that vote buying imposes on some citizens and on societies at large (not to mention the other problems laid out earlier), one may conclude that there must be better ways to reduce these expenditures. What are the inefficiencies? First, for the vote sellers. Even under the probabilistic selective incentives model, they are selling their votes because, in a narrow sense, doing so yields greater value to them than they would get from conditioning their votes on programs or government performance. But notice that they may sell their votes to one party, hoping that another party wins.[14] An unemployed woman who lives in a country with no unemployment insurance might sell her vote for a bag of food and hope that a different party, one that promises to deliver unemployment insurance, wins. Furthermore, against the narrow sense in which vote sellers benefit, one must weigh the loss of consideration of the interests of this voter and of the class of others who are likely to have similar interests. Vote buying, for reasons I have explained, tends to have the effect of lopping off the lower end of the income distribution from effective exercise of citizenship, thus skewing public policy in a direction that hurts vote sellers. Selling their votes for minor payoffs is in their interests only in a second-best sense. The first-best outcome for vote sellers would be to force parties to compete with programs and performance.

The last source of inefficiency that vote buying under the probabilistic selective incentives approach imposes is that it can contribute to the undersupply of public goods. Consider a setting in which a party wins every election by buying 51 percent of the votes with personal payments. The government has no (electoral) incentive whatsoever to pursue national defense or clean air or transportation infrastructure. All it needs to do is have enough in its coffers to pay off half of the electorate at the next election.

The Normative Implications of Alternative Models of Vote Buying

Norms of Reciprocity

I alluded earlier to an alternative approach to vote buying, where not the fear of losing particularistic benefits but the desire to reciprocate drives sellers to return the favor with a vote. Just as in the case of vote buying driven by probabilistic selective incentives, vote buying driven by norms of reciprocity deprives citizens of having their interests interpreted and made known. This model may appear less coercive because the voters' behavior is driven not by fear of retribution but by a norm, and one that seems to enhance social cooperation. Yet if parties use and promote this norm as a way of encouraging voters to support them even though withholding that support might be in their interest, the norm itself appears fairly coercive. And social psychologists have shown that people feel obliged to reciprocate even when favors are unsolicited and unwanted (Regan 1971; Cialdini 1984).

High Discount Rates

In another alternative model, poor voters prefer smaller rewards now over larger ones later, either because they discount future consumption heavily or because future rewards are less certain than ones they can collect now. If voters sell their votes because, with discounting, programmatic benefits are simply of less value to them, does vote buying violate Dahl's equal consideration principle? In a sense, it does not. The vote seller's interest lies in a quick, certain, immediate payoff, and that interest is being accurately interpreted by the party that buys the vote. Yet from a broader vantage point, democracy would be improved by finding other ways of dealing with the conditions that make vote selling appealing. Democracy suffers because the vote seller's interest in an immediate and certain payoff induces her not to weigh in, for example, on which public policies she would prefer were she able to afford the luxury of waiting for them. Even if vote sellers are really revealing their immediate interests, society as a whole suffers from efficiency losses of the kind described previously. It would be better for potential vote sellers to be paid, anonymously and from public monies, the equivalent of the price of their vote, in exchange for their using elections to voice preferences for public policies (see Karlan 1994).

Why Isn't the Use of Programs to Cultivate Constituents Equally Undemocratic?

If politicians use programs to appeal to voters, is vote buying really any less democratic than programmatic politics? To answer this question, first we need a clear rule-of-thumb to distinguish whether a personalized benefit is simply a public program delivered to an individual, or is in fact a "payment" for a vote. To decide, we must answer two questions: Does the benefactor-party choose the recipient *only* because, if given the favor, she is likely to vote for it? Or does the benefactor-party choose the recipient because she falls into some more abstract category? If the answer to the first question is yes and to the second question no, then the party is buying the vote.

Clearly, political parties frequently hijack purported "programs" for the purpose of buying votes. The programmatic justification becomes mere window dressing, and a misleading description of how resources are really distributed. Several studies rigorously document this hijacking, or political manipulation, of public programs. Norbert Schady (2000) shows that the Alberto Fujimori administration in Peru directed antipoverty programs toward communities, not because their poverty made them eligible, but because about half of their voters supported the official party in the previous election (they were, hence, "marginal" districts). Gabriela Pérez Yarahuán (2002), and Alberto Diaz-Cayeros and Beatriz Magaloni (2003), show that the Carlos Salinas administration in Mexico diverted funds from the massive national solidarity program (PRONASOL) to individuals and communities who did not deserve them or deserved them less than did others. Waikeung Tam (2003) shows how the ruling party in Singapore used public housing funds to reward its supporters. It would be naive to think that political manipulation of programmatic resources is a phenomenon only of the developing world. Stephen Ansolabehere and James Snyder (2002) document the political manipulation of public expenditures in the United States, where counties whose electorates favored the state governor's party received disproportionate funds.

These situations allow for an easy answer to the question I posed at the beginning of this section: to the extent that unemployment insurance is redirected to the pockets of employed people, or antipoverty funds to communities that do not best fit the fund's criteria, these cease to be programs and become efforts to buy people's votes.

Here's the tougher question: political parties have constituencies with certain abstractly definable characteristics, and they devise programs aimed at people with these characteristics in order to cultivate electoral support. Labor parties try to increase wages, business-oriented parties to reduce regulation; regional parties attempt to channel resources toward their regions. Do these practices not undermine democracy just as vote buying does?

Vote buying and cultivating categories of constituents with programs are similar but not identical. One difference is that in order to channel programmatic benefits to the kind of people who support a party, its leaders have to justify the programs by enunciating general, universalistic, and public policy–oriented reasons for them. A politician who wants to increase the minimum wage, or one who wants to reduce regulation, can't simply say, "We should do this because it will help me get reelected." He has to appeal to principles of fairness or efficiency or to the good consequences of the proposed programs. He must say things like, "Raising the minimum wage will lead to a fairer distribution of income," or "Reducing regulation will lead to economic growth." These imperatives improve the deliberative quality of democracy and may make actors more other-regarding (see, e.g., Cohen 1998). More relevant here, the beneficiaries of public programs are not trapped into supporting the benefactor-party. Like the vote seller, who is forced to condition his vote narrowly on the prospect of retaining or losing a valued payment, the beneficiary of a public program may well wish to vote for his benefactor. But because ongoing benefits don't ride on his particular vote, he is likely to consider the full range of a party's policies, actions, and performance. In this sense, the deployment of public programs to garner support among particular constituents makes these constituents more autonomous decisionmakers than does vote buying.

*   *   *

The hunch that we started with, then, has held up fairly well: vote buying is undemocratic. It is undemocratic whether voters sell their votes out of a fear of losing minor payoffs, or out of a feeling of obligation to reciprocate, or out of a desire to be sure of securing a desired benefit now. It is undemocratic whether elections are thought of as prospective moments of mandate definition or as retrospective moments of accountability. It is undemocratic in that it keeps vote sellers from having their interests accurately interpreted and made known, and in that it makes them less autonomous than are the recipients of politically motivated public programs. In addition to being undemocratic, it has bad consequences: it skews public policy, creates inefficiencies, and reduces the supply of public goods. In light of these conclusions, the imperative is to search for ways to reduce vote buying in today's developing democracies.

Notes

My research is supported by the National Science Foundation's Political Science Program, SES-0241958, and by a fellowship from the John Simon Guggenheim

Memorial Foundation. I am grateful to Frederic C. Schaffer and Andreas Schedler for their comments.

1. For normative treatments, see Epstein 1985; Karlan 1994; Kochin and Kochin 1998. The question is not whether vote buying is incompatible with a formal, Schumpeterian definition of democracy. Rather the hunch of many, which I flesh out in the final sections of the chapter, is that it conflicts with a richer understanding of democracy, as laid out by theorists such as Robert Dahl. This richer understanding incorporates the basic equality of voters' political rights, including an equal right to express preferences regarding public policies.

2. I do not claim that my model necessarily accounts for vote buying in all settings. It is driven by my own research in Latin America, and by secondary accounts of vote buying in other regions. There are two senses in which my model may not "travel." First, it amounts to a series of "if-then" propositions, and the conditions ("ifs") generating the outcomes ("thens") may not be present in all settings. Second, it is possible that the same conditions will generate different outcomes in different settings, if, for example, some contextual features also need to be present for a particular condition to have the effect I predict.

3. Note that the mechanism I specify here that links vote buying to poverty—the diminishing marginal utility of income—is different than one frequently specified: poor voters' presumed risk aversion and the presumed inherent uncertainty of public goods. In Chapter 7, Scott Desposato, for instance, focuses on the latter mechanism. Ultimately the appropriateness of one or the other mechanism will have to be decided empirically. As an initial proposition, I find the diminishing marginal utility of income the more psychologically tenable one: poor people's life experiences probably train them to be patient and to tolerate a lot of uncertainty.

4. A preponderance of empirical studies associate vote buying with poverty. My own research in Argentina (Brusco, Nazareno, and Stokes 2004) finds that low incomes, low educational achievement, and poor housing quality (as assessed by survey interviewers) all powerfully increase the probability that a person will be the target of vote buying. Yet some studies find contrary evidence. Frederic Schaffer (2004), for example, reports survey evidence suggesting that candidates for office in the Philippines offer money to voters in roughly the same proportions across income groups. Schaffer notes that Filipino parties are weak organizationally; it may be that they lack the level of insertion into social networks to monitor voters, and that therefore vote buying in the Philippines is necessarily less strategically targeted.

5. Strictly speaking, vote buying need not rely on clientelist *parties*. As long as there are grassroots actors who have the capacity to monitor voters and enforce the vote buying contract, they can sell their service to candidates from different parties. "Freelancing" by grassroots monitors has been observed in some settings (see Schaffer 2004). Parties probably prefer "in-house" to freelance monitors, because agency problems arise between candidates and monitors, and because it is less costly for parties to monitor party than freelance operatives. For one thing, party operatives who are imbued with loyalty to the party and zeal for its ideology and program are less likely to shirk; for another, parties can offer their grassroots operatives promotion within the party in return for efficient monitoring, whereas freelancers might be indifferent to such incentives.

6. Interview with "Ana," a pseudonymous Peronist organizer in the city of Córdoba, conducted in January 2003 by Valeria Brusco, Marcelo Nazareno, and Susan Stokes. My translation.

7. The number of type I and type II errors grows as parties move away from individual and toward collective payoffs and punishments. In 1985, in response to

electoral advances by the opposition, the national development minister from Singapore's ruling People's Action Party (PAP) explained that districts that had supported the PAP would benefit from public housing upgrades, whereas districts that had voted for the opposition would not. "This is a very practical political decision. . . . I make no apologies for it. As a PAP government, we must look after PAP constituencies first because the majority of people supported us." When an opposition member of parliament pointed out the unfairness of the policy to PAP supporters in opposition-majority constituencies, the minister replied, "It's regrettable, but it can't be helped" (cited in Tam 2003, 14).

8. My assumption here is that what a government has done is not self-evident to voters; if it were, incumbents would not have to invest in communicating their achievements. This is true if voters are "rationally ignorant" of the details of governments' actions: it may not be worth it to them to make the substantial investment in acquiring information that it would take to know this in detail (see Stigler 1975). Or they may not be able to handle the information cognitively, or just not care.

9. A simple numeric example: Country A has three inhabitants, whose incomes are 1, 5, and 12. Country B has three inhabitants, whose incomes are 5, 6, and 7. Although inequality is greater in A than in B, the two have the same total (18) and hence average (6) incomes. Assume that a party has, as the total amount it can spend on buying votes, one-third of the average income, or 2, and that to win a person's vote, the party's payment has to increase the voter's income by at least 20 percent. In Country A, the party gives one unit of income to 1 and one unit of income to 5, thus increasing their incomes by 100 percent and 20 percent respectively. It wins both of their votes and the election. In Country B, the party gives one unit of income to 5, the poorest voter, increasing her income by 20 percent and winning her vote. It gives the remaining one unit of income to 6, and increases his income by about 17 percent, failing to win his vote. Vote buying succeeds in the more unequal country, but fails in the more equal country.

10. Of course, all else may not be equal. In Chapter 3, Fabrice Lehoucq proposes that, in nineteenth-century Britain, candidates turned to vote buying when they could not use their prestige or influence to capture votes, and that prestige and influence were more effective in small constituencies. Hence his proposition that the smaller the constituency, the less the vote buying.

11. Even with voice voting, a party that wants to monitor individuals' votes so that it can influence them with inducements needs organizational capacity to keep track of who voted how.

12. All of this treats parties as unified actors. But in many settings the mix of program and vote buying seems in part driven by struggles within parties. Local organizers control the information needed to monitor voters and to channel payments appropriately; to the extent that their party relies on vote buying, their position is enhanced. Turning to party leaders, as long as their ability to win office is not compromised, they prefer more centralized organizational structures, direct communication with voters unmediated by local bosses and operatives, and programs that make use of the intellectual talents that abound at the apex and are less prevalent at the grassroots. Hence, for example, when mass communications become cheaper, party leaders may jump at the opportunity to shift from vote buying to programmatic appeals.

13. The list is familiar: voters' policy preferences must be single-peaked; if there is more than one policy dimension, then voters' preferences must be symmetrical; and spatial models only make sense if voters can be arrayed, according to their preferences, along a continuous dimension. The last condition is violated, for exam-

ple, if issues have "valence"—everyone wants them (prosperity) or everyone doesn't want them (corruption; see Stokes 1966); or if issues have "sides"—everyone knows which side of an issue they're on but not where they are on a dimension (see Rabinowitz and McDonald 1989).

14. For an even starker example, see Kochin and Kochin 1998.

7

How Does Vote Buying
Shape the Legislative Arena?

Scott W. Desposato

There is widespread agreement that vote buying reduces the quality of democracy. Central to democracy is the participation and influence of voters in making collective decisions and solving collective problems. Citizens participate in collective decisionmaking by voting for candidates that share their opinions on the great questions of the day, be they taxation, security, or the environment. Politicians respond to voters knowing that they will be judged in subsequent elections by the quality of policy delivered. But as we see in Chapter 6, vote buying at its worst eliminates both participation and influence. Voters do not participate in public decisionmaking, instead trading their votes for private gains. Politicians have no incentives to deliver desired and high-quality programs, because voting decisions are not made on the basis of policy performance.

In this chapter, I examine an understudied but important second-tier effect of vote buying. Specifically, I examine how vote buying can shape the legislative arena. I argue that politicians' behavioral incentives are very different in vote buying compared to programmatic electoral markets. The primary mechanism is that the two kinds of electoral markets make very different demands on ambitious legislators. These demands lead to different kinds of political parties, coalition formation, and interbranch relations.

I demonstrate this relationship by comparing behavior in two legislative systems: one where private goods play a large role in elections, and one where public goods play a much larger role. Specifically, I compare the state legislatures of Piauí and Brasília in Brazil. These make a particularly nice laboratory for exploring such questions. They share identical formal institutions—electoral systems, internal rules, and governmental structures. They also face similar macropolitical and economic environments. But there are distinct societal differences across states, including dramatic differences in the nature of electoral markets. I take the "most different"

101

approach by comparing one of the most modern states, Brasília, with one of the most clientelistic, Piauí.[1]

I begin by presenting a theory of clientelism and legislative behavior, arguing that there are important differences in incentives faced by legislators in clientelistic versus programmatic systems. Subsequently, I introduce the two state assemblies examined in this chapter and review the extent of clientelism—which in Brazil often takes the form of vote buying—in each. I then present evidence to test my theory, and finally discuss the implications of my findings.

Vote Buying, Policy, and Legislative Behavior

My core argument is that the behavioral incentives of elected officials are very different in systems where vote buying is the norm than in systems where elections are determined by policy platforms. Where vote buying determines electoral outcomes, legislators' primary challenge is the immediate delivery of such goods to constituents. Where policy preferences drive voters' decisions, legislators' primary challenges are position-taking and credit-claiming. These differences reflect the different nature of public and private electoral goods, and shape legislative behavior in many areas, including policy participation, legislative oversight, and party formation. I proceed in four steps, characterizing the nature of electoral markets, explaining first voters' then legislators' calculus, and demonstrating the implications for legislative behavior in vote-buying and programmatic electoral markets.

Characterizing Electoral Markets

For the theoretical discussion, I work with an extreme dichotomy of electoral market types: purely vote buying markets, in which votes are exchanged exclusively for private goods, and purely programmatic markets, in which votes are cast in favor of public goods that are only delivered after an election (see Chapter 1).[2] Vote buying exchanges involve trading private goods for votes. Private goods are rival and exclusive—controlled and consumed by individuals. In the political sphere, these typically include cash, baskets of food, and clothing. In some cases, politicians effectively capture government resources and deliver them as if they were private goods. For example, a politician might give a "scholarship" that allows a child to attend a technically free public school.

At the other extreme are programmatic elections, in which politicians promise to provide public goods in exchange for votes. Public goods are nonrival and nonexclusive—one individual's consumption does not preclude another's doing the same, and enjoyment or ownership of the good cannot be restricted.[3] Examples include clean air, lower corruption, and public services available to all.[4]

Note that the theoretical implications and empirical evidence of this chapter are not confined to the two extremes of purely vote buying systems and purely programmatic systems. The theory I present has implications for many shades of clientelism, from cash payments, to the provision of local public goods, to the delivery of purely public goods. Consequently, purely cash-based vote buying is one extreme on a continuum of electoral market types. Similarly, the two cases I examine represent very different, but not idealized, extreme cases of cash vote buying and programmatic voting. However, in one case, private-goods campaigns are common, including vote buying, and in the other case, programmatic politics are much more the norm. For simplicity's sake, however, I will build the theory from the stylized extremes (see Desposato 2001 for more details).

Public- or Private-Goods Elections?

Explaining the existence or absence of vote buying would require a lengthy discussion and is well addressed by other contributors to this volume, but a few comments will help frame the link between electoral markets and legislative behavior. The phenomenon is both demand- and supply-driven. Social structure, particularly poverty and inequality, help drive demand, making private goods an optimal choice for voters. Institutions, resource availability, and other contextual factors influence the extent to which candidates respond to that demand.

At first glance, the exchange of private goods for votes may appear to be a paradoxical choice, since the private goods promised by politicians are usually much less valuable than those promised by programmatic politicians. For example, a candidate might pay US$25 or give a limited supply of a medicine, while a programmatic politician might offer a new public hospital or an income subsidy. Why would anyone choose a small supply of medicine over a new hospital, or a onetime payment of US$25 over a permanent income subsidy?

The answer has to do with timing and uncertainty. Vote buyers make well-defined offers and deliver goods almost immediately. Voters clearly understand the value of a cash payment, basket of food, or new trash can. Further, delivery is prompt. In some cases, candidates deliver payments the day before the election; in others, immediately after a vote is cast; and in still others, shortly after the election results come in. Consequently, voters in private-goods systems often receive payment before the election is over—so they receive benefit even if their candidate isn't elected.

Contrast this with high-value programmatic goods. Their value and delivery are both very uncertain and in no way guaranteed. *If* a candidate is elected, he or she *may* work hard to deliver a new hospital or income subsidy, and eventually, perhaps, a program or reform will be approved, though its final form may vary greatly from a candidate's campaign proposals. For example, a candidate might run on an environmental platform, which could include protecting wetlands from development. The candidate obviously cannot deliver said policy without being elected. Further, with the natural give-and-take of politics, a politician's effort to pass new legislation might be successful, might fail completely, or might result in some minor changes in development policy. The point is that voters have substantial uncertainty about the expected value of programmatic goods being offered and when they will be available.

The implication is that voters who are risk-averse or who heavily discount the future should place a higher relative value on immediate private goods than on long-term and uncertain public goods, than do risk-seeking voters with lower discount rates. Effectively, such voters have higher relative expected utility for private goods delivered immediately than for public goods possibly delivered sometime in the future. Which voters are these? Marginalized and impoverished voters, on average, should have higher utility for immediate private goods than for delayed public goods. This should be confounded for rural voters, whose access to basic public services and political information may be reduced. Such voters have short-term survival needs that lead them to heavily discount the future. They often live in areas that lack the basic public services and infrastructure that assuage short-term survival concerns. They also may lack the information resources or ideological frameworks with which to evaluate the expected value of complicated policy proposals.

In contrast, voters with higher income levels, higher education levels, and greater access to public infrastructure do not discount the future as heavily. Wealthy voters are less impressed by the small payment or basket of food offered by a candidate. Voters with more access to political information may more successfully evaluate the potential benefits of a fight for or against globalization, reducing the uncertainty about expected payoffs. Finally, voters with access to basic social services also have lower discount rates for future goods. Public social services provide a safety net that dramatically reduces the relative appeal of vote buyers.

The implication is not that poor, less-educated, rural voters are "guaranteed" to be vote sellers, or that richer, more-educated, urban voters are "guaranteed" to vote for programmatic policies. Certainly, demand and supply are both powerfully, but not deterministically, shaped by social structure. Inequality, poverty, and underdevelopment all suggest private-goods electoral markets. Development, wealth, and equality facilitate public-goods markets.

But these relationships are not guaranteed. Culture, political mobilization, and local norms could easily change voters' relative valuations of public and private goods. Marginalized voters could have strong cultural values against vote selling, or be highly politicized for many other reasons. Similarly, wealthy, educated voters may be happy to sell votes for small prices.

Finally, some previous work has treated vote sellers as being "inferior" to programmatic voters.[5] My discussion treats all voters equally. If the cash value offered for votes fell low enough, all voters would cast policy-oriented votes. Similarly, if the cash value rose high enough, all voters, rich and poor, would sell their votes. The point is simply that, all else being equal—culture, values, norms, and institutional frameworks—we would expect that poor voters in rural areas should have rational reasons to value private goods more than do wealthy voters in urban areas; this basic point is widely corroborated in previous research. Politicians face a similar calculus when choosing what type of good to provide. The two most important considerations are availability of resources for delivering private goods, and voters' prices. As prices rise or resource availability falls, fewer and fewer candidates will be able to use private-goods strategies, and will instead resort to promises of future public goods. Where prices are very low, candidates might use their own resources, but their preferred strategy is to use state or supporters' resources or programs (Desposato 2001).[6]

Other factors also directly affect the feasibility of private-goods candidacies. A larger electorate makes vote buying less likely, as purchasing enough votes for election becomes excessively expensive (Cox 1987). Similarly, as many vote buying schemes are illegal, the existence of a substantial "clean election" movement may make the risks of punishment for illegal campaigning unacceptable to candidates. Finally, changes in the mechanics of voting that increase the secrecy of the ballot can make voters' promises to support a candidate less credible.[7]

Electoral Markets and Legislators' Incentives

Private-goods and public-goods electoral markets create fundamentally different incentives for ambitious legislators. As stated previously, all politicians have two central challenges: providing desired goods and claiming credit for their efforts. In different kinds of electoral markets, however, the nature of each challenge varies dramatically. In private-goods electoral markets, delivery is the primary challenge; in public-goods electoral markets, credit-claiming is the primary challenge.

This follows directly from the discussion of the nature of electoral markets and voters' preferences. Consider first the case of private-goods electoral markets. An essential characteristic of private electoral goods is their immediacy. Vote-selling citizens heavily discount future benefits; this heavy discount makes the present value of a small cash payment greater than the future value of a beneficial policy program. This makes prompt delivery an essential part of private-goods markets. If delivery of private goods is not guaranteed and immediate, small cash payments lose their advantage over major policy programs.

Consequently, legislators should make obtaining and distributing private goods a top priority. The core implication is that whoever controls these government resources—party, political boss, or executive—will be an extremely important political actor. Negotiation with said actor will be a top priority for legislators seeking goods for their constituents.

In contrast, public goods do not have the same immediate, concrete requirements. Delayed delivery is offset by their higher value. Voters know that the promised balanced budget, lower taxes, and cleaner air may not all come immediately. Governments host multiple veto players, and policy formation is not the result of a single candidate's actions. Vermont's voters know that their socialist representative won't have much short-term effect; Oakland's Green Party assemblywoman was expected to work for change, but not expected to change everything overnight.

The priority for these kinds of politicians is credible policy development efforts. They should work to advance legislation that their constituents support, they should oppose contrarian positions, and they should vocalize positions and engage in debates—knowing that they won't get everything they want.

This leads to the second impact of goods-type on politicians' strategies. The two types of goods pose very different challenges for politicians' efforts to claim credit and reap the rewards of their delivery of promised goods. Credit-claiming is relatively easy in vote buying elections; it is extremely challenging in policy-based elections. The key mechanism is similar to that described above.

In private-goods electoral markets, voters have a clear idea as to whether or not candidates are complying with their promises. In many cases, promises are fulfilled immediately after elections. Evaluation of representatives' performance is thus greatly facilitated. Voters just ask, "Did I get the cash?" "Did I get the t-shirt?" "Did I get the promised medical treatment?" These questions are easy to ask and answer—reward or punishment for politicians follows swiftly at the ballot box. There are two implications here for politicians in private-goods electoral markets. First, credit-claiming will not be difficult (relatively, of course). Second, the concrete and easily measured nature of private goods *increases* the pressure to deliver private goods—voters will know whether or not a legislator is shirking.

In public-goods markets, credit-claiming is very challenging. As mentioned, a single legislator usually won't be able to balance the budget, increase educational spending, or lower taxes in a single term. A legislator can work hard to advance a promised agenda, but obvious and immediate evidence (clean air, lower tax bills, peace and prosperity) will be virtually nonexistent from the voters' perspective. To evaluate a representative's performance, voters need to carefully consider all aspects of her or his legislative behavior, including bill initiations, policy process participation, committee work, floor votes, and many others. Political scientists have not found ways to fully measure all these aspects; voters are far too smart to waste valuable time trying.

Politicians' challenge, then, is to overcome voters' immense information problem and demonstrate credible policy effort. They do this in many ways: legislators make speeches, send newsletters to constituents, cast public roll-call votes, write legislation they know won't pass, and constantly seek media attention for their efforts. These different challenges—delivering goods and credit-claiming—lead to very different kinds of career strategies for legislators. There are many specific behavioral implications, but here I consider two in particular: vote buying's impact on position-taking and on party strength.

The basic mechanisms of this theory should work in all systems. In the rest of the chapter, I apply the theory to two Brazilian state legislatures. Several key characteristics of Brazil shape these predictions and deserve mention. First, Brazilian states have "presidential" forms of government, with separately elected governors and state legislatures. Like the national executive, state governors are very powerful political actors and have significant power over the spending of state funds—that is, state governors are the primary purse-holders. These government funds can support vote buying activities both directly and indirectly. Directly, legislators may receive government resources to distribute. Indirectly, legislators may take kickbacks from government contracts and jobs.

Second, political institutions in Brazil make individual politicians the primary agents of politics—not parties. This distinction is crucial to understanding my predictions and to generalizing my argument. Institutional rules in Brazil give political parties very little authority over their members, and very few mechanisms for disciplining their members. Parties do not control campaign finance; Brazil's electoral rules reward personalistic, not partisan, behavior, and until recently parties *had* to renominate incumbents for their electoral lists, regardless of their loyalty.[8] Note that several of these rules have recently changed, including legislators' guarantee of automatic renomination. However, the period covered by my study preceded those revisions. Consequently, the agents of interest are individual legislators. In other political systems, party leaders and organization are the primary decisionmaking agents. I reconsider my argument in such contexts at the end of the chapter.

These institutional arrangements have two testable implications. First, legislators in private-goods electoral markets face smaller credit-claiming challenges than do legislators in public-goods electoral markets. Consequently, we should see minimal credit-claiming effort in systems where vote buying is common, and extensive credit-claiming efforts where policy drives elections.

A second implication of this argument is that the two idealized system types create different incentives for forming strong and cohesive parties. When applied to the Brazilian context, the theory predicts very different party system types. In public-goods systems, there are both informational and delivery incentives to form political parties. Parties solve voters' overwhelming information problem. With cohesive, programmatic parties, voters do not need to know about representatives' proposals, committee action, or attendance records—they need only know that a candidate is a member of the Green Party, for example, or a member of the probusiness party. Party membership, in this case, provides a brand name that solves voters' information problem.[9]

Voters' information problem is legislators' credit-claiming problem. In public-goods settings, legislators face the challenge of demonstrating their sincere efforts to voters. Disciplined, cohesive parties solve politicians' credibility problem. Further, political parties aid politicians' efforts at delivery. One of legislative parties' main purposes is to act as legislative coalitions to support the advancement of members' like-minded proposals and agendas. Parties help legislators develop and push their proposals, and coordinate efforts to defeat other measures that their constituents oppose.

In contrast, in private-goods systems there are no informational incentives for party formation, because information about legislative behavior is easy to obtain. Note that private-goods electoral markets can provide other incentives for party formation. In particular, where parties themselves control access to significant resources for vote buying, politicians should be highly responsive to party directives. Candidates will not wish to jeopardize access to the party's trough. But in Brazil, the executive branch, not the party, controls state resources. Consequently, individual Brazilian legislators who wish to deliver private and local public goods will respond to the demands of the executive branch—not of their party leaders. A deputy in a disciplined party that is opposed to the governor will be unable to bargain for state resources for voters, limiting his future career advancement. Consequently, such politicians should avoid creating disciplined parties.

That governors should use their influence, first, to enforce discipline and cohesion on members of their coalition, and second, to attract additional support as needed from legislators of opposition parties, has two implications. First, government parties will be highly disciplined in support of the governor. Second, opposition parties will either split, with some members trading support for the governor for state resources, or simply cease to confront the governor.

As a result, in public-goods settings, politicians have more incentives to create disciplined, cohesive political parties than in private-goods settings. In such environments, parties solve credibility and delivery problems. In private-goods electoral markets, parties will effectively be replaced by resource-wielding governors, leading to apparently cohesive government parties, and to divided or subservient opposition parties.

Vote Buying in Piauí and Brasília

I apply predictions to a comparison of legislative behavior in two Brazilian state assemblies: Piauí, where vote buying and private goods were common, and Brasília, where such electoral purchases were rare. This comparison is especially effective because it allows us to hold nearly all institutional and macropolitical environmental factors constant, while allowing the type of electoral market to vary.

Subnational governments provide a powerful and often underutilized laboratory for social scientists. They usually share many societal and institutional frameworks, but have important differences that allow for robust theory-testing. In the case of Brazil, all of the subnational governments share a virtually identical institutional setting. All the institutions that have been identified as essential to shaping elite behavior are virtually identical across states: form of government and division of powers, electoral rules, and legislative procedures. States share the same basic structure of government: a presidential (governor) system with strong executives, constrained unicameral legislatures, and a weak judiciary. Each state also uses the same electoral system. For state legislative elections, they use open-list proportional representation; for the gubernatorial races, they use majority runoff. All state assemblies use similar internal rules.

There are minor institutional differences across states. In some states, assembly leaders can cast roll-call votes only in the case of ties; in others, they can always cast votes. But overall, the legislative procedures, including quorum, roll-call, and committee structures, are much more similar than different across states.[10]

While institutions are virtually identical across Brazilian states, electoral markets differ considerably, given great variances in culture, ethnicity, and political history. While private-goods campaigns, including vote buying, were still common in Piauí, the least developed state (demographically) in Brazil, they were virtually nonexistent in Brasília, the most developed state in the country.

In Piauí more than half of adults have less than a single year of education, 65 percent have incomes below the poverty line, and only 34 percent have access to running water.[11] Piauí was settled by cattle ranchers, and ranching became a central sector of a predominantly agricultural economy. A limited tax base means that federal transfers to the state are an important part of the local budget, and that many municipalities would scarcely survive without such inflows.

Politics in Piauí has been characterized as clientelistic and oligarchical. Tomaz Teixeira noted that during the campaign of 1978, the government's gubernatorial candidate bought votes in low-income neighborhoods through direct payments to voters, jobs, and deals with local leaders. Teixeira also listed several threats that the candidate made to encourage voters: "Whoever does not vote for our candidate will not drink from my well during the four years of my term. Whoever doesn't vote for our candidate will be fired. If you don't vote for my candidate we'll shut off the water and light to this city. If you doubt me just try it" (1985, 128).

Robert Gonçalves's recent work is the best and only serious analytic study of politics in Piauí. He characterizes the current system as oligarchical, showing that many of today's major political actors in Piauí come from traditional political families whose roots stretch back nearly two centuries. Further, he explains their continued domination as the result of the agricultural-based economy and extreme poverty.[12]

My interviews and observations concurred with a private-goods characterization of Piauí's politics. All deputies confirmed that vote buying was common, and all described electoral relations based on the provision of local public or private goods. One deputy told me that many deputies were directly purchasing votes. As he put it, "[The impoverished voter] wants a guardian angel that when he is hungry, when the rain is weak, the boss gives food and medicine. The boss resolves his principal problem: dying of hunger, or a child dying from disease" (Martins 1999). He also estimated that perhaps ten of the thirty state deputies would directly purchase votes with payments. But all deputies provided services to constituents— effectively private goods. For example, the deputy noted that health is a right of everyone guaranteed in the constitution—but that the healthcare system does not work properly. Consequently, there are long waiting lists for medical treatment. Politicians, he noted, take advantage of these governmental failures: they step in and obtain the medical exam, the medicine, or whatever the constituent needs. One of this deputy's own major accomplishments was getting a road built, but he noted that this wasn't enough to get himself elected. He also had to provide transportation for voters, medical care, and other private goods. That is, local public goods like roads weren't sufficient for securing an election victory—voters demanded private goods.

Other interviews were similar. Other deputies concurred, estimating that the cost of a vote, purchased in cash, was about 20 reais (1999), and that candidates spent up to US$1 million in their election attempts. Deputies also emphasized the importance of providing goods to voters or groups of voters. A politician might finance a graduation party, or pay for a musical group to perform for the community, or pay for a medical exam, x-rays, or other kinds of healthcare. These sorts of exchanges were obvious and institutionalized. During one interview with a deputy, a constituent burst in to ask for funds for medicine. The state assembly had several doctors on staff, and deputies could refer voters for medical care. Private goods, and local public-goods politics, were clearly central to politics in Piauí.

The other Brazilian state under study here, Brasília, is unique in three ways. The first is its combination of municipal and state government responsibilities into a single political institution. The second is its *lack* of history—the district is a relatively young political unit. The third is its relatively high indices of development: on most demographic measures, Brasília is the most developed state in the union.

Strictly speaking, Brasília is neither a state nor a city—it is classified as "the federal district." It differs in several ways from the other twenty-six Brazilian states. Brasília is physically smaller than all the other states, and within the district there are no cities; rather, there is a unitary government that provides both state and municipal services. For example, the district government resolves local planning issues as does a municipality government, but also acts within the sphere of state governmental activity, creating or privatizing state-owned industries and imposing state taxes. Reflecting this dual nature of the government, the district's legislature is called a "legislative chamber"—a combination of a "legislative assembly" at the state level, and a "municipal chamber" at the city level.

But aside from these differences, the federal district is, politically, virtually identical to the other states. The district has executive, legislative, and judicial branches. It elects three senators, and based on population, eight legislators to the national congress. The electoral rules, internal procedures of the legislature, and division of powers between branches of government are the same as those in the other states. And while the legislative chamber does have to resolve some strictly municipal issues—like zoning ordinances—it also confronts all the same issues that a state legislature faces, including the creation and privatization of state-owned banks and other industries.

The political history of Brasília is easy to tell—because there is almost none. Brazilians had been talking of moving their capital to the vast interior for hundreds of years, but the move finally happened under the direction of President Juscelino Kubitschek. Construction of the new district, built from scratch on the open, high plains of the interior, began in 1956; the capital was transferred from Rio de Janeiro in 1960.

Because it is so new, the federal district does not have any enduring political cleavages or traditions based on a historical path. Residents come from every state in the country. Even five decades after its founding, most residents of Brasília were born somewhere else—and many are only temporarily residents of Brasília.

Initially, the federal district had no political independence. An appointed governor administered Brasília, and a Senate committee provided oversight and acted as the district's legislature—basically just rubber-stamping the district governor's proposals. Brasília did have representation in Congress, and provisions were made for the election of a local legislature, but these plans were put on hold following the 1964 military coup.

It was not until democratization that Brasília began to acquire real political independence. In 1990, the first district elections were held for the governor's office and for the new legislative chamber. The legislature itself is in a temporary building at the northern end of Brasília's *plano piloto* (the master-planned center of Brasília), with plans to construct a permanent home in the center of the district.

The most important industry in Brasília is the federal government and the service industries that it creates. Because of the large, well-paid civil service sector, the district's nearly 1.8 million residents enjoy the highest social development indices of all the Brazilian states. In terms of income, education, and life expectancy, Brasília is ranked first among Brazilian states, with only 13 percent of the population below the poverty line, 88 percent having completed primary school, and 87 percent having access to running water. However, there is a growing lower-income segment of the population who live in the "satellite" cities outside the *plano piloto*. The lower-income sector includes descendants of the workers who came to build the capital in the 1950s and, more recently, migrants from the northeast and the neighboring state of Goiás.

Perhaps because of the high levels of political information, income, and education, as well as the lack of personal ties between the new citizens of Brasília and their elected officials, Brasilienense elections have not been characterized as clientelistic or private-goods oriented. One deputy noted, "Voters here won't let themselves be bought."[13] He went on to note that some voters will accept payments for their votes—but these voters typically will sell their votes to more than one candidate and vote for still another. Further, he noted that the regional electoral agency had been very rigorously enforcing campaign laws. Another stated, "Look, voters here are very demanding—but they don't ask for things in exchange for voting." He also stated that the few voters who request payment make these requests of all candidates—they try to get private goods from many candidates.

A few deputies disagreed, noting that in the poorest areas of Brasília, some voters could be persuaded to vote for private goods or local public goods. I personally observed many constituents seeking jobs and other assistance in the legislature. But these deputies also agreed that direct cash payments for votes were extremely rare.

Further, some deputies also noted that constituents do pay attention and ask about specific roll-call votes, which these deputies attributed to the higher levels of education in Brasília (Cauhy 1999). This may be further reflected in another feature of Brasília's politics: corporativist representation. Many deputies noted that many representatives are tied to a specific social or occupational sector. For example, one was elected by the police union, another by the electrical workers' union, and a third by evangelical church members.

This pattern of representation is likely a function of size and history. Brasília's small size and recent settlement set it apart from other states in Brazil. Most states are too large for statewide campaigns; instead, candidates focus their efforts on a small number of geographically proximate cities. Further, recent settlement means that voters are less likely to have ties to any existing political machines. Consequently, many candidates in Brasília have sought to represent sectors, instead of carving out geographical voting bases.

Brasília stands in contrast to Piauí. Deputies acknowledge that private goods and local public goods are still used in campaigns, but note that direct payments are almost extinct. Many voters simply will not sell their votes, and those who are willing to sell do not make credible voting commitments. Public-goods campaigns are more common and are likely reinforced by union and other sectoral forms of representation, where candidates are tied to specific collective interests.

Differences in Legislative Behavior in Piauí and Brasília

The contrast between Piauí and Brasília suggests that, if my theory is correct, we should observe substantial differences in legislative behavior in the two states. Specifically, in Piauí, legislators should focus on the delivery of private goods. This should translate into little or no position-taking, weak political parties, and a general deferral of policy functions to the executive branch. In Brasília, legislators should focus more on credit-claiming for their policy efforts, and less on the direct and immediate delivery of private goods. Consequently, we should observe substantial efforts to publicly take policy positions, stronger and more cohesive political parties, and increased conflict between the legislature and the state governor.

My theory predicts more credit-claiming and position-taking in public-goods markets, and much less in private-goods electoral markets. One way to measure this (though there are many others) is through the frequency of roll-call votes. In public-goods states, roll-call votes can be useful demonstrations of effort and position-taking or part of a legislative strategy. Deputies can use roll-call votes to demonstrate their effort on behalf of a public-goods agenda—support for a new environmental law, opposition for tax hikes, or effort to increase the salaries of public employees. Such votes can similarly be used against their opponents in future elections. Opposition deputies might seek recorded roll-call votes so they can criticize their opponents who supported any policy initiatives that failed or proved unpopular.

In contrast, in private-goods electoral markets, legislators have no need for frequent roll-call votes—they are simply a waste of time, since constituents do not care how deputies voted on tax reforms or environmental regulations. Voters' primary concern is the delivery of private goods, or local private goods. This delivery takes place through an executive-legislative pact: deputies trade support for the executive's legislative agenda in exchange for access to state resources, as described above. Note that in Brasília, this difference is *not* driven by access to technology to facilitate roll-call votes. All 8,000 roll-call votes in Brasília's legislature (1991≈1998) were recorded on paper by hand!

To explore differences in legislative behavior across the two states, I collected data on the frequency of roll-call votes in both Piauí and Brasília for two legislative sessions: 1991–1994 and 1995–1998 (see Table 7.1). The pattern strongly matches my predictions. In Piauí, there were just 11 votes in the first period and 9 in the second. Further, about half of these roll-call votes were on proposed amendments to the state constitution—where roll-calls were mandatory. So only about 5 roll-calls per term happen "optionally." In contrast, the legislature in Brasília votes on almost everything. Compared to Piauí, there were more than 200 times as many roll-call votes: over 2,600 in the first period and over 5,300 in the second period. The differences are immense and consistent with my theory's predictions. Vote buying legislators don't need to take policy positions or claim credit for legislative effort. Instead, they focus on obtaining the private goods that citizens want.

My observations and interviews in each state confirmed that these

Table 7.1   Roll-Call Vote Frequency, Brazil, 1991–1998

	1991–1994	1995–1998
Brasília	2,622	5,349
Piauí	11	9

Note: See the appendix to this chapter for details on data.

mechanisms were at work. In Piauí, legislators did not need to have roll-call votes—because the executive branch had taken complete control of state policy. Their bargain with the executive was simply to approve the agenda and seek state resources from the executive branch for their constituents. There were no electoral payoffs for position-taking, obstruction, or otherwise doing anything but trading legislative support of the executive for private goods for voters.

I discussed legislative strategy with opposition parties in both states. The internal rules of both legislatures allow any deputy to ask for a roll-call verification of a voice vote.[14] Why, I asked, did they not use verifications to obstruct the government's agenda?

In Piauí, some opposition deputies simply made reference to "negotiation" with the governor and majority, with no additional comment. I interpreted these comments as indicators of legislative-executive negotiations, the trading of votes for particularistic state resources. I also spoke with opposition deputies from parties that have a reputation for disciplined and ideological behavior (the Workers Party, for example). The few deputies in Piauí from such parties claimed that they did not know they could request verifications. Some seemed to quite like the idea and claimed they would begin to use this strategy in the legislature. This may generate roll-call votes for future scholars, or these responses might simply have been dishonest. Either way, the lack of roll-call votes suggests that public position-taking or moving forward with a legislative agenda have had little relation to legislators' career strategies in Piauí.

Brasília is clearly very different in this regard. The district's legislature acquired the norm of undertaking a roll-call vote on *every* bill that made it to the floor—it almost never held symbolic votes. One president of the legislative chamber did reduce the number of roll-calls during his two-year term. But the next president returned to the practice of holding roll-calls for all bills. Even obviously administrative or symbolic measures, like extending the legislative session for another half hour or declaring "The Week of the Miner," were subject to roll-call votes.

In Brasília there was at least some evidence of these votes being used as position-taking measures. Deputies reported that voters would ask them how they voted on the more publicized and controversial measures. This does not mean that voters in Brasília are fully informed about each roll-call—this would be unexpected in *any* democracy, especially in subnational government. Further, not all deputies used roll-call votes in campaigns or speeches, and not all faced criticism in their campaigns for their voting records. But the fact that roll-call votes are frequent and occasionally scrutinized in this state and not in Piauí concurs with the predictions of my theory.

I also predicted that in Brasília, the informational demands of public-goods markets should lead deputies to build more cohesive and consistent political parties, while in Piauí, the urgency of delivering private goods should lead to legislators abandoning partisan concerns to negotiate for resources with the executive branch.

I compared cohesion scores for parties in each of the two legislatures. While there are many problems with roll-call cohesion scores, alternatives, including spatial models, are not possible when dealing with very few roll-call votes, as in Piauí. Further, note that the prediction is not simply that cohesion scores will be higher in Brasília than in Piauí. The rush to vote with the governor in search of resources could actually make Piauí look, on average, more cohesive than Brasília. The appropriate comparison is between government and opposition alliances.

In Piauí, the governor's control of private goods means that all legislators in his party will vote with him—trading policy support for resources. In contrast, opposition parties will be torn, with some legislators voting against the governor, and others abandoning their party's positions to seek governmental resources. In Brasília, all parties should have relatively cohesive voting, reflecting the informational demands of working in policy-oriented electoral markets.

Table 7.2 reports government and opposition party cohesion scores for each state using two measures of cohesion—an unweighted score and a weighted score.[15] The results strongly support my initial hypotheses.

In Brasília, there is effectively no difference between opposition and government party cohesion. Using the unweighted score, both coalitions' parties averaged a cohesion of 0.86. Using the weighted score, they had slightly different cohesion values, 0.84 and 0.86. But this small difference was not significantly different from zero, even with thousands of roll-call votes.

In Piauí, the government parties are very cohesive, averaging 0.89 and 0.94 for the two scores, well above the average for Brasília parties. This result is expected: members of the government coalition should unconditionally support the executive branch. In contrast, opposition party cohesion is very low, only 0.55 and 0.48 for the two scores. Further, the difference

Table 7.2   Government and Opposition Average Party Cohesion in State Assemblies, Brazil, 1991–1998

	Unweighted			Weighted		
	Government	Opposition	Difference	Government	Opposition	Difference
Brasília	0.86	0.86	0.00	0.84	0.86	−0.02
Piauí	0.89	0.55	0.34*	0.94	0.48	0.46**

Notes: See the appendix to this chapter for details on data.
 * $p < 0.01$; ** $p < 0.001$.

between coalition means is significant, even with only twenty roll-call votes.

In Piauí, my interviews and observations suggested that the theoretical mechanisms I described above do in fact explain patterns of roll-call cohesion. After the 1998 elections, the governor actually only had a minority coalition in the assembly, fourteen of thirty deputies. I discussed this with the leader of the opposition parties, deputy Leal Junior of the Liberal Front Party. I asked him why the opposition—with a majority in the state assembly—did not challenge the governor's legislative agenda more aggressively. He simply answered, "We negotiate."[16] Although he was the majority leader, he went on to note that "being in the opposition in the northeast is tough" and that his party "can't get anything [from the government]."

His comments were a bit more forthcoming in a newspaper interview a year later, in March 2000. When asked about the opposition's decision to vote in favor of the governor's proposals, he noted, "Certainly there will be an opposition. We will continue just as firm as before, but we will be able to vote in favor of the government's proposals" (Coelho 2000). It turned out that deputies in his own party were publicly siding with the governor, and that others had simply switched into one of the governmental parties in exchange for "benefits." The Liberal Front Party had tried to strengthen its opposition to Governor Mão Santo, but failed, as its members sided with the governor.

Piauí fit with the expected pattern: in clientelistic settings, parties are replaced by governors as political organizers. The government party is highly disciplined and responsive to government demands. The opposition is fragmented and incapable of resisting the governor's pressure—even when the governor does not have a majority.

The dynamics were very different in Brasília. There, the opposition parties did not divide over support for the governor. Across multiple measures and codings of government and opposition cohesion, the opposition parties were usually at least as cohesive as the government parties, often actually more cohesive. Where the governor had a majority coalition, executives sometimes had conflict with their own party. And where the executive did not have a majority coalition, I observed highly conflictual legislative-executive relations.

Parties in Brasília were relatively cohesive, consistently about 85 percent. The data concur with predictions. Using unweighted scores, the government and opposition had almost identical cohesion; using weighted scores, the opposition parties were slightly more cohesive than were the government parties. These slight differences are not significant for either measure.

I also tried examining cohesion in Brasília separately for each of the two legislative sessions (1991–1994 and 1995–1998). I had expected the two periods to be very different due to the election of a Workers Party governor for the period 1995–1998. The Workers Party is known for disciplined, ideological behavior. Brasília's other parties are less ideological. Consequently, I expected the governing coalition to be more disciplined than the opposition for the period 1995–1998, since the most ideological party was in the government and the opposition parties were those typically considered "catch-all" parties. However, my theory held even when the Workers Party was in the government: the party's government coalition had lower cohesion than did the opposition. The implication is that the differences between Piauí and Brasília aren't simply a "Workers Party" effect.

Roll-call vote cohesion scores concur again with my predictions. In private-goods electoral markets, opposition parties collapse as legislators defect to join the governor's coalition. In more programmatic systems, both opposition and government parties were relatively cohesive. This does not mean that parties in Brasília are not perfectly disciplined. Several legislators noted that their party was "democratic"—that is, that they could have their own opinions and vote differently than the party. But the patterns of party cohesion in Brasília stand in stark contrast to those observed in Piauí.

Implications for Comparative Studies: Anecdotal and Theoretical Discussion

In this chapter I have argued that vote buying can dramatically change legislative behavior, by altering legislators' optimal career strategies. In electoral markets driven by private-goods exchanges, legislators focus primarily on short-term, immediate delivery of small goods. In programmatic markets, legislators focus on long-term policy strategies and on informing voters about their efforts. The different strategies have implications for many facets of legislative and interbranch politics.

I have explored these ideas by comparing legislative behavior in two Brazilian states: Piauí and Brasília. In contexts of frequent vote buying, legislators made no effort to take policy positions and were mostly unaware of mechanisms for so doing. In addition, political parties and their positions were much less important than alliances with the resource-controlling state executive. In more programmatic environments, legislators frequently and deliberately took policy positions and publicized their legislative efforts. In addition, parties were less subject to executive influence and showed more independent cohesion.

One of the important theoretical findings that comes out of this research is that even under virtually identical institutional environments, legislators can adapt fundamentally different political strategies in response to societal variables. Recent scholarship on Latin America, in particular, focuses on the central role of formal institutions. But all such research—and every theory of democratic institutions—rests on assumptions about voters. The assumption might be that voters don't matter, that voters cast fully informed ideological distance–minimizing votes, or that voters only care about private goods, but some assumptions about voters are always present.

This research shows that these assumptions matter. Whether elections are based on vote buying or on policy positions has a dramatic impact on the organization and activities of the legislature. In other words, the same institutions work very differently in different contexts. This suggests that theories of institutions should include voters' characteristics, and that institutional frameworks and theories cannot be applied indiscriminately across contexts. This does not mean that institutions do not matter. The analysis herein is embedded in the specific Brazilian context of weak partisanship, permissive electoral rules, and strong executives in presidential systems of government.

The basic mechanisms of credit-claiming and delivery challenges should translate directly across political boundaries to other countries, but some of their manifestations will vary with local contexts and institutions. For example, in any political system, legislators in programmatic electoral environments should invest more resources in credit-claiming than do their vote buying colleagues: sending newsletters, making speeches, calling for roll-call votes, and otherwise maximizing public exposure for their legislative efforts. Similarly, vote buying legislators should focus on obtaining deliverable goods for constituents.

Some of my findings do apply to party systems generally across countries; others will require some modification. The basic, first-level incentives should remain unchanged. In programmatic systems, there should be stronger incentives to form cohesive parties. Where vote buying is common, although informational incentives to form parties will not exist, there may be other incentives for party formation. In particular, legislative behavior will depend on who controls the resources that politicians need to advance their careers. In Brazil, weak partisanship, personalistic electoral rules, and gubernatorial control of resources mean that parties in clientelistic environments are weak. But if party leaders control cash and other goods needed to buy votes, then politicians should be extremely responsive to party directives. Examples include the Peronists in Argentina (Auyero 2000) and the Institutional Revolutionary Party in Mexico (Fox 1994).

Regardless, the most important lesson is that vote buying has serious second-level effects on the nature and quality of politics. There are clear normative concerns with the impact of vote buying on participation and representation. A substantial body of literature explores the impact of vote buying on citizenship and participation, builds explanations for the emergence and persistence of vote buying, and offers solutions to prevent vote buying and ensure full democratic participation to all voters. The findings in this chapter show that vote buying has ripple effects throughout the political system, reaching far beyond the confines of elections.

Appendix: Details on Data and Measurement

All roll-call votes were collected directly from the archives of the state legislatures. In the case of Brasília, the nearly 8,000 roll-call votes were entered manually into a database and audited with the help of undergraduate and graduate research assistants. In the case of Piauí, legislative staff searched the legislative daily record for roll-call votes and typed them into a report. I am indebted to the generous and professional assistance provided by the staff at the Legislative Assembly of Piauí, the Legislative Chamber of Brasília, and the faculty and students of the University of Brasília, especially professors Luis Pedone and Paulo Calmon and master's student Moema Bonelli Henrique de Faria. Without their cooperation, this data collection effort would have been impossible.

Two cohesion measures were used: an unweighted cohesion score, and a weighted cohesion score. The first weights all votes equally but discards those with less than 5 percent voting in the minority. The second weights all votes by one minus the overall cohesion on the vote.

Calculation of party cohesion proceeds as follows. First, party j's cohesion on vote k, or C_{jk}, is calculated using the familiar Rice index:

$$C_{jk} = \frac{|Y_{jk} - N_{jk}|}{Y_{jk} + N_{jk}}$$

where Y_{jk} is the number of "yes" votes and N_{jk} is the number of "no" votes cast by party j's members on vote k. Average cohesion, over all parties and votes is thus

$$C_p = \frac{\sum_{j=1}^{n} \sum_{k=1}^{m} C_{jk} W_{jk}}{nmW}$$

where there are n parties and m roll-call votes. W_{jk} combines the vote-specific weight and the size of the voting party.

Finally, overall party cohesion, or C_p, is calculated as the weighted average of cohesion on all bills. The weight,

$$W_{jk} = \left(1 - \frac{\mid Y_k - N_k \mid}{Y_k + N_k} \right) (Y_{jk} + N_{jk})$$

adjusts for the contentiousness of the bill and the size of the group voting. The first part of the weight is maximized when the legislature is equally divided (value of 1) and minimized (value of 0) on unanimous votes. The second part of the weight varies directly with party size.

My recent work has shown how small parties' cohesion scores can be artificially inflated, and offers possible corrections for that inflation (Desposato 2005). In this application, that inflation is biased *against* my alternative hypothesis. Hence, using uncorrected cohesion scores makes my findings even more robust.

Notes

Thanks to Barbara Geddes, Jim Robinson, Fred Schaffer, and Andreas Schedler for comments; special thanks to Moema Bonelli for excellent research assistance.

1. Since the writing of this chapter, the frequency of vote buying appears to have fallen in response to increasingly rigorous enforcement of electoral rules, especially on the part of the federal prosecutors and courts. Increased party competition and improvements in living standards for Piauense citizens have also likely played a role.

2. In many ways, elections can be considered markets where votes are exchanged for promised policy outcomes. Politicians offer goods—tax cuts, education programs, or cash payments—and voters maximize their utility by "spending" votes on candidates. There are of course important differences between electoral markets and markets as usually understood. Politicians do not have legally binding commitments to provide specific goods, and if not elected will usually provide nothing. Secret ballots limit voters' and candidates' ability to make binding commitments. In all cases, interesting mechanisms have evolved to overcome these limitations.

3. See Pearce 1992 for more details.

4. There are other goods between these two extremes, including local public goods and club goods.

5. See Banfield and Wilson 1963 for some examples.

6. Why use private goods when programmatic goods are more efficient? Ultimately, the answer depends on markets and competition. If voters' private-goods prices are low enough, candidates that idealistically pursue programmatic campaigns will simply lose to private-goods campaigners.

7. This brief discussion does not begin to do justice to the richness of our knowledge of electoral markets; I defer to the other contributors to this volume for more details.

8. See Ames 2001; Mainwaring 1997; Carey and Shugart 1995.

9. See Aldrich 1995; Cox and McCubbins 1993; Snyder and Ting 2001.

10. One significant difference between Piauí and Brasília is that while Piauí is

composed of self-governing municipalities, Brasília, as the federal capital, does not contain any municipalities. This difference is discussed in some detail later.

11. Data from the 1990 Brazilian census. Censo Demográfico, 1991 [Disquete]: variáveis selecionadas (Rio de Janeiro: Instituto Brasileiro de Geografia e Estatística, 1991).

12. See Gonçalves 1997, 1998/1999.

13. Adaão Xavier, interview with Scott W. Desposato, Brasília, July 1999.

14. Piauí's rules are discussed in the 1998 *Internal Regimen of the Legislature (ALEPI)* (chap. XIII, sec. VI, art. 182); Brasília's are discussed in the 1998 *Legislative Chamber of the Federal District (CLDF)* (chap. X, sec. II, art. 164, sub-secs. 1–2). Note that Brasília's legislative chamber imposes several restrictions. Any deputy can request a verification of a vote, but this must occur within a one-hour period; the first request will be honored, and subsequent requests require the approval of one-third of the deputies. This would be problematic except that the legislative chamber almost always has roll-call votes, and the minority coalition within the chamber is generally larger than one-third of the deputies.

15. The difference between the two is in how scores are aggregated. With the unweighted score, votes with less than 5 percent opposition are discarded and all others are weighted equally. With the weighted score, each vote is weighted by its contentiousness.

16. Leal Junior, interview with Scott W. Desposato, Teresina, Piauí, May 1999.

8

How Does Vote Buying
Shape the Economy?

*Jean-Marie Baland
& James A. Robinson*

In many situations, political institutions may allow political parties or political entrepreneurs to engage in vote buying. One obvious such situation will arise when there is no effective secret ballot (see Chapter 3). In this case, voting behavior may be observable, and the possibility of an enforceable "exchange" between the voter and someone else wishing to buy his or her vote emerges.[1] Such exchanges can take many forms. In Chile in the "parliamentary period" before the reforms of 1925, political parties operated booths outside of polling stations and directly purchased with money the votes of citizens (Millar Carvacho 1981). "The urban voter . . . sells his votes. The buying of votes in the cities became a system in which all political parties were engaged. . . . There were even candidates that offered to pay more for votes than any other candidate in printed ads" (Heise González 1982, 228–229).

In Palermo in the 1970s, the Christian Democratic Party distributed public sector employment and free spaghetti and shoes in exchange for support. Judith Chubb noted that "a substantial part of politics revolves around the *posto* [job or position] and . . . when all is said and done, a job signifies a vote and vice versa." At election time, other incentives were used. For instance, "in Palermo . . . in every quartiere the arrival of the truck of pasta, accompanied by thousands of ballot facsimiles with the candidate's name and number, is still the high point of every electoral campaign" (1982, 91, 170).

In nineteenth-century Brazil, landowners took their workers to the polling stations and directed them how to vote. Richard Graham discussed the position of *agregados,* "poverty-stricken agricultural workers." He quoted a description from 1879 of how landowners manipulated the political behavior of such workers: "By their dependence on the owners these agregados constitute an enslaved class, which, although not subject to any tribute in money or labor . . . [are subject to] the electoral tax [i.e., their vote],

123

which they pay at the right moment at the ballot box, or else risk eviction" (1990, 20–21).

In this chapter we investigate the implications of vote buying and electoral corruption for the economy and for economic policy. Building on our previous research (Baland and Robinson 2003a, 2003b), we emphasize the idea that vote buying may be direct or indirect, and that either form can lead to distinct types of inefficiencies in resource allocation and public policy. The distinction between these activities can be seen in the previous examples. In Chile before 1925, individuals directly sold their votes to political parties. This is direct vote buying. In Palermo and Brazil in 1879, however, although vote buying was endemic, individual voters often implicitly contracted away their votes when they entered into particular employment relationships. After these relationships were created, the votes of employees were sold, or "controlled," by their employers. This is indirect vote buying—the votes of individuals are not sold by themselves, but rather by others to whom the voters have ceded, or contracted away, their political rights. Contracting took place directly with politicians if the voters were public sector employees, or with landlords if the voters worked for them or depended for their livelihood on access to their land. In these cases an individual did not sell his or her vote at the time of an election.

Why is it that some individuals are prepared to contract away their right to vote to others? Why are some able to control the votes of others? This possibility arises whenever an economic relationship generates rents for one party. A rent is a return received in excess of the minimum needed to attract workers to that activity. Such rents arise in many circumstances—for example, when there is asymmetric information, when individuals bargain over the surplus from an exchange or contract, or when there are market frictions. When a relationship generates rents and one party has the ability to terminate the relationship, then the threat of termination can be used to control the behavior of others. This connection has been noted in the informal literature on electoral corruption and clientelism. For example, James Wilson, in his discussion of how political machines in the United States used public sector employment as a way of securing political support, defined "patronage jobs" as being "all those posts, distributed at the discretion of political leaders, the pay for which is greater than the value of the services performed. This 'unearned increment' permits the machine to require that the holder perform party services as well" (1961, 370). Previously (Baland and Robinson 2003b), we provided the first formal analysis of how the threat of taking rents away from an individual can allow his or her political behavior—voting—to be controlled, and we developed the implications of this connection.

The fact that such control exists gives an added incentive to form organizations or relationships where such rents exist, even if it is not socially efficient to do so. In the next section we discuss in more detail the most tangible example of this in the context of the agrarian economy. Here the existence of a political profit from indirect vote buying leads to an increase in the demand for land and, when there are imperfect capital markets, an increase in land concentration. When land concentration is inefficient, as it is often thought to be in the absence of scale economies, this creates socially inefficient patterns of land concentration. Thus large farms form, not because this is economically desirable, but rather as a way of controlling the political behavior of workers. Indirect vote buying therefore leads to economic inefficiencies because the payoff to controlling the votes of others creates incentives to organize economic activities or structures of asset ownership in such a way as to facilitate this control.

When relationships exist that allow votes to be sold indirectly, it is the preferences of those who do the actual selling that are relevant for political parties. In trying to design policy platforms to win power, parties will aim to please those with the votes. James Scott made exactly this argument in his discussion of electoral corruption. He referred to individuals whose votes are controlled by others as "locked-in electorates" in which "the voter was connected to the larger political system through his agent-patron whose control over his political will was a function of his control over his means of subsistence." In such a system, "There was no sense in parties or candidates appealing directly to 'locked-in electorates.' By definition, these were voters who could be mustered most easily by coming to terms with their landlord, their employer, or their master who could deliver their votes in the election" (1972a, 98–99). This immediately implies that public goods will be undersupplied, because the benefit that these have on the utilities of those whose votes are sold is discounted. Instead, parties will want to target their policies to those selling the votes (Baland and Robinson 2003a).

Indirect vote buying therefore can lead to two distinct types of inefficiencies. In addition, direct vote buying can lead to inefficiency in the provision of public goods when citizens have unequal political power. In this case, rational politicians attempt to target their policies at the most powerful citizens, and because public goods cannot be targeted, they are undersupplied so as to make more resources available for buying the votes of these pivotal individuals.

The study of the implications of political institutions for the economy is of course not new. A large literature has examined how regime types, particularly democracy and dictatorship, and variations in democratic institutions, influence the economy. Most of this research focuses on the implications of political institutions for public policy and hence the economy.[2] To our knowledge, our work represents the first attempt to develop formal models to study the microfoundations and the economic implications of vote buying. There is a large literature by historians, sociologists, and political scientists documenting the incidence of political corruption and vote buying, but this literature has not suggested systematic implications for economic organization or the allocation of resources, with the exception of William Summerhill (1995), who developed a simple model of the idea that political rents accrue to landowners, and tried to estimate the impact of electoral reform on the economy using data from nineteenth-century Brazil. This literature does argue that vote buying and control typically benefit some political groups and elites, for instance the Junker landlords in nineteenth-century Prussia, or the Coroneis of rural Brazil, and would naturally tend to favor the policies preferred by those groups. For instance, Scott noted that "the normal effect of [political] corruption is to cement together a conservative coalition and hold back or cancel out the effects of growing collective demands" (1972a, ix). Nevertheless, this literature does not make clear predictions about how vote buying influences public policies or the economy.

A related literature in economics (e.g., Buchanan and Tullock 1962) suggests the idea that allowing votes to be bought and sold promotes social welfare, because it takes advantage of unexploited gains from trade. Our research shows that in models with natural market imperfections and restrictions on fiscal instruments, this intuition is incorrect.

Our idea that vote buying leads to the inefficient undersupply of public goods is related to the ideas of Robert Bates (1981), Tortsen Persson and Guido Tabellini (1999), and Alessandro Lizzeri and Nicola Persico (2001), who show that public goods may be undersupplied because they cannot be targeted. Our contribution is to suggest that buying votes is the finest sort of targeting imaginable and thus generally leads to even lower levels of public goods.

Indirect Vote Buying and the Employment Relationship

In the absence of a secret ballot, one can imagine many ways in which votes can be exchanged or cast. Individuals can in principle sell them to each other, although in the absence of third-party enforcement, such a contract is not necessarily incentive-compatible (indeed, one hardly finds evidence of such activities in the historical record). More likely, individuals will sell votes to "patrons," political parties, or entrepreneurs who, if payment takes place before voting, are able to wield some sanctions if voters do not vote as stipulated. Alternatively, if payment is made after voting, then the vote buyers have sufficient reputational concerns that they will pay for the votes as promised. Despite these possibilities, however, the preponderance of evidence is that when there is no secret ballot, votes are delivered indirectly by individuals who are able to use coercion or sanctions. In such situations, nothing is given to individuals for their votes; rather it is the threat of losing something that they already have that leads individuals to vote as demanded.

What is it that people might lose? An obvious thing is rents from any economic relation. We previously developed a model of an agrarian economy in which worker effort is valuable in production but imperfectly observed (Baland and Robinson 2003b). Instead, employers observe output, which is an imperfect signal of effort. When landowners hire a worker, they enter into a principal-agent relationship and need to design a labor contract that gives the worker an incentive to work hard. Since exerting effort is unpleasant for workers, they will only do so if they find it to be in their interests—if they are given incentives. This is therefore a classic situation in which the employment relationship is subject to moral hazard.

Since the employer cannot directly observe whether or not the worker has actually worked hard, wages have to be conditioned on output, which is observable. The optimal way to give workers incentives is to use a carrot and a stick, so that good output levels are rewarded, while bad ones are punished. Usually, however, such optimal contracts are not possible, because they entail that when output is low, workers actually have to transfer income to employers. This is unlikely to be feasible, either because workers can quit or because they have insufficient wealth. This limits the use of sticks. To compensate, employers must give an even larger carrot when output is bad, and it is this that gives workers rents. Workers are prepared to work hard because of the fear of losing these rents.

Imagine, then, that employers are conceding rents to workers as part of an optimal labor contract in the presence of moral hazard. Now introduce voting behavior and imagine that workers prefer one party, while the employer prefers another. We have shown (Baland and Robinson 2003b) that, because the employer is already giving rents to the worker, the threat of withdrawing these rents allows the employer to control the voting behavior of the worker. Employment does not simply generate profits; it also gives power to control the behavior of others. Controlling votes may be valuable for many reasons. Either the landlord can simply force the workers to vote for whom he or she prefers, thus increasing the chance that the political party will win an election, or the landlord can sell the votes to a political party in exchange for money, favors, employment, or political access.

Controlling votes gives an extra incentive to hire labor, since now there is a political profit in addition to any economic profits. The desire to attain power over others and the benefits it brings may significantly influence the way the labor market functions and also, due to the complementarity of factors of production, the markets for capital and land. We have shown (Baland and Robinson 2003b) that the political profits from selling workers' votes drive up the demand for labor, and that, since land and labor are complements in production, this increases the demand for land. This increase in demand drives up the price of land and leads to land concentration, even if this is socially inefficient.[3]

It is useful to illustrate these ideas with a simple model. Consider an economy with n agents: l employers, and $n - l$ workers. All employers and all workers are identical, so that each employer hires exactly $((n - l) / l)$ workers. To each worker, this employment yields an employment rent, equal to R, which adds to his or her opportunity cost of time, w, so that the worker's total income, y_w, is given by

$$y_w = w + R$$

Employers earn a profit (π) from each worker they employ. They are always in a position to dismiss a worker and terminate the employment contract.

The agents also have ideological preferences, so that each agent obtains an increase in utility, equal to σ, when they can freely vote for the party or politician of their choice. Political parties buy votes, and propose a price per vote, equal to p, which we consider as being exogenously given in this example. As discussed above, one should think of the types of favors that can be exchanged for votes quite generally. Only in some cases will a favor actually be a transfer of income. Here we use p as a reduced form for all of these other possibilities.

The presence of employment rents, R, gives employers the opportunity to control their workers' votes in that, if employment rents are large, a worker will vote the way his employer tells him to if the latter threatens to fire him for noncompliance. Indeed, if the worker obeys the employer, he earns $w + R$, while if the worker does not comply, and sells his own vote to the party of his choice, he earns $w + p + \sigma$. As a result, as long as

$$w + R \geq w + p + \sigma$$

the control of a worker's vote is costless for the employer, since the threat of removing the employment rent is enough to induce the worker to vote the way the employer tells him to vote. Note that without the rent, the inequality can never be true, and thus employers would have no political control. The benefit to the employer from selling the vote of a worker to the employer's own preferred party is $p + \sigma$, so that the employer's total rents from hiring one worker is $\pi + p + \sigma$.

However, it may be the case that

$$w + R < w + p + \sigma$$

so that the rent given to the worker is not large enough to discipline him. To do so, the employer has to transfer the worker an extra rent, R^p, such that R^p

$\geq p + \sigma - R$, that is large enough to induce the worker to vote as stipulated. Note that it will be optimal for employers to pay the smallest amount necessary, so that $R^p = p + \sigma - R$. It is interesting to note that, by doing so, employers are able to extract from the worker his employment rent, R. Indeed, while in the absence of vote buying the employer earns π per worker, the employer now earns $\pi + p + \sigma - R^p$, which is equal to $\pi + R$.

We have thus shown that, even in a situation in which parties buy votes at the same price from any voter, the mere fact that employment yields some rents to the worker, no matter how small, allows the employer to control the worker politically. By doing so, employers earn political rents from each employment relationship they create, which gives them an incentive to provide more employment than the efficient level.[4] This has two consequences, as noted above. On the one hand, it tends to distort downward the ratio of land to labor, or the ratio of capital to labor. On the other hand, it increases the demand not only for labor, but also for complementary inputs, such as land. Though we have modeled political control in terms of voting (Baland and Robinson 2003b), our analysis extends to other types of political activities (such as types of protests, riots, demonstrations, and other forms of collective action). The results of such a model would be similar to those of the model we present.

A Case Study: Chile

The model sketched in the previous section has several important empirical predictions with respect to the impact of political reform on land prices and concentration and voting patterns. If political reform that stops electoral corruption and the selling of votes occurs, then the incentive to employ people to control their voting vanishes, and employment and land concentration should fall. Moreover, as the demand for land falls, so should its equilibrium price. Finally, we should observe large changes in voting behavior, as workers whose votes were previously sold can now vote freely.

Here we examine these implications by considering the electoral reforms that took place in 1958 in Chile. Many scholars have claimed that, before the reforms, there was widespread electoral corruption and control of voting behavior in the countryside, to which the successful introduction of the secret ballot in 1958 put an end. We therefore collected data on land concentration, land prices, the employment of *inquilinos* (dependent agricultural laborers), and voting outcomes before and after the reform to determine whether the implications of our model would be consistent with what happened.

After independence, Chile adopted republican institutions, and elections were used to allocate political power. After 1874, these elections were even based on universal male suffrage. Nevertheless, as in all other Latin

American democracies in the nineteenth century, in Chile the franchise was only partially effective, because voting was not secret. Fraud, coercion, and electoral corruption were all used to systematically influence the outcomes of elections (see Posada-Carbó 2000; Lehoucq and Molina 2002). Even the end of open voting with the electoral law of 1925 did little to restrict corruption, because even though the law stipulated that ballots were to be issued by the government, each party had a separate ballot (Castro 1941, 35; Cruz-Coke 1984, 27–29). To vote for a particular party, a voter had to request that party's ballot, thus making it possible to know for whom he or she was voting. This practice was finally stopped in 1958, with an electoral law promulgated on May 31 that introduced the full Australian ballot.

On the basis of these institutions, Chile formed a relatively stable, though restricted, democracy. After 1932, democratic stability was based on an explicit compromise between the growing power of urban groups and the power of the traditional landed elites (Valenzuela 1978, 26; Scully 1992, 108–109). Landlords systematically controlled rural voting until the late 1950s. James Petras and Maurice Zeitlin documented that, "until 1958, elections were carried out with each political party having a separate ballot. . . . Thus the patrones often simply gave the ballots for the party of their choice to the inquilinos, and provided them and nearby peasants with transportation to and from the polling places" (1968, 510) (for more evidence, see Kaufman 1972; Bauer 1975; Loveman 1976). René Millar Carvacho's evidence (1981, 172) is similar. The control of rural votes by landlords was made possible by the relatively good working conditions of the inquilinos compared to the possible alternatives, and the available evidence shows that they earned rents (Baland and Robinson 2003b; Bauer 1995, 27–28).

By the 1950s, the political landscape in Chile was dominated by several main parties. The traditional nineteenth-century parties, the Conservatives, the Liberals, and the Radicals, were all still effective. The Conservatives and Liberals were furthest to the right, and were united in most things except in their attitudes toward the Catholic Church (the Conservatives were closely associated with the church, while the Liberals tended to be anticlerical). The Radicals were oriented more toward the center politically and were strongly anticlerical. Also in the center, though in very small numbers in the 1950s, were the Christian Democrats. To the left were the Socialists and then the Communists (the latter were officially banned from 1948 to 1958, though they competed under different names). The landed oligarchy provided the traditional constituency of the two right-wing parties, the Conservatives and the Liberals (see, e.g., Gil 1966). The existing party system was shocked, however, by the return of former dictator Carlos Ibáñez as a populist presidential candidate in 1952. Ibáñez formed a very heterogeneous coalition of mostly leftist groups and capitalized on the general disillusionment with the traditional parties.

We focus here on the 1957 parliamentary elections (all of Congress and half of the Senate), as they allow a more direct comparison to the parliamentary elections that occurred after 1958 (the 1961 and 1965 elections). The landed oligarchy in Chile dominated the Central Valley provinces, particularly the provinces of Aconcagua, Colchagua, and O'Higgins, and it is in these three provinces that the proportion of votes in favor of the two right-wing parties was the strongest. As Table 8.1 shows, the share of right-wing votes in 1957 was 70.2 percent in Colchagua, 58.5 percent in Aconcagua, and 47.4 percent in O'Higgins; these shares were all much higher than the national average (33 percent) as well as the scores obtained in the other rural provinces.

We focus here on the fifteen rural provinces of the Central Valley and the Frontier region, which are relatively homogenous in their physical characteristics. We therefore omit the arid and semiarid provinces of the far north and the far south, because land concentration tends to be very high given the economic activities undertaken there—mostly ranching. (However, as shown in Baland and Robinson 2003b, the relationships highlighted here remain remarkably similar if we consider instead all Chilean provinces, or even all Chilean municipalities.) Across these provinces, the relationship between right-wing votes and the patron-inquilino system is striking, as shown in Tables 8.1 and 8.2. For example, the correlation between right-wing votes and the proportion of inquilinos in the agricultural labor force is as high as 0.64. Provinces in which the inquilino system was more developed tend to exhibit stronger support for the right-wing parties. The correlation between the proportion of right-wing votes and land concentration is 0.64, while the correlation between the latter and the proportion of inquilinos is 0.80.

As column 4 of Table 8.1 shows, the introduction of the secret ballot had an immediate impact on the balance of political power in Chile. Brian Loveman noted: "The introduction of a public ballot meant that landowners could no longer effectively control the votes of rural labor. The electoral hegemony of the Right in the countryside thus gave way to forces that advocated social change in the rural areas. . . . In 1958 the performance of the FRAP (Socialists and Communists) in rural districts left little doubt that landowners' control over rural votes had considerably declined" (1976, 219).[5] Interestingly, however, despite these changes, Jorge Alessandri, of the Conservative Party, won the presidential election in 1958, principally on a platform emphasizing conservative monetary policies as a response to the populism of the Ibáñez regime.[6]

Compare now the electoral results of 1957 to the average of the electoral results in 1961 and 1965. Across the fifteen Central Valley and Frontier provinces, the fall in the right-wing votes occurred in provinces with higher initial right-wing votes (p = –0.71), larger proportions of

Table 8.1 Voting Patterns in Chile's Central Valley Provinces Before and After 1958 (percentages)

Province	Proportion of Right-Wing Votes			Change in Right-Wing Votes	Proportion of Votes for Christian Democrats and the Left			Change in Votes for Christian Democrats and the Left
	1957	1961	1965	1957 vs. 1961–1965	1957	1961	1965	1957 vs. 1961–1965
Colchagua	70.2	45.8	22.1	−36.3	6.6	33.2	63.4	41.7
Aconcagua	58.5	38.6	19.0	−29.4	6.9	37.2	70.0	46.7
O'Higgins	47.4	29.6	14.0	−25.6	14.5	40.7	67.8	39.8
Other Central Valley rural provinces	32.2	31.7	16.9	−16.0	11.0	16.1	68.3	31.2
Other rural provinces	27.0	26.5	14.1	−8.5	22.8	37.9	57.7	25.1
Total	33.0	30.4	12.5	−11.5	20.1	37.5	65.0	31.1

Source: Baland and Robinson 2003b.

Table 8.2 Land Distribution and Agrarian Relations in Chile's Central Valley Provinces Before and After 1958 (percentages)

Province	Share of Total Agricultural Area Operated by Farms over 200 Hectares			Proportion of Inquilinos in the Agricultural Labor Force			Change in Share of Total Agricultural Area Operated by Farms Over 1,000 hectares, 1955–1965
	1955	1965	Change, 1955–1965	1955	1965	Change, 1955–1965	
Colchagua	79.7	71.7	−8.0	20.4	12.0	−8.4	−8.7
Aconcagua	94.9	88.9	−6.0	19.3	11.0	−8.3	−6.0
O'Higgins	73.6	53.1	−20.5	20.2	11.0	−9.2	−23.7
Other Central Valley rural provinces	66.0	60.8	−5.2	15.2	9.9	−5.3	−4.1
Other rural provinces	70.5	73.6	3.1	8.0	5.6	−2.4	−4.2
Total	71.4	69.5	−1.9	12.4	8.4	−4.0	−1.1

Source: Baland and Robinson 2003b.

inquilinos per worker (p = –0.78), and larger land concentrations (p = –0.58, for the area operated by farms larger than 200 hectares). The fall in right-wing votes was dramatic in the Central Valley provinces. Even the absolute number of right-wing votes fell in that area, despite the large increase in registered voters. Therefore, while the right-wing parties lost 11.5 percent of votes in 1961–1965 compared to 1957 in Chile, the fall was 36.3 percent in Colchagua (from an absolute majority of 70.2 percent of the votes in 1957 to barely 22.1 percent in 1965, and 23.1 percent in 1969!), 29.4 percent in Aconcagua, and 25.6 percent in O'Higgins. Simultaneously, the rise in Christian Democrats and left-wing votes was equally dramatic in those provinces, as it increased by 41.7 percent in Colchagua (from 6.6 to 48.3 percent of the votes), by 46.7 percent in Aconcagua, and by 39.8 percent in O'Higgins, more than in the other Central Valley provinces (31.2 percent) and in the other rural provinces (25.1 percent).

Between 1955 and 1965, the pattern of land distribution changed significantly. Thus, while the general fall in land concentration over Chile was almost negligible (the area operated by farms larger than 200 hectares fell by 1.9 percent over the period), the change was far from homogeneous (see Table 8.2). In fact, the share of large farms actually increased in nine provinces, and the increase was larger than 10 percent in five of them (Antofagasta, Aysen, Atacama, Osorno, and Chiloe). Across the fifteen Central Valley and Frontier rural provinces, land concentration on average fell by 5.7 percent, and land concentration rose in the border provinces of Osorno, Cautin, and Llanquihue. Falling land concentration is associated with a fall in right-wing votes (p = 0.36), a fall in initial land concentration (p = 0.30), a fall in the initial amount of right-wing votes (p = 0.37), and a fall in the proportion of inquilinos in the agricultural labor force (p = 0.21).

In the landed oligarchic provinces, the fall in land concentration and in right-wing votes was accompanied by a corresponding fall in the proportion of inquilinos in the agricultural labor force (1965 versus 1955). The correlation between those changes across the Central Valley and Frontier provinces is notably high. For example, the correlation between the change in the proportion of inquilinos and the change in right-wing votes is 0.47, while the correlation with the fall in land concentration is 0.55. Clearly, the 1958 ballot reform dealt a fatal blow to the strength of the landed oligarchy.

Our model also predicts that the electoral reforms of 1958 should lead to a fall in the price of land. To examine this issue (see Baland and Robinson 2003b), we collected data from the most important national Chilean newspaper, *El Mercurio,* from August 1956 to December 1960, by recording nationwide announcements of farms offered for sale. Because the electoral reform law was promulgated on May 31, 1958, we first looked at the average price of one hectare of land before and after this date according to the province location. Table 8.3 summarizes this information. While it appears that land prices in real terms may have fallen after 1958, the fall was much more pronounced in exactly those provinces that we have already singled out: Aconcagua, Colchagua, and O'Higgins. Also noticeable is the hierarchy in land prices, with land being the most expensive in the Central Valley urban area (Santiago and Valparaiso), followed by Aconcagua, Colchagua, and O'Higgins, then by the other Central Valley provinces, and finally by the other provinces (the Frontier, the North, the Lakes, and the Canals), in the latter of which prices fell by about 7 percent. However, the difference in prices in Aconcagua, Colchagua, and O'Higgins compared to prices in the other Central Valley provinces disappeared after 1958.

In interpreting the results given in Table 8.3, we did not properly control for the size of the farm, or for the quality of land. As a result, we turned to regression estimates, in order to investigate the existence of a structural break on May 31, 1958. The results obtained (Baland and Robinson 2003b) were striking. We showed that there was a structural break in farm prices before and after the electoral reform: prices fell by about one-third after May 31, 1958. Most interesting is that the fall was more pronounced in precisely the three Central Valley provinces of Aconcagua, Colchagua, and O'Higgins, and probably also in Santiago and Valparaiso. It seems hard to imagine that there is a plausible alternative story that can explain our correlations between what happened before 1958 in Chile and what happened afterward. However, we did consider a series of alternative explanations that may account for different parts of the evidence (see Baland and Robinson 2003b). Our conclusion, however, is that all of these explanations are less consistent, and some are starkly inconsistent, with the totality of the evidence compared to our theory.

Indirect Vote Buying and Public Policy

Indirect vote buying does not lead to the misallocation of resources simply because of the incentives it creates to structure the economy to take advantage of it. It also has a profound influence on public policy. Consider a situation (following Baland and Robinson 2003a) in which the state budget is equal to B, and two political parties, party 1 and party 2, compete for office by proposing an allocation of this budget between expenditures on a public good, G, and political rents given to the voters. These rents are used to purchase votes with a price per vote, to be determined endogenously, of p. Parties thus compete by proposing political platforms (G_j, p_j) for $j = 1,2$, to the voters, under the condition that the government budget constraint must be satisfied, or

Table 8.3 Land Prices in Chile's Central Valley Provinces Before and After 1958

Province	Before 1958			After 1958			
	Average Land Price (thousand pesos per hectare)	Number of Observations	Median Farm Size (hectares)	Average Land Price (thousand pesos per hectare)	Number of Observations	Median Farm Size (hectares)	Change in Average Land Price (percentage)
Urban central (Santiago and Valparaiso)	275 (202)	40	128	236 (172)	21	100	–14
Aconcagua, O'Higgins, and Colchagua	211 (201)	22	179	135 (154)	21	214	–36
Other Central Valley provinces	151 (156)	41	280	107 (111)	43	240	–29
Other provinces	66 (48)	53	500	61 (66)	37	594	–7
Total	162 (175)	156	243	127 (138)	107	210	–22

Source: Baland and Robinson 2003b.
Note: Standard deviations are shown in parentheses. The grouping of provinces is identical to the groupings in Tables 8.1 and 8.2, except that (the few) observations from the province of Concepcion have been included in "Other provinces."

$$G_j + p_j n \leq B \tag{1}$$

where n is the total number of voters in this economy.

We assume that the objective of the political parties is to maximize their expected vote share. However, as is the case in many standard models of political competition (for instance in the probabilistic voting model, in which all groups or individuals have equal political power; Lindbeck and Weibull 1987; Coughlin 1992), this objective boils down to maximizing a utilitarian social welfare function—the sum of the utilities of voters. There are two types of agents in this economy, l employers and $n - l$ workers, and we use a subscript i to refer to a representative individual. Employers earn an income y_e while workers earn an income y_w. Employers are identical, so that each of them employs $((n - l) / l) \geq 1$ workers. All agents have the same utility function, which is quasi-linear. Hence

$$U_i = c_i + v(G), \text{ where } c_i = y_i + \Delta_i \text{ for } i = e, w$$

Here c_i is consumption; Δ_i represents the political rents accruing to agent i from selling votes to a political party. Here $\Delta_i = p_j$ if individual i sells his or her vote directly to party j; $\Delta_i = 0$ if individual i's vote is controlled by someone else; and $\Delta_i = p_j(((n - l) / l) + 1)$ if individual i is an employer who sells the votes of his or her workers to party j. Here $v(G)$ is the utility each agent derives from the provision of G units of the public good, which we assume to be strictly concave, with $v'(G) > 0$ and $v''(G) < 0$, indicating diminishing marginal utility. For simplicity, we only allow public goods to directly affect utility here, but in a more general model they could also represent infrastructure and other things that directly increase income. None of this alters the results we present here.

We first consider a situation in which votes can be freely bought and sold, but in which employers do not control the votes of their workers, so that parties can buy only one vote per individual. In such a situation, competing parties choose G_j and p_j to maximize the following objective function:

$$l(y_e + p_j + v(G_j)) + (n - l)(y_w + p_j + v(G_j))$$

subject to equation 1 above. In equilibrium, parties will choose (G_j, p_j) such that the budget constraint is satisfied with equality, so that $p_j = ((B - G_j) / n)$. Substituting this into the parties' objective function, we find that

$$l(y_e + ((B - G_j) / n) + v(G_j)) + (n - l)(y_w + ((B - G_j) / n) + v(G_j))$$

and maximizing this with respect to G_j, we derive the first-order condition:

$$1 = nv'(G_j) \tag{2}$$

Equation 2 is one equation in one unknown, the level of G_j that maximizes the vote share of party. Notice that in models of this type, there is a unique strategy that a party must adopt to maximize their vote share, and this strategy is the same for each party, in the sense that it involves offering the same level of public goods and the same price per votes to each individual. The fact that equation 2 only involves the public-goods level of one party demonstrates that this equilibrium strategy is a dominant strategy. The level of G_j that solves equation 2 corresponds to the socially efficient level of the public good. We denote this G^*. This is such that the marginal cost of providing the public good is equalized to the sum of its marginal benefit across all agents in the economy (the so-called Lindahl-Samuelson rule).

Consider now another situation in which employers control the $((n - l) / l)$ votes of their workers, so that they can sell $(((n - l) / l) + 1)$ votes to the political parties. In this situation, all votes are sold by the employers, and as a result the preferences of the workers are irrelevant for determining the outcome of the election. It is the preferences of the employers that will determine which party wins. This being the case, parties propose political platforms (G_j, p_j) that maximize the utility of employers. In particular, they now maximize

$$l(y_e + p_j(((n - l) / l) + 1) + v(G_j))$$

Using the government budget constraint as before, it is easy to derive the first-order condition that implicitly defines the optimal choice of public goods for political parties to offer:

$$1 = lv'(G_j) \tag{3}$$

In the latter expression, the marginal cost of the public good is now equated to the sum of the marginal benefits across all employers, thereby ignoring its impact on the workers. We denote the solution to equation 3 by G^c. The amount of the public good provided is thus too low compared to the socially optimal level. To see this, note that

$$v'(G^*) = (1 / n) < (1 / l) = v'(G^c), \text{ since } l < n$$

and thus

$$v'(G^*) < v'(G^c) \text{ and, since } v'' < 0, G^* > G^c$$

The key intuition behind this result is that when some votes are sold indirectly, the parties need to propose platforms that please only those agents who sell the votes, and can safely ignore the preferences of those whose votes are sold.

Direct Vote Buying, Targeting, and Public Policy

We now develop a simple extension of the model of the previous section to show how, once groups of voters have different amounts of political power, underprovision of public goods arises when vote buying is direct. This occurs when vote buying can be targeted more finely than taxes and transfers.

In the previous section, we implicitly assumed that when votes were being bought, political parties had to buy all votes at the same price. This is without loss of generality when all individuals have the same political power. However, when individuals or groups of individuals differ in this, parties will typically wish to buy only the votes of the most powerful individuals. What do we mean by political power? Our model is consistent with various interpretations. A group may have power if it consists of a lot of "swing voters" who are willing to switch from one party to another. Alternatively, a group may have power if it has solved the collective action problem while other groups have not (Grossman and Helpman 2001). On the other hand, a group may have more power if it has a relatively high marginal utility of income (i.e., if it is poor), since in this case politicians can buy votes relatively cheaply (Dixit and Londregan 1996).

As previously, we consider here a situation in which the state budget is given, equal to B, and in which two political parties compete for office by proposing an allocation of this budget between expenditures on a public good, G_j, proposing a uniform transfer to all agents in the economy, t_j, and buying the votes of individual voters. However, we now allow the price paid for a vote to differ across voters of different types. This setup is meant to illustrate the idea that buying votes may allow politicians to target policies more effectively than can standard fiscal policies. This can be politically attractive when some groups of voters have a lot of political power (see Chapter 6 for more on these issues in the context of vote buying).

No agent sells the votes of other agents, so that only one vote may be bought directly from each individual agent. More specifically, we assume that there are two types of agents in this economy, A and B, so that party $j = 1,2$ pays price p_{jA} for the vote of an agent of type A, and price p_{jB} for the vote of an agent of type B. There are $(n / 2)$ agents of both types, and they have identical preferences:

$$U_i = c_i + v(G), \text{ where } c_i = y + p_i + t_j$$

The key difference between the two types of agents is that agents of type A have more political power than agents of type 2. Otherwise they are identical—in preferences and in incomes.

Parties compete by announcing to the voters political platforms $(G_j, p_{jA}, p_{jB}, t_j)$ for $j = 1,2$ that must satisfy the government budget constraint:

$$G_j + p_{jA}(n / 2) + p_{jB}(n / 2) + t_j n \leq B \tag{4}$$

Given this constraint, and the preferences of the agents, the socially efficient level of the public good, once more denoted G^*, again satisfies equation 2. As before, we assume here that the two parties maximize their expected vote share. As a result, they maximize the weighted sum of the welfare of all voters, where $\phi > 1/2$ is the weight given to agents of type A, and $(1 - \phi)$ is the weight given to agents of type B. The parameter ϕ parameterizes the relative power of group A: because $\phi > 1/2$, this means that A has more power and obtains more weight in the objective function of the party.

Parties thus simultaneously choose $(G_j, p_{jA}, p_{jB}, t_j)$ to maximize

$$\phi(n / 2)(y + p_{jA} + t_j + v(G_j)) + (1 - \phi)(n / 2)(y + p_{jB} + t_j + v(G_j)) \tag{5}$$

subject to equation 4. As $\phi > 1/2$, it directly follows from equation 5 that political parties should buy the votes of type-A voters only, as the marginal impact of a dollar increase in the price of votes paid to agents of type A always increases the expected vote share of the party more than giving an extra dollar to voters of group B. Technically, the optimization problem has a corner solution where $p_{jB} = t_j = 0$, and where the level of public goods satisfies

$$1 = (n / 2)v'(G_j) \tag{6}$$

and

$$p_{jA} = (2 / n)(B - G_j)$$

Here political parties undersupply public goods in order to free up resources to target them to the group with the most political power (it is immediate that G_j defined by equation 6 is smaller than G^*. As discussed, there are many ways that votes may be bought. An obvious way, in the spirit of this analysis, is through public sector employment (which helps to motivate why the cost of buying votes appears in the government budget constraint). A job is as targeted a form of redistribution as one can imagine, since it benefits just one individual.

Conclusion

In this chapter we have developed some general ideas about vote buying that suggest, along with the evidence from Chile, that electoral corruption has pervasive, first-order effects both on the way the economy is organized and on the efficiency of public policy. In our view, there is little to sustain the type of optimism expressed by James Buchanan and Gordon Tullock (1962) about the prospect that votes can be bought and sold.

From this point of view, the introduction of political institutions that stop corruption and vote buying, such as the Australian ballot, appear to be as significant a step in the process of political development as the construction of electoral democracy itself. Indeed, as our evidence on Chile suggests, the Australian ballot has dramatic political ramifications. In Chile, it led to a complete rearrangement of the party system, ultimately playing a central role in the rise of Salvador Allende and the Augusto Pinochet coup of 1973. There are other examples along the same lines. For instance, in Argentina, universal male suffrage was introduced in 1862, but radical political change came only with the Saenz Peña legislation of 1912, part of which was the introduction of the Australian ballot. This innovation resulted in the rise of the urban Radical Party and the collapse of the traditional rurally based Conservatives, and culminated in the coup of 1930. The political fallout from these reforms included the unraveling of the political coalition that underpinned the prosperity of the Argentine export economy, and the rise of Peronism in the 1940s. Nevertheless, the introduction of the secret ballot does not always induce coups and dictatorships. In Britain after 1872, it helped to induce large expansions in socially desirable policies, such as education and public goods.

Notes

1. When individual voting behavior is not observable, it may still be possible to observe how aggregates of voters behave.

2. Examples of work comparing the policies and economic implications of dictators and democrats include McGuire and Olson 1996; Acemoglu and Robinson 2001; Przeworski et al. 2000. Recent research on the implications of different democratic institutions (electoral laws, presidential versus parliamentary institutions) for economic policies includes Persson and Tabellini 2000, 2003; Austen-Smith 2000; Milesi-Feretti, Perotti, and Rostagno 2002.

3. A large empirical literature has argued that there is an inverse relationship between farm size and productivity, and that large farms tend to be relatively inefficient. See, for example, Berry and Cline 1979; Binswanger, Deininger, and Feder 1995.

4. This example, however, leaves unanswered two related issues. First, there is the question as to what mechanisms lead some agents to become employers and oth-

ers workers. Second, the way ideology is modeled here is overly simplistic and, in particular, we may think that employers care not only about the votes of the worker whom they themselves bring to their preferred party, but also about the votes brought by other employers. This, however, creates a public-goods type of problem, which we ignore here.

5. See Baland and Robinson 2003b for a discussion of why the secret ballot was introduced in 1958.

6. Allesandri polled only 33,416 votes more than Salvador Allende, the candidate for the Socialist-Communist alliance (out of 1,235,552 votes cast).

Part 3

Is Reform Possible?

9

How Effective Are Institutional Reforms?

Allen D. Hicken

Vote buying is a widespread practice in democratic polities, as this book demonstrates. Almost as common are attempts to eliminate (or at least curtail) the practice of vote buying. These anti–vote buying campaigns run the gamut from voter education efforts (see Chapter 10), to electoral reform, to efforts to change cultural mores.[1] In this chapter I focus on one particular set of anti–vote buying tools available to election officials and legislators, namely institutional reforms. These are reforms that seek to adjust the incentives and ability to buy and sell votes by altering the political-institutional environment in which voters, candidates, and parties interact.

I argue that institutional reforms can and do have predictable effects on the prevalence of vote buying. However, two factors often limit the efficacy of institutional reform efforts. First, because wholesale, coordinated reform is politically difficult, institutional reform often happens in an ad hoc or uncoordinated manner. When this occurs, reform in one area can be undermined by the lack of reform (or conflicting reforms) in another area—for example, stricter anti–vote buying laws without concomitant enforcement, or greater enforcement efforts without changes to candidate and voter incentives to exchange money for votes. Similarly, if institutional reform occurs in a vacuum—that is, without supporting changes in the socioeconomic or cultural environments[2]—this may reduce the reform's impact.

I begin by briefly reviewing some of the factors, identified elsewhere in this volume, that can support vote buying. In connection with each factor, I discuss institutional remedies that could alter the incentives and the ability of candidates and voters to buy and sell votes. I then turn to the case of institutional reform in Thailand. Vote buying has been a well-known feature of Thai elections since the 1970s. In 1997, Thailand adopted a new constitution with the primary goal of bringing about an end to vote buying and money politics. I analyze how the constitutional reforms may alter the incentives and capabilities of voters and candidates to trade votes for

145

money. Drawing on evidence from the 2000 and 2001 elections, I argue that some features of the new electoral system, along with greater (potential) monitoring and enforcement of anti–vote buying rules, suggest reduced incentives for vote buying. However, the broader picture is less clear. The new electoral system is not likely to eliminate the incentives for vote buying, and the future role of the Election Commission of Thailand (ECT) is in some doubt. Finally, many of the underlying structural factors that feed vote buying remain unaddressed.[3]

Remedies for Vote Buying:
A Menu of Institutional Reforms

Among the factors that facilitate or encourage vote buying are several for which there are plausible institutional remedies. The list below briefly summarizes four factors that can contribute to vote buying, along with possible remedies from the menu of institutional reforms. This list is certainly not exhaustive, but it is representative of the types of problems that scholars have identified and the institutional solutions that have been proposed or applied in countries around the world.

1. *Strong incentives to cultivate a personal vote.* The types of strategies candidates adopt in their effort to win office vary depending on the surrounding institutional and political environment. Candidate-centered electoral systems, especially those with intraparty competition, generate strong incentives for candidates to cultivate a personal vote. One strategy for cultivating such support is via vote buying. Thus, vote buying is more likely in countries with extremely personalized electoral and party systems, and less likely in countries where parties are stronger and party labels are more valuable to voters and candidates (see Chapter 4).

Institutional remedies. Reduce incentives to cultivate a personal vote by eliminating intraparty competition. Strengthen incentives to pursue a programmatic campaign strategy and invest in and protect a party label. Possible reforms include restricting party switching, requiring candidates to belong to a political party, adopting a closed-list proportional representation system, or adding a party-list tier to the legislature.[4]

2. *A supply of surplus votes.* As discussed in Chapter 4, electoral systems differ in their propensity to produce a supply of surplus votes. When voters can cast multiple votes, they may discount the value of some of those votes, reserving some for the sincere expression of their preferences while considering others as extra votes that are available for sale. All else being equal, vote buying is more likely where there are multiple and potentially surplus votes, than where voters cast a single vote.

Institutional remedy. Reduce the potential supply of surplus votes by moving from a multiple- to a single-vote system.

3. *Small number of votes needed for victory.* The number of votes needed to ensure victory is another variable that may affect the expected utility of vote buying. Where the number of needed votes is small, vote buying may be a viable strategy. But as the number of votes a candidate has to win in order to ensure election rises, candidates face incentives to abandon individual-level strategies such as vote buying and adopt strategies aimed at larger numbers of constituents (e.g., pork barreling, policy position taking, public-goods provision).

Institutional remedies. Increase the number of votes needed to secure election by increasing the size of the district electorate. Reduce the number of competitors in a given district by raising barriers to entry. These include requirements that candidates belong to a political party or that parties meet certain thresholds of support (e.g., a minimum vote percentage in the past election, a requisite number of members, candidates, or branches).[5]

4. *Low probability of detection or costly punishment.* The degree to which anti–vote buying regulations exist and are enforced has a direct effect on the expected utility of vote buying. Laws outlawing vote buying are not sufficient to deter vote buying. All three of the following additional conditions must accompany anti–vote buying legislation: a high probability of detection, severe penalties for engaging in vote buying, and a high probability that enforcement of the penalty will be carried out. If any of these three conditions is lacking, anti–vote buying legislation is not likely to deter candidates.

Institutional remedies. This area of institutional reform is the most frequent target of anti–voting buying campaigns. Taking the responsibility for monitoring and enforcement out of the hands of politicians and placing it under an autonomous or semiautonomous agency is one common strategy for increasing the probability of detection and punishment. Strict campaign finance regulation and reporting requirements, together with incentives for whistleblowers, can also help raise the probability of detecting violations.

Vote Buying and Institutional Reform in Thailand

Vote buying has been a regular and much lamented feature of national elections in Thailand throughout its (semi)democratic history. In fact, to some vote buying is *the* defining feature of Thai elections. Depending on the survey, 31–70 percent of Thai voters admit to being offered money for their votes (Pasuk et al. 2000). It is nearly impossible to find an analysis of Thailand's political system, either in the popular press or in the academic literature, that doesn't make some mention of vote buying. Several studies of vote buying in Thailand have focused on the mechanics of the exchange, which by now are fairly well understood (see, e.g., Murashima 1987; Sombat 1993; Arghiros 1993, 1995; Callahan and McCargo 1996; Callahan 2000). Other studies have taken vote buying as an independent variable and used it to explain certain political or policy outcomes. Daniel King (1996) argues that the importance of vote buying as a campaign strategy has increased the influence of big business in Thai politics, while James Ockey (1991, 2000) demonstrates that vote buying can be linked to the growth of organized crime. Efforts have also been made to explain why a market for votes exists in the first place (Arghiros 1995; Callahan and McCargo 1996; Callahan 2000). Explanations tend to focus on a variety of structural and socioeconomic factors, such as pervasive patron-client relationships, low levels of development, and bureaucratic neglect and corruption in rural Thailand. These explanations are especially valuable because they look beyond vote buying as an isolated phenomenon to be outlawed and eradicated. Instead, they treat vote buying as a reflection of an underlying socioeconomic, cultural, and political environment.

Continuing in the latter tradition, I argue that political-institutional factors have played a significant role in shaping the market for votes in Thailand. In the remainder of this section, I explain why Thai candidates in the prereform era had incentive to employ personal (as opposed to party-centered) campaign strategies, and why vote buying was a method of choice for many candidates as they sought to cultivate personal support networks. I then turn my attention to the effects of Thailand's new constitution on this market for votes.

The Market for Votes in Prereform Thailand

As discussed throughout this volume, there is no single root cause of vote buying. Socioeconomic factors, such as income levels, education, and urbanization, along with societal patterns and culture, can affect both the demand and the supply side of the vote buying relationship. Vote buying is also located in a larger political order. In Thailand, numerous scholars argue that vote buying is fueled by the chronic neglect and abuse of rural areas (Nelson 1998b; Sombat 1993, 1997; Anek 1997; Ammar n.d.; Callahan 2002).[6] Another important feature of that political order is the nature of Thailand's electoral and party systems.

For most of its democratic history, Thailand has used a block-vote electoral system. This type of majoritarian electoral system is uncommon.[7] Under the 1978 and 1992 constitutions, Thailand was broken down into 142–156 electoral districts (depending on the election year), which together were responsible for filling 360–393 seats in the House of Representatives.[8] Electoral districts were broken down into one-, two-, and three-seat districts. Most Thai districts had a district magnitude of three or two, while a few were single-seat districts. Seats were allocated by province *(changwat),* with each province receiving the number of seats commensurate with its population (one seat for every 150,000 people). See Table 9.1 for a summary of these data for the six elections prior to the new constitution of 1997.

If a province had a large enough population for more than three seats, the province was divided into more than one district, and the seats were distributed so as to avoid single-seat districts. Single-seat districts occurred only in provinces with a population under 225,000.[9] Voters were allowed to vote for as many candidates as there were seats in a district, and seats were awarded to the top one, two, or three vote getters on the basis of the plurality rule (block voting). Voters could not group their votes on one candidate (no cumulation) but panachage was allowed—voters could split their votes between candidates from different parties. Finally, voters were not required to cast all of their votes—they could partially abstain (known as plumping).[10] Parties were required to field a full team of candidates for any district they wished to contest (e.g., three candidates in a three-seat district), and to run a minimum number of candidates nationwide (one-fourth to one-half of the total House membership, depending on the elections year).

What are the implications of the block vote when it comes to vote buying? Thailand's block-vote system undermined the party cohesion and the value of party labels by encouraging factionalized parties and candidate-centered campaigning. One determinant of party cohesion is the degree to which the electoral system allows for intraparty competition (see Chapter 4). Thailand's system did not generate the degree of intraparty competition that occurs in systems where there are fewer seats than copartisan candidates in a given district, such as in single nontransferable vote or single transferable vote systems, but it did pit candidates from the same party against one another.[11] As a result, neither candidates nor voters could rely on party labels to help differentiate between candidates from the same party.

Table 9.1   Basic Electoral System Data, Thailand, 1983–1996

	1983	1986	1988	March 1992	September 1992	1995	1996
Total districts	134	138	142	142	142	155	156
Total seats	324	347	357	360	360	391	393
Three-seat districts	65	80	82	85	85	88	88
Two-seat districts	60	49	51	48	48	60	61
One-seat districts	9	9	9	9	9	7	7
Minimum required number of candidates	162	173	178	90	90	98	98

Source: Hicken 2002.

Instead, most candidates worked to develop a personal reputation and personal network of support. The fact that voters had multiple votes—an invitation to split their vote—and that votes were not pooled among copartisans further, strengthened the incentive to pursue a personal strategy.

There is an abundance of quantitative and qualitative evidence in support of the claim that in prereform Thailand, party labels carried little value, and that personal strategies were generally more important to candidates than were party strategies (see Hicken 2002 for a review of this evidence). However, the fact that candidates have strong incentives to adopt personal strategies does not necessarily imply that vote buying will be the preferred vehicle for pursuing that strategy. Indeed, as discussed in Chapter 4, a variety of means and methods can be employed by candidates in an effort to create personal support networks, including targeting particularistic goods and services to a candidate's constituents. In fact, candidates do rely on a mix of methods in Thai elections.[12] Yet vote buying stands out as the method of choice for most candidates, most of the time.[13] One reason is certainly the traditionally lax enforcement of anti–vote buying laws. However, there are other reasons why vote buying is attractive to Thai candidates.

First, the peculiar features of the pre-1997 Thai electoral system, combined with traditionally lax enforcement of vote buying prohibitions, render vote buying a feasible and alluring option for candidates. As discussed earlier, Thailand's block-vote system gave most voters two or three votes. Theoretically, voters might have assigned equal value to each vote. In reality, it seems that voters often treated their second and third votes as surplus votes (Sombat 1993, 1997; Callahan 2000; Party Interviews 1999, 2000). The following stylized account, while not universally applicable, is typical. In each district, voters needed one member of parliament (MP) to whom they could turn if they ran into trouble with the bureaucracy (e.g., if they needed to get a family member out of jail or obtain a permit or license). Usually, this MP was the candidate who had the strongest local ties and who was best known to individual voters—in short, a person whom voters could trust to be responsive to their needs. Even without vote buying, this was the candidate whom voters would most likely prefer. However, voters needed only one MP to perform these services. Thus the second and third MPs were not really "needed" from the perspective of voters. It was the second and third votes, then, that were typically for sale. Who received the second and third votes depended, in large part, on which candidate was willing to pay the most for those votes. Candidates, aware of the supply of surplus votes, designed campaign strategies to make the most of this supply. Voters were encouraged to vote for their most preferred candidate "first," and then to give their second (or third) vote to the candidate giving the money (Sombat 1997; Party Interviews 1999, 2000).

Another possible method for cultivating a personal support network is to (promise to) direct pork and other particularistic forms of government largesse to a candidate's constituents and supporters.[14] Indeed, this is a form of personal strategy that virtually all candidates for political office employ. Thai elections can be seen as battles over control of the government pork barrel. Once MPs are in power, it is expected that they will use their position to reward their political constituents and supporters (Christensen et al. 1993; Ammar 1997; Likhit n.d.). The flow of pork from elected representatives to their constituents is certainly not unique to Thailand. Pork provision is a feature of nearly every democracy, but especially those with candidate-centered electoral systems (e.g., the US system, and the single nontransferable vote system in Japan). In some of these democracies, the use of particularism is the personal strategy of choice, while the direct purchase of votes is rare. The question for Thailand is: Why, given the prevalence of pork barrel politics, did vote buying remain a major part of most personal strategies?

To answer this question in the context of Thailand, we must view vote buying and pork distribution not as potential substitutes for each other, but as complementary strategies. Pork and patronage and vote buying are the key components that hold together the candidates' personal electoral support network. Politicians use pork and patronage, not as their major tool to win support from voters (though they do some of this), but rather to protect and promote certain business interests (often including their own).[15] However, in order to help and protect these interests, politicians first have to get elected. Business interests cannot directly supply votes in sufficient numbers, so what do they give politicians in exchange? The answer is financial support, which politicians then use to buy votes (as well as fund other campaign activities).

In short, a symbiotic relationship has developed between most politicians and business interests—a relationship made possible through vote buying and pork and patronage. Politicians receive the resources necessary to buy votes and gain office, and in exchange, business interests acquire political connections, insurance against recalcitrant local officials, as well as specific economic benefits (government contracts, special licenses, etc.). Pork distribution, then, is a means by which politicians raise money to fund their vote buying. This relationship between pork and campaign funds is certainly not unique to Thailand. For example, recent research on Brazil supports the idea that the real aim of pork-barrel politics is money, not votes. David Samuels (2002) finds that pork-barrel expenditures are not directly linked to electoral support, but rather to a candidate's ability to raise money.[16]

To argue that pork and vote buying are complementary in the Thai political system is not to say that pork is not or could not ever be used to mobilize voters directly. However, the pre-1997 political system generated incentives against a greater reliance on pork-based voter mobilization. In order to effectively use pork as a personal strategy, it is not enough to be a member of parliament. The real goal is to be a member of a party within the governing coalition (and, even better, to be a senior minister within the coalition). Parties outside the coalition lack the access to government resources to reward supporters that parties in coalitions have.[17] However, Thailand's multiparty system makes coalition membership an uncertain prospect for any party.

Between 1983 and 1996, more than fifteen parties (on average) competed in each election (see Table 9.2). Of those parties, twelve succeeded in winning at least one seat (on average) in the House of Representatives.[18] Most of those parties present in the legislature were not part of the government coalition—the average size of the coalition cabinet was just over five parties. In other words, only about one in three parties that fielded candidates in an election could expect to win a cabinet seat.

Even when a party is fortunate to become part of the coalition cabinet, its seat at the table is anything but secure. Thailand's multiparty governments are notoriously short-lived.[19] Historically, Thai cabinets have lasted less than thirteen months (on average). Cabinets since 1978 have lasted slightly longer than the historical average—just over eighteen months.[20] (Minor reshuffling of cabinet portfolios among existing coalition members occurs even more frequently.) The type of pork-barrel initiatives necessary to win and maintain the support of voters, such as infrastructure projects, takes time to bring online. Given the level of government and cabinet instability, there is a very real chance that politicians would lose their access to resources before they could fully distribute and claim credit for constituency pork.[21]

The story that emerges is one of uncertainty. Candidates cannot be certain that their party will be part of the government—most will not. Even if their party joins the cabinet, the time horizon for carrying out pork-barrel projects is likely to be short due to cabinet and government instability. Business interests and voters are aware of this uncertainty and respond accordingly. Companies hedge their bets by funding all of the major parties and seeking favors that politicians can deliver immediately (licenses, government contracts, protection from bureaucratic interference, etc.). For their part, voters do not rely solely on promises to distribute pork once a candi-

Table 9.2   Party Data, Thailand, 1983–1996

Average number of parties standing for election	15.3
Average number of parties capturing a seat in the House of Representatives	12.0
Average number of parties in the government coalition	5.3

Source: Hicken 2002.

date is in office, and in fact tend to discount such promises.[22] This makes the immediacy of vote buying attractive to both voters and candidates.

In the final analysis, vote buying stood out as one of the most effective ways for candidates to pursue personal strategies in pre-reform Thailand. The electoral system ensured a ready supply of surplus votes available for purchase. The lack of enforcement, whether out of fear, negligence, or collusion, meant that the risk of being penalized for vote buying was negligible (Callahan 2000). Finally, an alternative strategy for mobilizing a personal support network—pork-barrel politics—worked best in tandem with vote buying.

The 1997 Constitutional Reforms

In 1997, Thailand adopted a new constitution. While the drafters had many goals, it is fair to say that they designed the constitution chiefly to combat vote buying and reduce money politics (McCargo 1998; Connors 1999; Prawase 2002; Sombat 2002).[23] To do this, the drafters overhauled the electoral system and election administration, and worked to "sever the link between elections and government ministries" (Callahan 2002, 4). By one measure they succeeded—the 2001 House elections did indeed see a reduction in the overall amount of vote buying (McCargo 2002; Croissant and Dosch 2001). In addition, a record number of candidates were charged and punished for vote buying. Yet the overall results of the reforms were mixed. Vote buying by no means disappeared, and candidates and parties exhibited impressive flexibility by adapting their vote buying to the new electoral environment (McCargo 2002; Croissant and Dosch 2001). For example, voters were paid to become party members, to join a candidate's "club" (it's interesting to note that the number of members recruited to the Thai Rak Thai Party [11 million—most of whom received some form of monetary reward for joining the party] approximates the number of votes for the party's list—11,634,495 [Nelson 2002, 7]). It is impossible to predict future trends based on just one election, and I will not attempt to do so here. Instead I will briefly discuss how the implementation of many of the reforms discussed earlier in the chapter affected the market for votes, and I will offer preliminary evidence from the 2000 Senate and 2001 House elections.

Consistent with the anti–vote buying campaigns in other democracies (e.g., Taiwan), one of the hallmarks of the Thai effort was reforms to increase the probability that vote buyers would be detected and punished. The new constitution created the Election Commission of Thailand to organize and oversee elections. Before 1997, elections administration was the job of the Ministry of Interior, which at times was far from neutral in its behavior (Callahan 2000). The ECT was designed to be an independent body, free from political and bureaucratic pressure. Not only was it charged with carrying out election organization and administration, but it was also empowered to investigate violations of electoral rules and to disqualify offending candidates (*Constitution* 1997; *Organic Law* 1998).[24] In both the 2000 Senate elections and the 2001 House elections, the ECT acted forcefully to disqualify candidates who were guilty of vote buying, and to hold new rounds of elections in districts where electoral fraud was particularly widespread.[25] In several districts, multiple rounds of elections over several months had to be held before the ECT would certify the results. Despite these successes, the ECT was criticized by those who felt it was overzealous, and by those who felt the ECT's emphasis on countering vote buying had come at the expense of other aspects of election administration (e.g., vote counting) (Croissant and Dosch 2001). Some complained that the ECT's anti–vote buying efforts merely caused candidates to switch "their energies away from risky vote-buying activities" in favor of simply buying local election officers (McCargo 2002, 250). In later elections (2005 and 2006) the ECT was less active and generally viewed as more beholden to the ruling party than in 2000 and 2001 (Somroutai 2002).

The 1997 constitution also overhauled Thailand's electoral system. Gone is the block-vote system. Following a growing trend (see Shugart and Wattenberg 2001), the constitution drafters established a mixed-member or two-tiered system in Thailand. Four hundred seats were elected from single-seat districts on a plurality basis. One hundred additional seats were elected from a single nationwide district via proportional representation. Each party was required to submit a list of candidates for voters to consider, and voters cast two votes: one vote for a district representative and one for a party list. Candidates chose between either running in a district or running on the party list.[26] The constitution also provided for an elected Senate, the first in Thailand's history. Finally, the constitution put new restrictions on party switching and made voting compulsory for all eligible voters.

The overall effect of electoral reforms on vote buying is ambiguous. Some of these reforms could potentially reduce candidates' incentives and ability to buy votes, while others push in the opposite direction. First, the drafters hoped that compulsory voting would expand the size of the electorate and make it too expensive to buy enough votes to win office. They were somewhat successful in this regard. Turnout for the first round of the 2001 election was higher than turnout for the 1996 election, but the effect of this expansion on vote buying is unclear. The number of votes bought seems to have declined, but the amount of money spent buying votes actually increased.

Another change was the move from block voting to single-seat, single-vote constituencies. This eliminated the ready supply of surplus votes that was available to candidates before 1997. Reducing the supply of votes also drives up the price of a voter's remaining vote, thus increasing the cost of vote buying (Party Interviews 2000). This may account for why, despite the reported decline in the number of votes being bought and sold in 2001 relative to previous elections, the estimated amount of cash spent on vote buying was actually higher than in previous elections (Kamol 2002). Thai banks reported that the increase of currency in circulation during the election campaign (a proxy for vote buying) was 25 billion baht (roughly US$1 billion), 5 billion baht more than during the 1996 election (Tasker and Crispin 2001).[27] In short, candidates bought fewer votes, but the votes they did buy were more expensive.

The drafters of the Thai constitution also adopted several institutional reforms designed to encourage candidates to abandon personal strategies (such as vote buying) in favor of more programmatic or party-oriented strategies. The move to single-seat districts brought an end to the intraparty competition that had helped fuel the need for personal campaign strategies. The constitution also placed new restrictions on party switching in an effort to encourage party building and party discipline.[28] Finally, the drafters also included a national party-list tier—hoping to encourage voters and candidates to place party before person. The effect of these reforms was already evident in the 2001 election. For the first time in recent memory, political parties, led by the new Thai Rak Thai Party, moved away from relying solely on personal strategies, in favor of coordinated, party-centered strategies.[29] Parties developed the beginnings of serious policy platforms and actually campaigned on those policies (Nelson 2002). However, this shift from personal strategies to nascent party-centered strategies was largely confined to the campaign for party-list seats. Campaigns for the 400 constituency seats generally remained candidate-centered affairs (Nelson 2002). Indeed, this is not surprising given the electoral system. Single-seat districts still generate strong incentives to cultivate personal support networks (although somewhat less than the block vote) (Carey and Shugart 1995). Over time, party-centered campaigning and party-centered voting may gradually have spilled over into constituency elections, but given the 2006 coup and uncertainly over what the next constitution will look like, we may never get an opportunity to find out.[30]

Another reason that personal strategies such as vote buying persisted in Thailand in constituency elections is that the reforms that the drafters of the constitution adopted did not all push in the same direction. Two sets of reforms, chosen for reasons apart from a concern about vote buying, may actually have undermined the constitution's anti–vote buying reforms. The first was a sharp net reduction in the number of votes needed to win a seat. The drafters hoped that smaller constituencies would allow candidates to develop loyal relationships without having to resort to vote buying (Borwornsak and Burns 1998). However, the combined effect of adding more seats to the legislature and switching from block voting to single-seat, single-vote districts was a dramatic reduction in the number of votes that candidates needed to win election (this despite the higher voter turnout in 2001). In the 1996 election, the average winning candidate garnered over 93,000 votes. In 2001, candidates won seats with an average of just under 33,000 votes—a 65 percent reduction in the number of votes needed to gain a seat. As discussed earlier, the use of personal strategies tends to be negatively correlated with the size of a district's voting population and the number of votes required to win an election. Fewer voters means that a fixed amount of money, patronage, or influence will buy a larger portion of the total votes, all else being equal.[31]

A second feature of the new constitution that suggested the continued importance of personal strategies in Thai election is the electoral procedure for the Senate. Senators were elected from districts comprising one to eighteen seats. Each voter cast a single vote, and seats were awarded via the plurality rule. This electoral system, known as the single nontransferable vote, is the epitome of a candidate-centered electoral system (see Carey and Shugart 1995; Grofman et al. 1999). Candidates in such a system must typically create personal support networks in order to win. However, Thailand's version of this electoral system went beyond most other examples. Senate candidates were constitutionally prohibited from belonging to a political party. They were also not allowed to campaign for office. The aim of the constitution drafters was to create a legislative body that would remain above the petty political squabbling that characterizes the House (Suchit 1999). The reality was very different. Candidates could not rely on party labels to distinguish themselves from other candidates, nor could they campaign on programmatic policy differences—no campaigning was allowed. Instead, they had to create personal support networks similar to those used by House candidates (many of the successful candidates were family members of prominent politicians and so were able to rely on existing support networks [Nelson 2002]). In fact, the reliance on personal strategies, specifically vote buying, was so common in the first Senate election that it took five months and several rounds of disqualifications, followed by new elections, to fully seat the Senate.

Conclusion

Vote buying does not exist in isolation. It is best understood as a product of a polity's underlying socioeconomic, cultural, and political environments. In this chapter I have focused on the prospects for institutional reform as a weapon in anti–vote buying campaigns. Both theory and evidence suggest that changing institutions can alter actor incentives and ultimately behavior.

However, in the case of combating vote buying, institutional reforms are not a quick fix. The reform of any particular rule or institution must be considered in light of the incentives produced by other rules and institutions, and by the broader political, socioeconomic, and cultural environments. The case of Thailand supports this view.

Thailand's prereform political institutions, especially its electoral system, provided candidates with strong incentives to pursue vote buying strategies. Significant portions of the 1997 constitution and the accompanying electoral reforms were designed to reduce these incentives. Nonetheless, the reforms had a mixed effect on the incentives and capabilities of voters and candidates to trade votes for money. The move to single-member districts decreased the supply of surplus votes, and compulsory voting increased voter turnout, consistent with decreased incentives for vote buying. In addition, the adoption of a party list, restrictions on party switching, and an end to intraparty competition combined to make party-centered strategies more appealing. However, incentives to pursue personal strategies still existed in the form of single-seat districts, a candidate-centered electoral system for the Senate, and a reduced number of votes needed to win a seat.

The most visible factor in the decline of vote buying during the 2001 elections was more stringent enforcement of campaign rules by the Election Commission of Thailand. However, even if the ECT had remained an active and independent agency (which was not certain), it could not be the sole solution to the problem of vote buying. Enhanced detection and punishment of vote buying, if not accompanied by serious attention to the underlying environment, are only partial solutions. Without deeper structural changes to the political, socioeconomic, and cultural factors at the root of vote buying, greater enforcement will merely be a catalyst for greater creativity as candidates and parties work to find ways around the law.[32] While the constitutional reforms brought about some changes in the underlying political environment, many issues remained unaddressed. Until efforts are made to tackle factors such as the socioeconomic gulf between Bangkok and rural Thailand, or the extreme centralization of political and bureaucratic authority, vote buying is likely to continue in one form or another.

Notes

1. In an attempt to change the cultural norms that support vote buying in Thailand, specifically the norm of reciprocity, a senior Buddhist monk declared that it was not immoral to take money from one candidate and vote for another.
2. Or if these changes take time to develop.
3. A military coup in September 2006 did away with the 1997 constitution, thus bringing an end to the episode of reform discussed in this chapter.

4. On the latter, see Shugart and Wattenberg 2001.

5. Lowering district magnitude while keeping the size of the electoral constant would also increase the number of votes needed to win, all else being equal. However, the effect of changing district magnitude on incentives to cultivate a personal vote is conditional on the type of electoral system in use (see Chapter 4, and Carey and Shugart 1995).

6. For an analysis of the power relationships that underlie vote buying, see Callahan 2002.

7. Most majoritarian systems use single-seat districts in which voters have only one vote. Other countries that have used electoral systems similar to Thailand's include Mauritius, nineteenth-century Great Britain, the Philippines (Senate elections), and the United States (some local elections).

8. Thailand has a bicameral legislature consisting of an elected House and (until the 1997 constitutional reforms) an appointed Senate.

9. Each additional 75,000 people above 150,000 were counted as an additional 150,000. A province with 200,000 people would receive one seat, while a 225,000-person province would receive two seats.

10. See Cox 1997, 42–43, for a general discussion of cumulation, panachage, and plumping.

11. See Hicken 2002 for more details.

12. On the use of pork, see Christensen et al. 1993; Ammar 1997. On the use of patron-client relationships, see Arghiros 1993, 1995, 2000. On violence and intimidation in elections, see Ockey 1991, 2000; Callahan 2000; Anderson 1990.

13. As for why more voters don't accept money from one candidate and then vote for whomever they wish anyway, see the discussion of surplus votes later, and the literature on the cultural norms and social structures that support vote buying in Thailand (Arghiros 1993, 1995, 2000; McVey 2000a). For a critique of some of these arguments, see Nelson 1999. Candidates also attempt to devise methods for minimizing such defection (Sombat 1993, 1999).

14. I use Gary Cox and Mathew McCubbins's definition of pork (2001). They divide pork into public goods that are directed or allocated on the basis of political rather than economic calculations (morsels), and rents that are extracted from the government.

15. Former prime minister Banharn Silapa-acha, a rural businessman who grew rich off of state contracts, stated that he could not afford to be out of government and quipped, "those in the opposition are certain to be starved" (Banyat 1992).

16. For the story of why and how this relationship between pork-barrel politics and vote buying developed in Thailand, see McVey 2000a; Hicken 2002; Pasuk and Baker 2002.

17. Until 1998, each MP had access to an MP development fund that could be used to finance projects in the MP's constituency. Each MP, including opposition MPs, received the same amount of funds (about 20 million baht per MP in 1997) (Hicken 2003).

18. The average effective number of legislative parties is six over the same period. The effective number of parties (ENP) is defined as 1 divided by the sum of the weighted values for each party. The weighted values are calculated by squaring each party's seat share (s_j): ENP = $1 / (\sum s^2_j)$ (Laakso and Taagepera 1979).

19. As are constitutions. Constitutions have an average life expectancy of four years, three months (Hicken 2002).

20. Cabinet duration figures are my calculations, based on data from Chaowana 1998.

21. On the other hand, rapid cabinet and government turnover means that all parties have a reasonable chance of being in government. The fact that no party faces the prospect of being shut out of government for an extended period of time may explain why one or more disciplined, programmatic national parties did not emerge in pre-1997 Thailand. In other candidate-centered democracies (e.g., Japan, Italy, Brazil), there is often at least one party that rejects the norm of candidate-centered campaigning in favor of a party- and policy-oriented strategy. However, these parties have usually been those that, having been shut out of power for extended periods of time, lack the resources necessary to cultivate personal votes. See Chapter 4 for more details.

22. There is variation on this point. Some candidates have developed reputations for consistently being able to win a seat at the table (often through the strategic use of party switching) and then using their position to bring home the pork. For example, the province of Suphan Buri is sometimes referred to as "Banharn Buri," after former prime minister Banharn Silpa-archa. This is due to the large number of pork-barrel projects (many bearing his name) that he has brought to his constituency over the years.

23. Ironically, reforms adopted in the late 1970s and early 1980s designed to clean up elections and restructure parties are actually credited with exacerbating the problem of vote buying (McCargo 2002, 7). For more on the frequent attempts in Thailand at reform via constitutional change, see Girling 1981; McCargo 1998.

24. Actually, the ECT's authority to disqualify was ambiguous, and there was considerable debate on the point. A backlash against the ECT's disqualification of candidates for the 2000 Senate elections eventually culminated in a decision by the Constitutional Court that the ECT did not have the power to disqualify candidates (Nelson 2000). The ECT eventually found a way around this, by relying on its ability to disfranchise those guilty of electoral violations (*Organic Law* 1998, sec. 85/1). According to Sections 109(3) and 106 of the Organic Law, those who are disfranchised cannot stand for election (see Nelson 2002, 15, for more detail).

25. For details on the ECT's activities during the 2000 and 2001 elections, see the ECT website, http://www.ect.go.th, and Nelson 2002.

26. The two tiers are not linked in any way—that is, votes from one tier don't transfer to the other tier.

27. Using the change in currency in circulation as a proxy for the extent of vote buying in an election is worth exploring as a means for more thorough comparisons of vote buying in the future. See Anusorn 1995 for a discussion of the usefulness of this proxy.

28. The constitution suspended this rule for the inaugural 2001 election.

29. This does not mean they abandoned more traditional campaign strategies, as the earlier account of Thai Rak Thai membership recruitment suggests.

30. As the recent experience of Japan demonstrates, it is also possible that the personalism of constituency races can bleed over into the party list race (McKean and Scheiner 2000).

31. Note that this greater purchasing power may be partially offset if, as argued earlier, the price of votes has risen due to a decreased supply.

32. There were numerous examples of such creativity in the 2001 election (see Croissant and Dosch 2001; Nelson 2002).

10

How Effective Is Voter Education?

Frederic Charles Schaffer

Election watchdog groups, public-minded corporations, government election bodies, reformist political parties, and other civic educators sometimes try to curtail vote buying by implementing "demand-side" reforms intended to alter the behavior of voters. This type of reform often takes the form of civic education.

Many civic educators around the world have kept the message simple and palatable to voters: accept the money, but vote your conscience. In Bulgaria, the party representing the Roma told their supporters to "eat their meatballs but vote with your heart." Civil society groups in Zambia urged voters to "eat widely but vote wisely." Jaime Cardinal Sin, archbishop of Manila during the twilight years of Ferdinand Marcos, advised voters to "take the bait but not the hook."

Other civic educators have taken other tacks, perhaps realizing that this kind of message may encourage voters to ask for money. Prior to the 1989 election, reformers in Taiwan produced stickers with the message "my family doesn't sell votes," and asked voters to display them on their houses. In Brazil, the slogan of a national ad campaign was "votes don't have a price, they have consequences." In Mexico, Catholic bishops distributed pamphlets informing parishioners that "your vote is free . . . it cannot be bought or sold." Radio spots broadcast in Guinea told voters that "your voice is sacred, so no material goods should influence your choice." Civic educators in South Africa advised: "Do not vote for a party which offers money or food for exchange for your vote. One who tries this is corrupt."

How have voters responded to these educational campaigns? Empirical data are scattered and thin, but what we do know is not encouraging. A researcher in Taiwan discovered that not everyone reacted to the "my family doesn't sell votes" sticker as civic educators had anticipated: "In 1991 I interviewed an opposition party activist in a southern Taiwanese village who said she wouldn't dream of using the sticker, which she found embarrassingly self-righteous. She gave me the sticker as an example of how out of touch activists in Taipei were with conditions in the countryside" (Rigger 2002, 5).

In Thailand, voter education campaigns also produced unintended consequences. During the 1995 election, for instance, public service ads inspired the very behaviors they were trying to discourage—in schoolchildren, no less. One observer explained:

> To promote the elections, mock polls were organized in many schools. But in one primary school there were unexpected results: "one team bribed the others with candy, while another straightforwardly stuffed papers with their candidate numbers into the hands of younger pupils." This was not seen as a natural thing for Thais to do. Rather, as the assistant principal told the press, it was the product of modern media culture: "They did not know they were doing anything wrong. They saw anti-vote-buying advertisements on TV but did not get the whole message. They thought bribery might help them win, so here we got plenty of candy today." (Callahan 2000, 133)

Children were not the only ones to draw the "wrong" lesson from voter education campaigns. A network of Thai election monitoring organizations hosted a series of educational forums in Chiang Mai province in 1999, with funding provided by the National Democratic Institute for International Affairs. A primary goal of the forums was to teach voters not to sell their votes. After interviewing some 1,700 attendees, evaluators found that, perversely, "there was a slight increase after the forum in the number of participants who believed that it was wrong to sell their votes and not vote for the buyer" (Thornton 2000, 29). In other words, the forums (like the anti–vote buying ads to which the school children were exposed) reinforced or produced the very beliefs they were designed to dispel.

During the lead-up to the 2001 elections in the Philippines, poll-watching groups like the National Citizens Movement for Free Elections (Namfrel) and the Parish Pastoral Council for Responsible Voting (PPCRV) sponsored a variety of radio, television, and newspaper public service ads on the evils of vote buying. They also distributed flyers, pamphlets, and posters, while several corporations placed their own newspaper ads. One Namfrel handout challenged voters: "Ask yourself, why is the candidate treating your vote as a commodity or an item in a sari sari [corner convenience] store?" A Namfrel newspaper ad reminded voters: "Your vote is valuable. It does not have a price." Still another asked: "Do you love the country or the money?" A full-page newspaper ad placed by 3M Innovation (the maker of Post-Its) told voters: "Don't be blinded by money. Vote with your conscience." Another newspaper ad paid for by Red Horse Beer warned voters: "A little pocket change won't put you ahead. Don't get bribed. Vote for the right candidate." Pagbabago@Pilipinas—a group of artists, educators, businessmen, and professionals dedicated to social reform—distributed a song through Namfrel and parish offices called "You Can't Buy Me" *(Hindi Mo Ako Mabibili)*. The song contained the following lyrics: "You can't buy me. I won't make that mistake again. You think because I'm poor, you can fool me. . . . What do you think, I don't have self-respect? No, you can't buy me."

To gauge the effectiveness of this kind of advertising, I put together a team of interviewers. We showed three print ads to 160 randomly selected voters in five communities around the country where vote buying is common.[1] Only 14 percent of the respondents, we found, thought that someone in "a community like theirs" would change his or her mind about accepting money from a candidate upon seeing the Namfrel "your vote is valuable" ad, 22 percent upon seeing the Red Horse Beer "pocket change" ad, and 29 percent upon seeing the 3M "blinded by money" ad. The ads, furthermore, elicited strong negative reactions among many respondents, making nearly one in five feel, in their words, "manipulated," "humiliated," "insulted," and the like. Also worth noting is that a number of respondents thought that some of the ads would encourage, not dissuade, people from selling their votes. Typical is the reaction of a farmer who remarked that "this ad says not to accept pocket change, so it means: go for the highest bidder!"

When we asked another fifty-four voters in Metro Manila (the city of Manila itself plus surrounding cities and towns)—including twenty-four voters who had accepted money—whether seeing the ads would have had an effect on *their own* behavior, only one man said that seeing these ads would have changed his mind about taking money (but not about his choice of candidates).[2] All others responded that the ads would have had no effect whatsoever. Indeed, nineteen of the fifty-four people had seen one or more of these ads during the 2001 election campaign, and reported that the ads did not influence their choices at that time. Just as significant, one of every three voters who did not accept any money was downright offended by the ads, calling them "hurtful" or "insulting." One indignant retiree snapped, "They think I can be bought for pocket change? Don't they know I wouldn't accept even a large sum of money?"

Anti–vote buying education campaigns, as far as we can tell, have not proven to be tremendously effective in either the Philippines or Thailand, nor is the anecdotal evidence from Taiwan auspicious. The rest of this chapter explores some of the reasons for this apparent ineffectiveness. It focuses on the Philippines, where, unlike Taiwan or Thailand, voter education has been the cornerstone of efforts to curb vote buying.[3]

To preview the argument, this chapter makes the case that it is in part the upper-class character of the civic education movement in the Philippines that has hamstrung efforts to convince poor voters to stop selling their votes. Civic education campaigns present an upper- and middle-class view of vote buying that does not match up well with how the poor themselves experience it.

These differences in how the upper and lower classes view vote buying are embedded within larger differences in how the rich and poor see each other and their respective roles in democratic politics. To understand how class affects the effectiveness of civic education, it is thus necessary to first examine these broader differences.

Class in the Philippines

Because class is a key category for this analysis, a few words on its meaning in the Philippine context, and its relation to civic education, are in order. Class distinctions are important and real to most Filipinos, though precise class boundaries are hard to delimit. There is a long-standing debate among academicians about the structural attributes of "the middle class" or "the bourgeoisie." Opinion pollsters and market researchers distinguish five classes: A (very rich), B (moderately rich), C (middle class), D (moderately poor), and E (very poor). Estimates of the class composition of the Philippines using this schema vary somewhat. Depending on the survey, classes A, B, and C—the middle and upper classes—together make up 7 to 11 percent of the population, class D 58 to 73 percent, and class E 18 to 32 percent.

The use of these lettered categories has notably spread beyond the polling and marketing industries. Journalists writing for the daily papers regularly talk about the "ABC crowd." People in urban centers sometimes also use these categories to designate themselves and others. Residents of Metro Manila are familiar enough with these categories that pollsters can ask interviewees to place themselves into one of them.

There are, of course, still other categories that ordinary Filipinos use to designate class. When speaking about wealth, speakers of Tagalog (the most widely spoken language in the country) sometimes distinguish *mayayaman* (the rich) from *mahihirap* (the poor). When speaking of politics and social order, they might differentiate *elitista* (elites) from *masa* (the masses). In the realm of taste or culture, they differentiate those who are *burgis, sosyal,* or *coño* (from the upper class, but more broadly classy, smart, chic, snooty) from those who are *bakya* (literally "wooden clog," meaning poor, tacky, cheesy, old-fashioned) or *jologs* (crass, low-class). These categories, to be sure, are not completely overlapping. Not everyone who is wealthy is a *coño* sophisticate. Not everyone who is poor has provincial *bakya* taste. It is also noteworthy that an awareness of "middleness" is growing, no doubt because the number of managers, teachers, and other white-collar workers has itself has grown in the past few decades.

For the purposes of this analysis, the middle and upper classes—however loosely we must content ourselves with defining them—will be grouped together. One reason is that the number of people who belong to these classes is relatively small. Consequently, pollsters typically group the rich A and B classes together with the middle-C class when presenting their findings. The few quantitative data that are available thus do not often permit finer distinctions.

Another reason for grouping the middle and upper classes together is that civic educators tend to be drawn from both strata. Among the most active participants in election watchdog groups are middle-class white-collar workers, educators, and church leaders; upper-class local capitalists and corporate managers who perceive their business interests to be damaged by the lack of transparency and accountability in government; and middle- and upper-class students attending elite universities or private high schools.

The two most prominent voluntary organizations involved in cleaning up elections are Namfrel, which conducts a "quick" parallel vote count to deter and detect vote padding and other forms of "wholesale" cheating, and the PPCRV, which fields poll watchers on election day to deter intimidation, vote buying, and other forms of "retail" malpractice. In the 2001 elections, Namfrel claims to have fielded more than 150,000 volunteers nationwide, while the PPCRV reports that it fielded more than 450,000. Both organizations also engage in voter education.

While a wide array of civic associations and church groups—from the Women's Action Network for Development to the National Council of Churches in the Philippines—belong to Namfrel, big business plays the leading role. The general secretary of Namfrel, Guillermo Luz, is also the executive director of the Makati Business Club, whose membership consists of chief executive officers and senior executives representing the largest corporations in the country. The national chairman of Namfrel, Jose Concepcion Jr., is also chairman of the board of the Concepcion family-owned RFM Corporation, the country's second largest food and beverage conglomerate. The national secretariat of Namfrel, tellingly, is located in the RFM corporate headquarters. The list of business and professional associations that have donated labor, money, and materials to Namfrel reads like a who's who of the Philippine corporate world. Among them are the Philippine Chamber of Commerce and Industry, the Management Association of the Philippines, the Bankers Association of the Philippines, the Integrated Bar of the Philippines, and the Federation of Philippine Industries. Business and professional organizations have leadership roles in the organization's most dynamic provincial chapters as well. As one observer noted, "'free and fair elections' is the new business of business" (Hedman 1998, 166; see also Hedman 1999).

As for the PPCRV, its origins can be traced to a small breakfast hosted by the archbishop of Manila in 1991. Among the guests were Haydee Yorac, board member of the Commission on Elections (Comelec), and Henrietta de Villa, national president of the Council of the Laity of the Philippines. As the conversation turned to the upcoming 1992 elections, those present decided to initiate, in words attributed to Yorac, a "big organized systemic endeavor" to "repel the evil" of goons, guns, and gold (Bacani 1992, 40). The PPCRV was officially launched five months later by the archdiocese of Manila, and it soon spread nationwide. While the seven members of the board of advisers are all bishops or archbishops, the PPCRV is a lay organization. The national chairman comes from the laity, as do most members of the national executive board. The PPCRV relies, furthermore, on the (lay) parish pastoral council of each parish to supply coordinators and volunteers.

The lay membership of the PPCRV is disproportionately middle-class. As the PPCRV noted in its report to Comelec on the 1992 elections, "the involvement of the poor, as deduced from the data, was not clearly manifested" (de Villa 1992). The same concern—that "volunteers belong to the middle class, less from grassroots"—was echoed in a 1996 national conference report (Parish Pastoral Council for Responsible Voting 1996).

If civic educators come mostly from the middle and upper classes, vote sellers are concentrated among the poor. According to one national survey, in the 2001 national and local elections, 8 percent of voting-aged adults in the ABC classes were offered money, as were 9 percent of the D class and 7 percent of the E class. Though people in each of these three categories received offers in roughly the same proportion, there are far more people in the D and E classes, which together make up no less than 89 percent of the population. Thus, in absolute numbers, many more poor people were offered money. The poor were also more likely than the better-off to accept what was offered: 68 percent of class-D respondents and 75 percent of class-E respondents accepted, compared to only 38 percent of ABC respondents.[4]

Philippine Democracy Viewed from Above

Many in the middle and upper classes, it might not be an overgeneralization to say, find elections to be a source of both frustration and anxiety. Election after election, politicians whom they perceive to be inept, depraved, or corrupt are returned to power. Actors, entertainers, and sports heroes with little or no experience in politics routinely do well in the polls. In the May 2001 elections, a child rapist serving a life prison sentence won a congressional seat, as did a candidate fighting extradition to the United States on charges of wire fraud, tax evasion, illegal campaign contributions, and conspiracy to defraud the government.

Consequently, many in the middle and upper classes are left with a feeling of electoral powerlessness. The ABC classes, when grouped together, make up no more than 11 percent of the electorate, which means they do not often decide electoral outcomes. Whoever wins the vote of the D and E classes wins, period. Such was the (successful) strategy of presidential candidate Joseph "Erap" Estrada, who ran in 1998 on the platform *Erap para sa mahirap* (Erap for the poor). Winning 38 percent of the class-D vote and 48 percent of the class-E vote, he was not hurt by weak support among the ABC classes (only 23 percent). Going into the election, Estrada knew that he did not need their votes, and therefore he did not court them. Some ABC voters were reported to have said that they would leave the country if Estrada were to win. His reply, broadcast on national television, was an indifferent "they can start packing" (Laquian and Laquian 1998, 111).

Most politicians thus work hard, as Estrada did, to cultivate the poor vote. They sponsor community "projects" such as school building, street lighting, well digging, and drainage cleaning. They also provide more direct payoffs to voters by supplying potential supporters with food, money, free medical care, scholarships, discounted funerals, and the like. To protect this pool of votes, politicians also take measures to prevent the relocation of poor voters to areas outside their bailiwicks. In Quezon City, for instance, a congressional representative tried to postpone the completion of a major roadway until after the election, so that "his" squatters would not be resettled elsewhere.

Many in the middle and upper classes are troubled by the kind of patronage politics that results. They are also troubled by the pivotal role played by poor voters who allow themselves—in the words of one journalist—"to be herded, fed, and paid" (Espina 2001). As a result, many better-off Filipinos not only feel contempt for "dirty" or incompetent politicians, but also have misgivings about the poor who keep reelecting them. Not *all* wealthy Filipinos have such feelings, of course. Crony capitalists who bankroll vote buying politicians, and members of the higher classes who distance themselves from reform groups, among others, surely hold different opinions. Still, misgivings about the poor can be heard in sitting rooms, coffee houses, and office buildings across the country, and read in almost all of the major newspapers.

These apprehensive feelings toward the poor intensified during the turbulent five months leading up to the legislative and local elections of May 2001. The period began with an aborted impeachment trial of President Estrada on charges of graft, bribery, and corruption. A massive popular demonstration soon followed, which resulted in his forced resignation and subsequent arrest. This provoked another, even larger, counterdemonstration in his support, which culminated, just two weeks before the elections, in a violent attempt to storm Malacañang Palace and remove from power the new president, Gloria Macapagal Arroyo. Underlying this tumult was a gaping class divide: those who sought to remove Estrada from the presidency were drawn largely from the middle and upper classes, while those who tried to defend or reinstate him were for the most part poor.

Middle- and upper-class apprehensions found a particularly high-tech but lowbrow outlet during the pro-Estrada demonstrations, commonly referred to as "Edsa 3,"[5] in text messages exchanged by people who disapproved. Text messaging is wildly popular in the Philippines among those wealthy enough to afford cellular telephones (in 2001, subscribers sent at least 70 million messages daily). The many critics of Estrada exchanged an enormous number of text messages containing disparaging jokes about the poor who attended these demonstrations.[6] The political power of text messaging became evident during the oust-Estrada "Edsa 2" rallies, when anti-Estrada jokes, news flashes, and instructions were sent around frenetically. Many observers believe that this texting played a pivotal role in mobilizing and organizing demonstrators. The power of text reappeared during Edsa 3, though this time the messages took aim not only at Estrada, but also at the poor who gathered to support him.

Some text messages questioned the motives of those who went to Edsa 3 by mocking their hunger and poverty. One message read: "Edsa 1: free the nation from a dictator. Edsa 2: free the nation from a thief. Edsa 3: free lunch, dinner, breakfast and snacks too . . . let's go!" In other words, those who participated in Edsa 1 and Edsa 2 were moved by their principles; those who gathered at Edsa 3 were there for the handouts. Other messages derided those who went to Edsa 3 for being stupid: "The world's looking at the Philippines again. The rally at Edsa will be in the Guinness Book of World Records for the largest gathering of fools, idiots and imbeciles ever." Still other messages disparaged those at Edsa 3 for being unclean: "Calling all the filthy and ignorant, the toothless and unclothed, let's prove we have no brains—go to Edsa, please pass." This form of derision was not confined to texting. In the Tagalog-language media, the poor who rallied at Edsa 3 were referred to as *mabaho* (smelly) and *hindi naliligo* (unbathed). In the English-language media, the poor were called, more poetically, "the great unwashed."

This focus on dirt reveals the journalists' and texters' class anxiety rather than their powers of observation. As anthropologist Mary Douglas (1966) has taught us, "dirt" is something that is not in its proper place. In the eyes of many better-off voters, the poor have been literally "out of place"—both at Edsa and in the electoral arena. It is because the poor hold undue influence, many of the better-off believe, that politics is stinking and rotten.

The power of this "dirt" construct can be seen in the skewed reaction of President Arroyo when organizers of the Edsa 3 protest played over loudspeakers a ribald drinking ditty called "Gloria Labandera" (Gloria the

Laundrywoman) in an attempt to deride her. To their surprise, the president embraced the image. With pride, she revealed to the nation that she was, in fact, the granddaughter of a laundrywoman. Soon after, the National Food Authority began selling discounted rice and sugar from Gloria Labandera rolling stores. A detergent manufacturer even proposed to the president using the name Gloria Labandera for a new line of soap.

The new president, in a metaphorical sense, was poised to launder the "dirty" nation (see Figure 10.1). But getting rid of dirt requires more than metaphorical cleansing or promotional gimmicks. Cleansing requires real action. "Filth is precisely that which we are taught to renounce and repel forcefully," writes Filipino scholar Vicente Rafael (2001), "while the inability to separate oneself from it is taken to be a pathological sign of immaturity and perversion that requires corrective intervention." As Rafael suggests, there are at least two ways to clean that which is morally dirty: it can be repelled or corrected. Middle- and upper-class reformers in the Philippines have contemplated both strategies.

To repel dirt is to push it back to where it belongs. For instance, some in the Philippines have suggested barring the poor, or some portion of the poor, from participating in elections at all—an idea that has even attracted the attention of the lofty Newsmakers Breakfast Forum. One proposal is to disfranchise those who do not file tax returns; another is to require voters to pass a competency test to limit the franchise to the better-educated, who also happen to be the better-off.

Figure 10.1
President Gloria Macapagal Arroyo, "This is what I use!"
Philippine Daily Inquirer, July 24, 2001

Neither of these solutions have been implemented. Nor is it likely that either will be adopted anytime soon, since each would face serious political and constitutional challenges. Thus most reformers—for practical, political, or ethical reasons—have banked on a different way to put the poor "in their place": corrective intervention. That is, they have tried to "discipline" the poor, to train them to vote "correctly." As one columnist observed, "We call the poor dumb for not voting wisely, which is just another way of saying for not voting the way we want them to" (de Quiros 2001).

Voter education, however, requires knowledge about those to be educated. To effectively teach people how to vote "wisely" requires understanding the reasons why they vote "unwisely." After Edsa 3, there was a new awareness among members of the middle and upper classes that they did not really understand those whom they wanted to educate. "Isn't it amazing that in this day and age there still exist undiscovered islands in our archipelago?" writes one commentator. "In early May we discovered one such island: a colony of smelly, boisterous and angry people. They are the poor among us" (Coronel 2001).

Philippine Democracy Viewed from Below

How, then, do the poor—this "undiscovered colony"—understand Philippine democracy, and their place in it? To explore this question, I and two research assistants conducted 139 interviews with a random sample of registered voters in four areas of Barangay Commonwealth, Quezon City.[7] Quezon City, located within Metro Manila, is the largest city in the country. It has a population of over 2 million (the population of Manila itself is only 1.5 million). Barangay Commonwealth is the largest barangay in Quezon City, with a population of about 120,000 (a *barangay,* or community, is the smallest administrative unit in the Philippines). The people who live in Barangay Commonwealth are predominately poor. The four areas in Commonwealth under study, with a total population of about 14,000 registered voters, have no class-A or class-B residents, and only 10 percent belong to class C. The vast majority fall within the D and E classes. Barangay Commonwealth is thus a typical urban poor community.

What we learned from the interviews was that, to many residents of Barangay Commonwealth, a major problem with Philippine democracy is that the poor are not shown kindness or respect, that those with power and money act in ways that are rude, hurtful, or unlawful. As a dressmaker explained to us, "There is no democracy at this time because they [the rich] don't listen to the poor. The way they look at us is really ugly." One woman described her own personal experience: "The rich treat us so inhumanely. They look at us as if we were rats. When I used to work as a house helper my employer used to beat me. . . . Someone called on the phone, and she accused me of giving out the number. She started hitting me all over. She was rich so she felt she had the right to do that." This kind of treatment understandably leads to feelings of insult and indignity. Such feelings help explain why Edsa 3 received such widespread support from residents of Barangay Commonwealth. To them, the demonstrations represented, above all, a plea or demand on the part of the poor to be noticed, to be heard, and to be treated with humanity.

In terms of electoral politics, this moral calculus leads many voters to choose candidates whom they perceive to be caring, kind, and helpful. To give but one example, consider the reasons why this unemployed elderly widower voted for then-congressman Sonny Belmonte to be mayor of Quezon City:

> He's very helpful to fellow human beings. He helps the poor. He helped me personally. When my wife was dying, I asked for his help. I told him I didn't have the money to pay the hospital bills, and he gave me 5000 pesos. I had first gone to [congressman] Liban [another candidate for mayor]. The people in his office told me to go to the Quezon Institute, or to go ask Belmonte. They told me to go here; they told me to go there. My gosh, they made me feel so stupid!

This man chose not to vote for Liban because Liban's staff had refused his request for assistance. Worse, they had given him the run-around. To him it had been humiliating and shaming. Belmonte, in contrast, had helped the man, and had treated him with dignity.

Politics, then, for many among the poor in Barangay Commonwealth, is a politics of dignity. "Bad" politics is a politics of callousness and insult, while "good" politics is a politics of consideration and kindness. In contrast, many in the upper and middle classes tend to view "bad" politics as a dirty politics of patronage and corruption, while they see "good" politics as a clean politics of issues, accountability, transparency. Interestingly, the personalized distribution of material rewards from candidate to voter figures prominently in both lower- and upper-class characterizations, but the value placed on this distribution is inverse: lauded in one but reviled in the other.

Class and the Meaning of Vote Buying

Viewed in this perspective, it becomes easier to see how the fight against vote buying—and more broadly the effort to replace dirty politics with clean politics—is disproportionately a middle- and upper-class project. What is less obvious is that this class character of reform has consequences.

Perhaps most important, it has led reformers to misunderstand the electoral practices they seek to curtail.

Many in the middle and upper classes share the opinion, voiced here by a newspaper editorialist, that "the *masa* [masses] treats elections as mere fund-raising circuses" (Bondoc 2000). Votes, in this view, are simple commodities that the poor exchange for money, without any moral or political reflection. "Ignorant" voters literally chase after the money of corrupt politicians (see Figure 10.2). It follows that an important way to combat vote buying is to provide poor voters with a moral education to, in the words of one journalist, "rescue" them "from the bondage of ignorance" (Olivares-Cunana 2001).

Many of the 2001 advertisements discussed at the beginning of this chapter—ads that exhorted the poor to vote their conscience, love their country, or have self-respect—issue from the same worldview. Moreover, these public service ads echo, in a more polite form to be sure, the same assumptions present in the derogatory Edsa 3 text messages. The poor, in both cases, are presumed to be desperate, shortsighted, and lacking in moral or political discernment. Just as the text messages assume that the poor went to Edsa for the free meals and not out of principle, these ads assume

Figure 10.2
Philippine Star, July 1, 2002

that the poor participate in elections simply as a way to come into some fast money.

But do the poor—even those who accept money from candidates—really use their votes in that way? I was able to place a few questions on the topic of vote buying in a national, postelection survey of 1,200 Filipinos.[8] Responses from that survey show that "vote selling" is more complex than a simple exchange of votes for money—and this should come as no surprise if we remember the language used by the residents of Barangay Commonwealth.

In the national survey, only 38 percent of poor voters (classes D and E) who accepted money reported voting for the candidate, or roster of candidates, on whose behalf the money was offered. Of those 38 percent, one in five said they would have voted the same way had they not been offered anything. Thus money appears to have influenced decisively the vote of only about 30 percent of the poor voters who accepted it. In other words, most voters who received money still apparently exercised their freedom of choice.

Furthermore, those who accepted money had mixed sets of motives for doing so. To be sure, economic motives are sometimes powerful. In the national survey, 29 percent responded that they accepted the money because they needed it. But there were other, more morally saturated reasons as well, including a desire not to embarrass the person who did the offering (9 percent), and a belief that it's an obligation of candidates to give money or things to their supporters (9 percent).

When these survey responses are put into the context of the open-ended interviews we conducted with poor voters in Barangay Commonwealth and other areas of Metro Manila, a still more complex picture emerges. There we found that many people accept money because they do not see all forms of money-giving as attempts to purchase their votes. Local ward leaders who actually distribute the money often say it is simply a "handout" that does not obligate the voter to the candidate. Indeed, many voters that we talked to distinguish giving money with strings attached (what they call "vote buying") from giving money without such strings (what they call "goodwill" money). And most people we spoke with see goodwill money as less problematic than vote buying. In the words of one unemployed voter: "It's definitely not okay to buy votes! That's against the law. But to spend money for the purpose of spreading the candidate's name and goodwill, I guess that's okay."

Goodwill money is given as a gesture of generosity on the part of a candidate. It carries no explicit understanding that the voter will cast a ballot for that candidate. What it may do is to demonstrate to the voter that this is indeed a candidate who cares, who pays attention to the poor. It seemed to have this effect on a laundrywoman we interviewed, who explained to us that "there were no conditions attached to the money that they gave me so I didn't feel I had any obligation to them. But I voted for them just because they bothered at all to give me something."

It appears, then, that to many urban poor voters, the moral calculus involved in deciding whether to accept money or gifts is embedded within, and derived from, the politics of dignity described above. It is all right to accept gifts if they come from candidates who are showing consideration, paying attention, and offering help.

These observations suggest that voter education materials that tell people not to treat their votes like commodities miss the mark of how most poor voters think of their votes. The resulting friction between reality and representation generates much of the antipathy felt by many poor voters toward the education materials:

> I find this ad irritating; they think that when I vote it's because of the money. (market woman)

> Automatically this ad impresses upon you that you can be bribed. I find that insulting. (nurse)

> The words hurt; they see voters as greedy. (domestic helper)

> This ad makes it seem that elections only focus on vote buying. It is insulting to those who don't accept money. (fisherman)

It is the portrayal of the poor as driven only by material need, as people without principles, that seemed to pique several of the respondents.

Most poor voters we interviewed do not like the feeling of being bought. Their reasons for accepting things from candidates are complex, and are often tied to their vision of what good politics ought to be, or how good politicians ought to behave. Voter education materials that ignore this reality, and instead reproduce middle- and upper-class stereotypes of the poor, do not appear likely to change the behavior of those who accept money from candidates.

Comparative Perspectives

Under what conditions are middle and upper classes likely to embark on anti–vote buying civic education campaigns? Under what conditions are such campaigns likely to fail or backfire? Space permits here only two comparative reflections.

First, reformers typically turn their attention to the behavior of individual voters only when elections are truly competitive. Where the middle class—or fragments of the middle class—are still fighting for competitive democracy, their reformist energies tend to be focused more on loosening administrative restrictions or curtailing government abuses than on changing the behavior of the poor.

To limit our focus to Southeast Asia, this fight for democracy is still ongoing in both Malaysia and Cambodia, and was only recently (and provisionally) won in Indonesia. Consequently, groups like the Malaysian Citizens' Election Watch or the Cambodian Committee for Free and Fair Elections (Comfrel) have not really devoted their resources to voter education (though the Comfrel did distribute in the run-up to the 2003 elections copies of a leaflet called "The Consequences of Vote Buying"). In Indonesia, election watchdog groups are still in the early stages of organizing themselves, most having experience only with the 1999 and 2004 polls.

Within Southeast Asia, Thailand and the Philippines are the countries where electoral competition has been the most open over the past decade (until a 2006 coup put an end to democratic rule, at least temporarily, in Thailand). So it is not coincidental that it is in Thailand and the Philippines where the most aggressive voter education campaigns were mounted.

Interestingly, in Thailand it was the middle class who worked most actively to promote clean elections. PollWatch, by far the largest poll-watching group in the country, drew most of its volunteers from this class: one survey found that 64 percent of PollWatch volunteers in the 1992 elections belonged to the middle class (LoGerfo 2000, 228–229). Indeed, PollWatch preferred to recruit its members from the middle class. As one scholar observed during the 1995 elections, "Since low education levels are seen as one of the main supports of election fraud, PollWatch actively recruited 'educated people'—students, teachers, business people, lawyers, civil servants—to work at the volunteer level" (Callahan 2000, 9). Thus, as in the Philippines, there was a class dimension to clean election reform: urban middle-class organizations such as PollWatch tried to discipline how the rural poor vote. As one scholar commented on the 1992 election, "These middle class stalwarts were acting to ensure that Thailand's largely rural electorate would choose only 'good' politicians who did not buy votes" (LoGerfo 2000, 229).

As in the Philippines, the poor in Thailand sometimes reacted to the educational efforts of PollWatch and other civic educators in ways unanticipated by reformers. Recall the reaction of schoolchildren to the anti–vote buying television ads, or the reaction of those who attended the educational forums in Chiang Mai province. Both the forums and the television ads generated the very beliefs and behaviors they were designed to forestall.

The second comparative point is that voter education seems most likely to have unintended consequences when it is undertaken by middle classes in formation, by middle classes who are trying to define themselves in contrast to the poor. Such was the case in both the Philippines and Thailand.

Class, it is important to recall, is in part a cultural construction that requires active work of self-definition. While class no doubt has something do to with wealth and one's place in the economy, it is also constructed out of shared values, tastes, habits, and (most important for our inquiry) political commitments (Bourdieu 1984). The problem is that the task of self-definition often becomes transformed into a project of hegemony as new classes attempt to impose their recently created "superior" lifestyle on the poor (Frykman and Löfgren 1987). In this context, then, we should note that sizable middle classes in both Thailand and the Philippines are fairly new, products of the Asian miracle of the 1970s–1990s (Hewison 1996, 139–145; Pinches 1996, 115–123). As a consequence of this newness, the middle classes in both countries are culturally inchoate. In the Philippines, "the newness of the middle classes gives rise to *homines novi* in search of a format and a culture" (Mulder 1997, 115), while in Thailand, "diverse fragments and diverse constructions . . . have not yet been conflated into a single social class" (Ockey 1999, 245).

The incipient nature of middle-class culture has led to much storytelling by middle-class intellectuals in both countries as they try to work out what it might mean to belong to the middle class. In Thailand, such cultural work has resulted in an ongoing effort "to construct the Thai middle class in terms of political practice and ideology" (Ockey 1999, 240). In the Philippines, it has produced what one historian called "'burgis [bourgeois] projects'—efforts on the part of middle upper class intellectuals to construct and display Filipino society and culture mainly to themselves" (Cullinane 1993, 74). As in Thailand, there is a strong political and ideological component in that construction.

Public service ads that describe the evils of vote buying appear to be part of these middle-class storytelling projects. Political education campaigns, in other words, might not just have been intended for the poor; they may also have served to remind middle-class Thais and Filipinos of who they are and how they are different from—and morally or politically superior to—the poor. One scholar thus described the drive to curb vote buying in Thailand as an unintended form of "middle-class cultural imperialism" that has resulted from attempts to construct a class ideology. "The unfortunate side-effect of these attempts," he wrote, "has been to consolidate a conviction among the middle classes that democracy belongs to the middle class, and that the lower classes are incapable of effective participation in a democratic system. The middle class frustration with the common practice of vote-buying is the most dramatic indication of this attitude" (Ockey 1999, 245–246). The same could have been written of the Philippines.

It may thus not be coincidental that in the Philippines, many of the anti–vote buying print ads produced for the 2001 elections ran in the English-language newspapers, which are read mostly by the middle and upper classes, just as if not more frequently than they did in the less expensive Tagalog-language tabloids. The ad placed by the makers of Red Horse Beer, for instance, appeared only in English-language newspapers (even if the ad itself was in Tagalog). It is also suggestive that the agencies involved in crafting the Philippine ads did not, as they usually do, submit their ideas to focus-group testing. Instead they relied, in the words of one ad executive who coordinated the Namfrel campaign, on their "own observations and personal experiences." This comment shows the extent to which the ad makers relied on their own conventional views of "the poor" when crafting their messages. Whatever the intent, the effect was to communicate higher-class sensibilities to a variety of class audiences. The problem, of course, is that the resulting stereotyped images, however reaffirming to the self-image of higher-class Filipinos, stood little chance of changing the behavior of the poor, and sometimes aroused instead their indignation and resentment.

Conclusion

Efforts to reduce vote buying through public education campaigns were not effective, as far as I can tell, in either Thailand or the Philippines. That failure, I have argued in this chapter, was a result of the class character of reform, or more precisely, a clash of moral codes that pitted higher-class reformers against lower-class "wrongdoers." Such class-based clashes are likely to originate, more speculatively, in attempts of new middle classes to build a political culture of their own, and in the distorting effect that this culture-building project has on how higher-class reformers perceive, and act upon, the poor and their politics.

To the extent that clean election reform in general, and anti–vote buying campaigns in particular, have been undertakings of middle and (sometimes) upper classes around the world today—from Taiwan to Brazil to Mexico—the problem of class-bound misperception may extend beyond Southeast Asia. Even where anti–vote buying campaigns are not class projects, this examination of civic education in the Philippines and Thailand highlights the importance of adequately understanding the practices one wishes to reform. Vote buying carries different meanings to different people, and these meanings can vary not only by class, but also by religion, ethnicity, levels of education, and the like. Civic education campaigns will be unlikely to succeed if they are not sensitive to these lived meanings.

No doubt, this variability of lived meanings raises a set of thorny normative questions. Should reformers be aiming to "correct" voters, to eliminate vote buying, if indeed it is not the amoral, shortsighted economic transaction they imagine it is, but rather something else, something involving moral judgment and political reasoning? Relatedly, has vote buying really been a serious defect of the Philippine and (now defunct) Thai electoral systems, or have efforts to discipline vote sellers reflected instead middle-class fantasies and anxieties blown out of proportion? One scholar went so far as to argue that in Thailand "vote-buying is not as big a problem as is our obsession with it" (Callahan 2002, 24). Could he have been right?

As an incomplete answer to these questions, let me make only the briefest of observations. Different types of vote buying surely have differential implications for various aspects of democracy, not the least of which is accountability. There is a difference, to return to a theme articulated in Chapter 2, between a candidate who literally purchases votes and a candidate who performs favors as an ostensible gesture of caring. In the former case, accountability may run no deeper than the demand for a periodic electoral payoff. In the latter case, it can take the form of ongoing demands for help. Certain forms of vote buying, then, impose a kind of accountability on politicians, and provide important sources of help for poor and vulnerable people. These forms of vote buying may well be more consonant with norms of democracy and social welfare than are vote-for-cash market transactions.

Still, no matter what meanings people attach to vote buying, or how much accountability it might entail, or how much help individuals receive, there are certain ills that typically go along with vote buying that make it a less than benign practice. To give but one example, in both Thailand and the Philippines, vote buying has been tied intimately to organized crime. Politicians need to raise large sums of money to buy votes, and because vote buying is illegal, the sources of those funds must remain clandestine. Often politicians turn to smugglers, gambling kingpins, drug syndicates, and kidnap-for-ransom rings to provide those untraceable funds. In Thailand, much of the money came from provincial, mafialike "godfathers" (Ockey 2000). In the Philippines, the chairman of the House Committee on Dangerous Drugs estimated in 2003 that one-quarter of all elected officials received money from drug barons (Romero and Crisostomo 2003). The number of bank robberies, illegal gambling operations, and kidnappings-for-ransom in that country spike just before the beginning of each election season (*Philippine Daily Inquirer* 2002, 2003a, 2003b).

If vote buying candidates who raise funds in such ways are elected, criminals get their financial support repaid in cash, cronyism, and protection. Vote buying thus not only fuels robbery, murder, and trafficking, but also extends the reach of organized crime by expanding the political influence of the criminal financial backers on which candidates rely. Thus, whatever benefits may accrue to individual voters, or whatever moral rationality they may be exercising, the criminality and the criminalization of politics caused by vote buying impose heavy societal costs that may well justify efforts to curb it. The open question is whether civic educators—working within a logic that makes sense to the poor and respects their dignity, principles, and autonomy—can find ways to convince those who accept money that vote selling is not in their own, or their community's, best interest.

Notes

Much of the fieldwork for this chapter was conducted in the Philippines from January through August 2001. That research was made possible by a grant from the Fulbright Scholars Program. Funding for additional fieldwork in 2000, 2002, and 2003 was provided by the Center for International Studies and the School of Humanities, Arts, and Social Sciences at the Massachusetts Institute of Technology. I would like to thank the Institute of Philippine Culture and the Political Science Department at Ateneo de Manila University for providing me with an institutional home. I am also indebted to Alfredo Metrio Antonio, Marion Ravinera Pantaleon, Jorge Rivas Alberto, and E-Anne Enriquez for their inspired research assistance. I am also grateful to Myrna Alejo, Suzanne Berger, Jenny Franco, Ben Kerkvliet, Carl Landé, Tony Moreno, Michael Pinches, and Andreas Schedler for their comments on earlier drafts of this chapter. Finally, I thank the *Philippine Star*, and Jess Abrera and the *Philippine Daily Inquirer*, for permitting me to reproduce the cartoons included in this chapter.

1. These communities were located in the National Capital region and the provinces of Quezon and Catanduanes in Luzon, Iloilo in the Visayas, and North Cotabato in Mindanao.

2. In addition to the Namfrel "your vote is valuable," the Red Horse Beer "pocket change," and 3M "don't be blinded by money" ads, interviewees were asked to comment on the Namfrel "do you love the country?" ad.

3. On the significance of vigorous law enforcement in Taiwan, see the conclusion to this volume, Chapter 11. On the importance of institutional reform in Thailand, see Chapter 9.

4. The survey (contained in Pulse Asia 2001) was commissioned by me. Data were gathered through face-to-face interviews with 1,200 adult respondents nationwide, chosen using multistage probability sampling for an error margin of ± 3 percent.

5. Edsa is the main thoroughfare that runs though Metro Manila. It was the site of the mass demonstrations that culminated in the ouster of Marcos in 1986, an event commonly referred to as "Edsa 1." It was also the focal point for the disproportionately middle- and upper-class "Edsa 2" protests that led to the ouster of Estrada in January 2001 (a Pulse Asia survey found that 65 percent of the adults who rallied at Edsa 2 came from the ABC classes; if class-D rallyists with some college education or middle-class occupations are included, then the total middle- and upper-class representation jumps to 74 percent [Bautista 2001, 8]). Edsa was again the place where hundreds and thousands gathered in late April and early May 2001 to protest Estrada's arrest, an event many call "Edsa 3."

6. Even though I did not engage in partisan politics while in the Philippines, I myself received dozens of such messages. Many were also reprinted approvingly by newspaper columnists.

7. We chose at random, from the voter registry, 2 percent of the people who were listed as living in each of the four areas. Of the people who actually still lived there—many had moved abroad or to the provinces after registering, and a few had died—our response rate was 81 percent.

8. Pulse Asia 2001 survey.

Part 4

Conclusion

11

Lessons Learned
Frederic Charles Schaffer

Vote buying is a global phenomenon: sporadic in some places, rampant in others. This concluding chapter offers a few broad conclusions about this widespread but ill-understood practice. One goal of the chapter is to provide a short synthesis of the main lessons learned in this volume. Another goal is to indicate areas most in need of further inquiry—areas where contributors to this volume disagree, where they are silent, or where their findings generate new puzzles to be solved. To structure this discussion, the chapter takes up six questions:

1. What are the organizational requirements of an effective vote buying campaign?
2. How dependable is vote buying as a vote getting strategy?
3. How expensive is vote buying relative to other electoral strategies?
4. Under what conditions does vote buying become an attractive electoral strategy?
5. What are the consequences of vote buying?
6. Can vote buying be "reformed" away?

What Are the Organizational Requirements of an Effective Vote Buying Campaign?

To be an effective electoral strategy, vote buying requires heavy investments of time, money, and personnel. As several authors in this volume note, candidates who wish to undertake even moderately successful vote buying campaigns need to know which voters are amenable to having their participation or abstention bought. Gathering this information requires extensive grassroots organizing, using local people with local knowledge. Candidates also have to obtain large sums of money to buy votes. Sometimes they can tap party or government coffers, or find wealthy backers. Other times they need to generate funds themselves, which they often do by participating in illegal revenue-generating activities such as bank robbery, the drug trade, gambling rackets, or kidnapping for ransom—all of which require dexterity, protection, and organization. The vote buying campaign itself necessitates hiring many operatives to both distribute electoral payoffs and monitor the compliance of vote sellers. Candidates need also to keep tabs on these operatives, to prevent, among other things, embezzlement or duplication of efforts. These tasks, to make the vote buying project even harder and more expensive, must be accomplished by means that go undetected or undisturbed by law enforcers. All of this requires skill and organization.

How candidates and parties manage these complex tasks is an area about which we know little. The pathbreaking work of Chin-Shou Wang and Charles Kurzman in Chapter 5 provides us with a rare look inside the vote buying machine of one local candidate in Taiwan. Among the key organizational features of this machine were a seasoned campaign manager with deep knowledge of local voters, political figures, and relationships; a network of supervisors to recruit a bevy of trustworthy grassroots vote buying operatives; precise vote buying target rates, with carefully calculated budgets and commissions; a system of bonuses to reward effective operatives; and careful coordination among operatives to prevent the duplication of efforts.

As Wang and Kurzman note, there are ways in which the organization of vote buying by this candidate in Taiwan differs from how vote buying is organized in other parts of the world. Relative to candidates in countries such as Brazil, Chile, Columbia, and the Philippines, the Taiwanese candidate deployed a high number of vote brokers. Relative to candidates in Mexico, the Taiwanese operatives were more likely to mobilize voters with trust and social obligation than with fear.

There are also ways in which the organization of vote buying in Taiwan is similar to how vote buying is organized elsewhere. Most notably, like many other vote buying campaigns around the world, the Taiwanese candidate tapped into local social networks to gain information about which voters were most amenable to having their votes bought.

These comparisons notwithstanding, our comparative knowledge of how vote buying campaigns are organized is thin. We have little detailed comparative knowledge about the recruitment of grassroots operatives, the bonuses and incentives offered to them, the strategies used to reduce embezzlement or wasteful spending, or the means by which candidates fund their vote buying campaigns. Wang and Kurzman show us how careful ethnographic work can shed light on such questions. Their work begs for replication in other parts of the world.

How Dependable Is Vote
Buying as a Vote Getting Strategy?

Despite the heavy organizational investments that candidates and parties are often willing to make in vote buying campaigns, they have few guarantees that voters will comply at the ballot box. As Andreas Schedler and I explain in Chapter 2, vote buying does not constitute a "normal" market transaction insofar as there are no legal sanctions to enforce vote buying agreements. Securing the compliance of voters without recourse to legal sanctions thus constitutes a fundamental challenge to any vote buying campaign. In this context, it is important to recall, as argued in Chapter 1, that unlike other strategies of manipulation, vote buying alone typically requires the willing complicity of voters.

Vote buyers use a number of strategies to boost the compliance of sellers. Such strategies include personalized normative inducements, informal sanctions, electoral surveillance, and contingency payments, as discussed in Chapter 2. Thus we might hypothesize that levels of compliance vary, among other things, with the degree to which these strategies are successfully deployed.

To focus only on electoral surveillance, where balloting is not secret (or the secrecy of the ballot can be easily circumvented or compromised), we should expect that voter compliance will be relatively high. Under the intimidating gaze of vote buyers and their agents, sellers are more likely to uphold their end of the agreement, lest they expose themselves to extralegal sanctions. Indeed, it is for this reason that Fabrice Lehoucq, in Chapter 3, notes that vote buying historically flourished in many places where the secrecy of the ballot was less than complete. The greater efficacy of vote buying under conditions of publicity also explains why Jean-Marie Baland and James Robinson, in Chapter 8, observe that vote buying declined dramatically in Chile when secret balloting was introduced in 1958.

However, when voters enjoy even a modicum of privacy while casting their ballots, many recipients of vote buyer goodies do not uphold their end of the bargain. One survey of Mexican voters found that only 37 percent of voters who "received a gift" from the ruling Institutional Revolutionary Party (PRI), and only from the PRI, voted for the PRI's presidential candidate in the 2000 elections (Cornelius 2004, 57). Survey data from the Philippines similarly show that among the poor, accepting material offers influenced decisively the vote of only about 30 percent of the people who accepted them in the 2001 elections (see Chapter 10). A survey of 1,920 people conducted in three provinces of Argentina indicates that only 16 percent of the people who received a handout during the 2001 election campaign were influenced by it in terms of their voting behavior (Brusco, Nazareno, and Stokes 2004, 70). Using a finer-tuned method, Wang (2001, 37, 54; see also Chapter 5 of this volume) compared the number of votes garnered by Kuomintang (KMT) candidates in one Taiwanese township to the number of voters who received money from KMT vote brokers (which he was able to determine by gaining access to the actual lists of names used by the vote brokers themselves). He found that no more than 55 percent of the people who received money voted for KMT candidates in the 1993 elections.

The KMT candidate won his race, the PRI presidential candidate lost his, and the survey data from Argentina and the Philippines do not tell us whether the votes gained there were enough to put individual candidates over the top. Whatever the electoral outcomes, high levels of leakage in all four countries suggest that vote buying is far from a surefire strategy—even when accompanied by a panoply of instrumental, coercive, and normative strategies to boost the rate of compliance among voters. Where balloting is at least intermittently secret, many people defect.

Of course, there are varying levels of secrecy. Carbon copies, cellphone videos, ballot marking, and voting assistants are among the tricks that vote buyers use to circumvent vote secrecy, even when balloting is nominally secret. Thus we might hypothesize that levels of voter compliance vary, among other things, with the degree of real privacy.

Among the most dependable forms of vote buying is "negative vote buying" (paying people to stay away from the polls)—a practice discussed by several contributors to this volume. Negative vote buying, or what some call "buying abstention," is more dependable than other forms of vote buying under conditions of vote secrecy, because it is easy to monitor and control the behavior of sellers, especially when the vote buyer can take physical possession of the seller's voting credentials (voter registration card, national identification card, and the like) and thus prevent the seller from casting a ballot.

While this form of vote buying has reportedly taken place in Guyana, Venezuela, Mexico, Kenya, Zambia, Malawi, and the Philippines, among other places, evidence suggests that it is not as widely practiced as one might expect, given its comparative advantage over other forms of vote buying. On the one hand, there are many countries in which this particular form of vote buying is largely unknown. On the other hand, negative vote buying is not particularly common even in those countries where it is most visible. In Mexico, for instance, the government began to issue photo credentials in 1992 in preparation for the 1994 federal elections. By the 2000 elections, local PRI officials were already adept at "renting" voter credentials to keep opposition supporters away from the polls, though this practice did not appear to be a common form of vote buying. A national postelection survey conducted by a Mexican academic institution found that, as reported by Wayne Cornelius, "only 5 percent of the 5 percent of respondents who had been exposed to some form of vote-buying or coercion had experienced it in that particular form" (2004, 53).

Why is negative vote buying not more widespread? Though the contributors to this volume do not address this question, we can nonetheless identify three factors that may well limit its scope. First, negative vote buying is most easily accomplished only in places where a single voting credential is required to vote, such as Mexico, Venezuela, Guyana, Zambia, and Malawi. By taking possession of that credential on election day, the buyer can have a reasonable guarantee that the seller will not be casting a ballot. Where no voting credentials are required to vote, or where different forms of identification can be presented, no such guarantee exists.

There are of course methods to keep sellers away from the polls that do not rely on taking possession of voter credentials. To prevent double voting, for example, voters in many countries are required to dip their fingers in indelible ink after casting their ballots. In the Philippines, party workers have exploited this requirement by paying registered voters to disqualify themselves from voting by staining their index fingers with ink prior to the opening of the polls.[1] There is little evidence, however, that this strategy is used widely in other countries, perhaps because of the many cases around the world of voters reportedly removing the ink stains with bleach, abrasives, or just soap and water. Allegations of removability have been made in Kenya, Mexico, Pakistan, Djibouti, Sri Lanka, Panama, Namibia, Guatemala, Afghanistan, and Papua New Guinea, among other places.

Second, negative vote buying seems only to occur in places where parties can easily identify rival supporters. The fact that partisanship in Guyana is largely race-based certainly facilitated that kind of identification. Electoral agents of the Indo-Guyanese ruling party could easily pick out Afro-Guyanese supporters of the opposition. Similarly, partisanship in Kenya, Zambia, and Malawi tends to run along ethnic or regional lines. The demographics of partisanship and its relationship to negative vote buying are more complex in both Mexico and Venezuela, though scattered evidence suggests that indigenous communities, where partisanship and ethnic identity tend to overlap, are particularly prone to purchasing abstention (Kornblith 2002, 14; Hernández Carrochano 2003, 2).

Third, where strong regional patterns of partisanship exist, the magnitude of negative vote buying may, paradoxically, be limited. When opposition partisans are clustered in discrete geographic locales, buying abstention can be dangerous for the operatives who are actually charged with seeking out people who are willing to sell their votes, since it requires venturing into towns or villages that may be hostile to them and their party. In Kenya, armed youth in one constituency assaulted six agents of the then-ruling Kenya Africa National Union days before a by-election. As reported by the British Broadcasting Corporation (BBC), the agents "were believed to have been offering people money in exchange for their voting cards when they were attacked" (*BBC News* 2001). In another incident, a Nairobi politician was almost killed during the 2002 election campaign "when a mob beat him for allegedly buying voters cards" (Central Depository Unit 2002, 42). For a variety of reasons, then, buying abstention is not a widespread form of vote buying around the world, even if it is the most reliable.

How dependable, then, is vote buying as a vote getting strategy? Different forms of vote buying vary in their degrees of dependability, and the more reliable forms of vote buying are not feasible under a broad range of conditions. Even with an array of compliance strategies at their disposal, most vote sellers in most places cannot guarantee that voters will uphold their end of the deal. Consequently, vote buying tends to be a strategy plagued by significant levels of defection.

How Expensive Is Vote Buying Relative to Other Electoral Strategies?

Vote buying campaigns in some places are massively expensive. As we saw in Chapter 1, they can cost millions of dollars. Candidates need to dole out goodies to voters. They must also, as Wang and Kurzman show in detail for Taiwan in Chapter 5, dispense large sums of money to build up vote buying machines, and there is little reason to believe that such organizational investments are unique to that country. How, then, do the costs of a vote buying campaign compare to the costs of other vote getting strategies?

This question is difficult to answer, especially relative to other strategies of manipulation.[2] Because manipulative strategies such as tampering with the voter registry or padding vote tallies are illegal, their costs (payoffs, operational expenses, and the like) are typically shielded from public view. Nevertheless, it does stand to reason that vote buying is potentially among the more expensive strategies of manipulation to the extent that, as we saw in Chapter 1, it is one of the few such strategies that requires votes to be picked up one at a time. Wholesale strategies of manipulation that require the co-option of a small number of individuals—even if that co-option requires substantial remuneration—may well be less expensive. Still, empirical evidence is slim, and scholarly attempts to calculate relative costs would be most welcome.

How expensive is vote buying relative to other strategies of mobilization? Allen Hicken in Chapter 4, Susan Stokes in Chapter 6, and Scott Desposato in Chapter 7 all identify campaigning on the basis of issues and ideology as an obvious alternative to vote buying. None of these authors, however, take up directly the question of relative cost, so a few words on this issue may thus be appropriate.

Available evidence suggests that mass-media issue campaigns cost much less per vote than do vote buying campaigns. As Michael Pinto-Duschinsky explains:

In 1996, the per capita costs of the elections in Thailand, where vote-buying was prevalent, were reportedly 4 to 5 times higher (relative to average incomes) than in the United States. Studies of Uganda and of Antigua and Barbuda, as well as my own informal interviews in Kenya, all indicate that traditional patronage politics imposes far greater financial burdens than television-based campaigning. The "mass distribution of imported hams, turkeys, and other giveaways" in the 1999 elections in Antigua and Barbuda meant that the cost-per-vote amounted to at least US$60 (the estimate offered by the ruling Antigua Labour Party) and may have been as high as US$300 (the opposition's preferred figure). Taking differences in income levels into account, these elections cost between 9 and 44 times more per capita than all the elections—state, local, and federal—that took place in the United States in 1996. (2002, 83)

This anecdotal evidence is backed up by data presented in this volume. Though systematic data on vote buying expenses is unavailable (due in large part to its illegality), the campaign expenses of the winning Taiwanese candidate in the 1993 county magistrate elections, studied by Wang and Kurzman in Chapter 5, do provide one point of comparison. The vote buying expenditures for this candidate (in the township under study) included not only 300 Taiwanese dollars (about US$10) for each of 14,090 voters (a total of 4,227,000 Taiwanese dollars), but also a 10 percent vote broker commission (422,700 Taiwanese dollars), and twelve performance bonuses that ranged from 30,000 to 100,000 Taiwanese dollars each (a total of 550,000). The candidate thus spent at least 5,199,700 Taiwanese dollars for the 7,691 votes he received, translating into a cost per vote of 676 Taiwanese dollars (about US$25).[3]

Contrast this to the United States, where the mass media are far more important in election campaigns. In the 1990 US gubernatorial general elections, the most analogous races in the US political system, the average cost per vote for each winning candidate was only US$3.30.[4] The cost per vote in Taiwan was thus seven times higher than it was in the United States. Even this figure is conservative: in Taiwan the cost per vote represents *only* the cost of buying votes (and thus excludes all other campaign expenses), while in the United States it includes *all* declared campaign expenditures. Thus the actual cost per vote in Taiwan was in all likelihood substantially higher.

The cross-national difference in cost becomes even more pronounced when one takes into account the greater wealth of the United States. The cost per vote, calculated relative to average national incomes, is at least seventeen times higher in Taiwan than in the United States. Also worth noting is that the US$3.30 average cost per vote in the 1990 US gubernatorial elections is not particularly low when compared to the cost in other democracies where vote buying is isolated or nonexistent. Campaigns in the Netherlands are among the least expensive. The average cost per vote in the Dutch 1982 elections was only US 33 cents (in 1990 dollars) (Koole 1989, 213).

Longitudinal data from Great Britain also support the conclusion that vote buying is a relatively expensive mobilization strategy. The cost per vote was substantially higher before the Corrupt and Illegal Practices Act put an end to most large scale vote buying in 1883: in the prereform elections of 1880, the cost per vote (using constant prices) to Conservative candidates was 7 times higher than in the postreform elections of 1910, 41 times higher than in the elections of 1929, and 230 times higher than in the elections of 1974 (Pinto-Duschinsky 1981, 15–29).

Vote buying, in sum, appears to be an expensive strategy relative to alternative methods of mobilization. It may also be more expensive than other strategies of manipulation, though on this point we can only conjecture.

Under What Conditions Does Vote Buying Become an Attractive Electoral Strategy?

Vote buying, as we saw in Chapter 1, is among the least-efficient strategies of manipulation, to the extent that it requires votes to be picked up one at a time, and it is among the least-dependable strategies in that it is the only one that (typically) requires the willing compliance of voters. Vote buying is also the least-efficient strategy of distributive mobilization (focused as it is on individuals and families rather than on whole neighborhoods, districts, or classes of people), and it is the only strategy of distributional mobilization that is unambiguously in violation of the law. As a tool of either mobilization or manipulation, vote buying would appear to have many drawbacks relative to the alternatives. Its organizational requirements are substantial, most forms of vote buying are not all that dependable, and relative to the alternatives its per-vote cost is potentially high. Under what conditions, then, does vote buying emerge as an attractive strategy?

Several authors in this volume address this question, none more so than Lehoucq in Chapter 3 and Hicken in Chapter 4. Lehoucq analyzes vote buying as a strategy of manipulation, and finds in his historical survey that candidates typically adopted this strategy only in places where other strategies of manipulation lost their potency or became less feasible logistically. For instance, where landlords retained their ability to coerce voters, as they did in nineteenth-century rural Ireland, no market for votes emerged. Only in places where voters became more independent—often because of urbanization— did vote buying proliferate, as it did in the cities of Ireland during the same period.

Hicken, in contrast, analyzes vote buying more as a strategy of mobilization than of manipulation. He finds that candidates tend to adopt this strategy where electoral systems (such as block voting or the single nontransferable vote) promote intraparty competition. To the extent that intraparty competition prevents candidates from distinguishing themselves on issues of ideology or program (on which partymates generally see eye-to-eye), vote seekers must instead use "personal" strategies of mobilization—such a pork-barrel spending, relying on fame, and vote buying—which permit them to stand out from the crowd. Hicken shows that a variety of conditions—ranging from cultural norms of gift giving, to weak law enforcement, to poverty and small electoral districts (both of which keep the cost of vote buying low)—might push candidates to favor vote buying over other personal strategies.

These findings are substantively interesting. They are also important theoretically, for they highlight the importance of understanding how vote buying gets framed (Schedler 2002b). How we understand the causes of vote buying varies depending on whether we see it as a strategy of mobilization or manipulation. Interestingly, neither Lehoucq nor Hicken states explicitly that he is operating within a particular frame. As is typically the case in the scattered literature on vote buying, the frames of mobilization and manipulation operate in the background, implicit but powerful all the same.

The point here is not to argue that one or the other frame is more "accurate" or "correct." Rather, the point is that vote buying is a strategy of *both* mobilization and manipulation, and we need to understand it in the context of both frames. Both Lehoucq and Hicken identify important and complementary conditions that give rise to vote buying. Vote buying, to synthesize and condense their insights, tends to emerge only in places where neither wholesale strategies of mobilization (ideological campaigns, allocational policies, pork-barrel spending, relying on fame) nor wholesale or coercive strategies of manipulation (vote padding, voter intimidation) are feasible or cost-effective. The conditions under which other mobilizational and manipulative strategies lose their comparative advantage is a question to which we will turn shortly; for now it is sufficient to note that the frames of mobilization and manipulation, taken together, offer a more comprehensive picture of vote buying than does either frame alone.

However complementary the two frames, we must nevertheless acknowledge that they do produce some findings that seem hard to reconcile. For instance, where Lehoucq sees urbanization—combined with the freedom it gives to voters—as one essential condition for vote buying to emerge, Hicken argues instead that urbanization "tends to undermine the incentives of candidates to buy votes," because, among other reasons, cities tend to lack the dense network of relationships on which the organizational infrastructure of vote buying campaigns are built.

When such contradictory arguments appear, it might be best to look more closely at context. That is, we might here recognize that urbanization is not a homogeneous process, and that urban communities differ, say, in the extent to which voters are embedded in social networks, or in how those networks function. From this perspective, it is probably not urbanization per se that is important, but rather the extent to which urbanization either liberates voters from the intimidating gaze of coercive overlords (thus making vote buying a comparatively attractive strategy of manipulation) or puts voters beyond the reach of solicitous grassroots party operatives (thus making vote buying a comparatively unattractive strategy of mobilization). Only under particular conditions will urbanization either intensify or reduce the incidence of vote buying.

Factors That Promote Vote Buying as a Strategy of Manipulation

Vote buying can become a relatively attractive strategy of manipulation, as Lehoucq shows in Chapter 3, in at least two circumstances. In some places, "harder" forms of coercion no longer work, because of social change or an opening of political space; in these cases, landlords and capitalists can no longer command voters. In other places, safeguards to or improvements in the administration of elections make it hard for candidates to stuff ballot boxes, pad the final vote tallies, or engage in other forms of "wholesale" fraud. Thus vote buying may emerge as an attractive strategy as a result of either broad sociopolitical transformation or more circumscribed changes in the administration of elections.

We know little about the specific historical forces that bring about the large sociopolitical transformations that are particularly conducive to vote buying. Among the many issues that might be investigated, let me here draw attention to just one. Vote buying would seem to require a peculiar kind of social environment—one that leaves voters independent, but not isolated. After all, in many places where vote buying proliferates, voters are free enough from their overloads that they cannot be blatantly coerced, yet enmeshed enough in existing social networks for candidates and parties to reach them. Thus for vote buying to emerge, social relationships must be revolutionized in one sense, but remain profoundly conservative in another. As discussed above, certain patterns of urbanization may meet these conditions.

We are similarly in the dark when it comes to the relationship of clean election reform to vote buying. Vote buying arises when elections are cleaned up unevenly—when wholesale forms of fraud are made more difficult to pull off than retail forms such as vote buying. Among the questions scholars might wish to investigate in the future: What are the political and institutional conditions that bring about this uneven progression of clean election reform? What are the political motives that might lead stakeholders to agree on reforms that make wholesale or coercive manipulation difficult, but leave open the possibility of vote buying? Are retail forms of manipulation inherently more difficult to control than wholesale ones?

Factors That Promote Vote Buying
as a Strategy of Mobilization

Vote buying, relative to other mobilizational strategies, is expensive. Under what circumstances does it become relatively advantageous? Certain institutional configurations, which Hicken neatly catalogs, appear to be particularly important. Among them are government resources that are easy for candidates to access, small electoral districts that put a cap on vote buying expenses, bans on mass-media political advertising, and candidate-centered electoral rules that generate intraparty competition and thus make it difficult for candidates to campaign on party platforms.

There are additional conditions that make vote buying a relatively attractive strategy of mobilization. One is a preexisting culture of gift giving, which is strongly present in Taiwan, among other places. Embedding vote buying within ritual gift exchanges helps engender feelings of obligation among recipients, and can thus lower the rate of defection. It may not be coincidental that of four countries for which we have data on leakage, the rate was lowest in Taiwan, since vote buying there often takes the ritualized form of gift giving.

Another condition is a highly unequal distribution of income. Surveys from several countries show that the poor are the favored target of vote buyers. Why the poor? Desposato argues in Chapter 7 that poor voters assign a higher value to immediate electoral payoffs relative to wealthier voters who can wait for the deferred delivery of pork or programs. Thus candidates gamble that even small, up-front outlays can sway the electoral choices of poor voters. Stokes argues in Chapter 6 that Desposato underestimates the patience of poor voters, and argues instead that candidates target poor voters simply because this strategy is more efficient. Because a poor person will be happier with a small payoff than will a rich person, the same amount of money will buy more votes among the poor than among the rich. We do not have enough hard evidence to assess the plausibility or accuracy of these two competing accounts. Why poverty is conducive to vote buying is a question that calls for more empirical work.

Note, however, that there is already one empirical finding that must be integrated into any theoretical account linking poverty to vote buying. If there were a simple, linear relationship between a voter's levels of poverty and the probability that this voter will be offered money, then we should expect the highest proportion of vote buying offers to be made to the poorest of the poor: the poorer the voter, the more likely she or he is to receive an offer. But surveys that differentiate the "poor" from the "poorest of the poor" show that this is not the case. In both Brazil and the Philippines, the poorest of the poor are no more likely to be offered money than are the poor (Pulse Asia 2001; Speck and Abramo 2001). This leveling-off might be explained by logistics (perhaps the severely poor are hard to reach), by instrumental calculation (perhaps vote buyers regard the severely poor as unreliable vote sellers), or by still other factors.

Another set of conditions that promote vote buying relates to party organization. Decentralized parties that do not allow party leaders to impose financial or ideological discipline on candidates, as Hicken notes in Chapter 4, are prone to vote buying. Vote buying is also made easier where there is an already established grassroots organization. In Taiwan, the KMT put together its network of vote buyers, wherever possible, by wooing already established local factions, as Wang and Kurzman explain in Chapter 5. In Argentina, as Stokes notes in Chapter 6, the legacy of Peronism and its appeal to the poor left dense party-linked social networks in place that formed the core of its grassroots vote buying machine. After the deaths of Juan and Eva Perón, and the fading of their party's charismatic appeal, the shift to electoral clientelism, including vote buying, was made easier by the grassroots organization the two leaders had constructed.

Contributors to this volume, then, identify a host of factors that encourage vote buying over alternative strategies of electoral mobilization and manipulation: particular electoral institutions (small electoral districts, bans on mass-media political advertising, candidate-centered electoral rules, and the like), a special kind of culture (strong norms of gift giving), certain social conditions (poverty), a specific kind of party organization (decentralization, preexisting grassroots networks), growing independence of voters from their overlords, and uneven electoral reforms that make wholesale manipulation more difficult but that do not sanction retail strategies such as vote buying. How these factors relate, interact, override, and reinforce one another is not altogether clear, and this question is ripe for future theoretical and empirical investigation.

Variation Within Countries

In examining the factors that favor vote buying over alternative strategies of mobilization and manipulation, we have thus far taken entire countries as units of analysis. This move is justified insofar as levels of vote buying in some places (say, late-twentieth-century Thailand) are on the whole much higher than in other places (say, nineteenth-century Germany), and thus call for explanations that can explain such aggregate differences. But we must also acknowledge that levels of vote buying can vary greatly *within* particular countries. As discussed above, there is often variation in levels of vote buying by class—the poor tend to be more likely to have their votes bought than the wealthy.

Variation can also sometimes be geographic, when, for instance, poverty overlaps substantially with electoral districts. In Brazil, vote buying is common in poor states like Piauí, but uncommon in rich states like Brasília (a fact that Desposato exploits to his analytic advantage in Chapter 7—though he is interested in examining the impact of vote buying, not its causes).

Levels of vote buying can also vary with the office being contested in the election. In the Philippines, to site only one example, senatorial candidates are far less likely to make vote buying offers than are candidates for local offices. For instance, voters were eight times more likely to receive money from mayoral candidates during the 2001 elections than from senatorial candidates (Pulse Asia 2001).

Given that levels of vote buying vary greatly within countries—across space, class, and the office being contested—we need explanations that can account for this variation. Since electoral rules are nearly identical across Brazilian states, institutional variables are apparently less salient in explaining regional variations in that country than are the various social, cultural, and organizational variables mentioned above. In contrast, institutional variables are plausibly important in explaining why senatorial candidates in the Philippines are not heavy vote buyers. Senators have a national constituency; they do not represent particular geographic districts. Senatorial candidates are thus forced to run national campaigns. The national scope of their electoral district means that the cost of vote buying campaigns for most senatorial candidates is prohibitively high, even if intraparty competition provides a strong incentive for candidates to adopt personal strategies like vote buying. Taking the Brazilian and Philippine cases together, we see that, in all likelihood, different combinations of factors carry different weights in different countries (and within different countries). In explaining the emergence of vote buying, there appears to be no parsimonious set of factors that applies universally.

What Are the Consequences of Vote Buying?

When widespread, vote buying can have far-reaching consequences, as multiple contributors to this volume show. It can fuel organized crime and the criminalization of politics. It can divert funds away from the provision of socially desirable public goods. It can also sharpen social inequalities (particularly in agrarian economies). In addition, vote buying can compromise principles of democratic equality, inclusive decisionmaking, and political autonomy. Vote buying is particularly damaging to the collective interests of the poor, which is ironic insofar as the poor are also its main beneficiaries: they are the ones who receive most of the electoral payoffs. But the payoffs come with a heavy price. The poor are the ones who suffer disproportionately from a loss of voice and autonomy, a dearth of public goods, and the intensification of inequalities. As well, vote buying alters the behavior of legislators: it provides a disincentive for them to take policy positions, and makes them more vulnerable to pressure from the executive, resulting in cohesive government parties, but fragmented or unassertive oppositions.

The repetition of "can" in the above paragraph is deliberate, and intended to underscore the conditional nature of particular findings. As contributors to this volume argue repeatedly, vote buying takes different forms, and these different forms sometimes carry different consequences. In other words, whose votes are bought, how they are bought, who does the buying, why voters accept payment, how compliance is achieved, and where the money comes from may all matter when it comes to plotting out the various consequences of vote buying.

Thus Stokes, when asking in Chapter 6 if vote buying is undemocratic, finds it necessary to distinguish different "empirical models" of vote buying. Particularly important to her are differences between the "probabilistic selective" and the "high-discount" models. In the former model, voters sell their votes simply because they value payoffs that are sufficiently high to them, while in the latter they sell their votes because they are deeply skeptical of programmatic promises. These different motives, Stokes argues, carry different implications for democratic equality, because they are different in what they reveal about voters' interests. Whereas probabilistic selective vote sellers disclose little about their interests, high-discount vote sellers expose an interest in a quick, certain payoff. Thus probabilistic selective vote buying is more damaging to the democratic principle of equal consideration of interests, because it carries less information about those interests.

Baland and Robinson, in Chapter 8, are similarly careful to specify the kind of vote buying that leads to the economic consequences they identity. They contrast direct vote buying (by which individuals sell their votes directly to parties) with indirect vote buying (by which voters cast their ballots as instructed by their employers, who sell their blocks of votes to parties). The authors show that there are economic consequences that are particular to indirect vote buying. Namely, it leads to the concentration of landownership, because farm owners, seeking to expand their political power, extend the size of their farms to bring under their political control larger numbers of workers.

While some consequences are specific to particular forms of vote buying, it is also true that other consequences have far more generic origins. Desposato, in Chapter 7, maintains that clientelism—whether it takes the form of episodic vote buying contracts or enduring patronage relationships—has similar implications for legislative politics. He argues that because the reelection of legislators in clientelist systems hinges on their ability to deliver goods that are "private" (available only to one's supporters) rather than "public" (available to all), their prime concern is to secure and deliver those private goods. The major challenge of legislators who seek reelection in "public-goods" systems, in contrast, is to claim credit for policies and programs. These divergent challenges lead to different kinds of legislative behavior, among other things. Legislators in clientelist systems tend not to take policy positions, and instead devote their energies to building alliances with resource-controlling state executives. Legislators in public-goods systems, in contrast, are more likely to advance policy proposals and take independent policy positions.

Taken together, the findings presented in this volume highlight the importance of distinguishing between three kinds of consequences:

- consequences particular to *specific types* of vote buying, such as probabilistic selective vote buying or indirect vote buying
- consequences that result from all forms of vote buying, but *not* from kindred forms of mobilization (such as patronage) or manipulation (such as voter intimidation)
- consequences that result from both vote buying *and* kindred forms of mobilization or manipulation

Past efforts to identify the consequences of vote buying were often insufficiently attentive to these distinctions. The contributors to this volume show why such distinctions are important. On the one hand, some forms of vote buying are more noxious than others. On the other hand, it sometimes does not matter whether mobilization takes the form of patronage or vote buying (whatever form the vote buying might take). Both lessons are important for those who seek not only to understand the consequences of vote buying on politics and society, but also to think about which practices are most in need of reform.

Can Vote Buying Be "Reformed" Away?

Efforts to reform vote buying may seek to change the behavior of either vote buyers (demand-side reform) or vote sellers (supply-side reform). Demand-side reform seeks to persuade voters to refrain from accepting money from or selling their votes to a candidate. Supply-side reform aims to alter the rules of electoral competition in ways that dissuade candidates from offering money in the first place. The efficacy of each of these two types of reform needs to be assessed separately.

Demand-side Reform

Demand-side reform often takes the form of voter education, and any education campaign must be premised on an understanding of why people sell their votes. Viewed from this perspective, vote buying constitutes an odd puzzle to would-be reformers: If vote buying is so bad—and so often bad, in particular, for the long-term interests of the very people who sell their votes—why do sellers sell? This volume helps us identify at least four generic categories of motivation. One is short-term economic need: a straightforward calculation of immediate individual benefit. The second is fear: apprehension about retaliation should the voter decline the offer, or vote differently than expected. The third relates to feelings of personal obligation to the vote brokers who actually buy their votes—to the local notables, friends, or family members who come knocking on their doors. The fourth is a belief that vote buying is a sign of virtue, the mark of a candidate who cares.

The third and fourth motives help explain why civic educators in some places have found it so hard to educate away vote buying. In various parts of the world, as I argue in Chapter 10, reformers have simply not understood adequately the moral nexus that sometimes binds vote sellers to vote buyers. When educators see—as they so often do—only narrow instrumental motives, and fail to acknowledge the social pressures and expectations that sometimes drive vote selling, this results in education campaigns that ring hollow or backfire. This fact may explain, in part, why we cannot identify any countries in which levels of vote buying have been substantially reduced as a result of voter education.

Supply-side Reform

Evidence on efforts to legislate away vote buying is more mixed. On the one hand, a simple reform—increasing the size of constituencies—appears to have greatly reduced vote buying in nineteenth-century Britain by making the practice too expensive. On the other hand, as Hicken explains in Chapter 9, the comprehensive set of supply-side reforms written into Thailand's 1997 constitution—including compulsory voting, which is functionally the same as increasing constituency size—met with only limited success in the postreform elections of 2000 and 2001. Provisions in the new constitution worked against one another, and candidates nimbly adjusted their vote buying strategies to circumvent the new constraints.

Part of the problem in Thailand, too, is that candidates found ways to generate large sums of money, removing the prohibition of cost that was so determinant in nineteenth-century Britain. Also damaging to the Thai reform effort was a lack of vigorous law enforcement. Taiwan, in this regard, offers an instructive contrast, and merits a short discussion.

In 1993, the president of Taiwan, Lee Teng-Hui, appointed as justice minister a young firebrand named Ma Ying-Jeou, who made a crackdown on electoral corruption his highest priority. Under the justice minister's direction, prosecutors indicted more than half of the members of the Taoyuan County assembly for selling their votes when electing the speaker and vice speaker of the assembly in early 1994. Investigations spread to other counties. Within five months, 436 politicians had been indicted, including 341 of the 858 newly elected councilors nationwide, and half of those indicted were convicted. These prosecutions sent a strong signal to politicians that a new era had begun, especially since almost all of those indicted belonged to Ma's own KMT party, including all of the 17 assembly speakers and 15 deputy speakers brought to court.

The crackdown soon extended to popular elections. In Tainan County, a record 981 people were convicted in a single case of vote buying during the 1996 legislative elections. Between 1995 and 1998, prosecutors won 4,375 local court convictions on charges of vote buying in southwest Taiwan alone, and 95 of those convicted were sentenced to prison. While political interference led higher courts to overturn convictions of several prominent KMT candidates during this period, many convictions stood (Wu and Huang 2004).

The campaign against vote buying picked up even more steam in 2000 with the defeat of the KMT presidential candidate by Chen Shui-Bian, the Democratic Progressive Party (DPP) leader who rode to power partly on his pledge to root out political corruption. Pledging in his inaugural address to "eliminate vote buying" and make "rule by the clean and the upright" his "topmost" priority, he appointed as justice minister Chen Ding-Nan, a former magistrate and legislator so respected for his integrity that he became known as "Mr. Clean." Under Minister Chen's watch, prosecutors made frequent use of wiretapping and forensic accounting techniques to track unusual movements of cash. They also expanded the role of local police in investigating suspected cases of vote buying, and provided rewards to arresting officers. Among the most effective tools was rewarding private citizens for information leading to the conviction of vote buyers. For the 2001 elections, rewards went as high as US$285,000. Among the most famous of informants was Tsai Pai-Hsiu, a water vendor and DPP activist who has earned enough money "ghost catching" to buy diamond rings, a Rolex watch, and three Mercedes Benzes.

These aggressive tactics led some vote buyers to abandon the practice, as we learn from Wang and Kurzman's careful ethnographic study in Chapter 5. Their observations dovetail with reports that vote buying declined over the course of the 1990s and into the 2000s, and with the proclamation by election watchers that the 2001 elections were the "cleanest in Taiwan's history."[5] Without the benefit of fundamental institutional reform (and with only a lackluster voter education campaign), the vigorous enforcement of law alone apparently had quite an impact, at least in the short run.

The reform of vote buying is anything but simple, and the long-term impact of the crackdown in Taiwan is not yet known. Still, the side-by-side comparison of Taiwan and Thailand does suggest that strong law enforcement is one essential element of any reform effort—at least in places where candidates are unlikely to give up the practice on their own. Where those who seek elective office can raise huge sums of money—and thus absorb the increased costs associated with larger constituencies, compulsory voting, or other reforms—heavy legal sanctions do appear necessary to change their behavior.

In sum, supply-side reform would seem to hold more promise than demand-side reform in the fight to reduce vote buying. In the application of supply-side reforms, furthermore, enforcing the rules of fair electoral competition would seem to be every bit as important as getting those rules right.

Conclusion

These conclusions are painted broadly. They gloss over much of the nuance and detail so carefully developed by the contributors to this volume. Still, these cursory remarks do bring to the fore a few central ideas running through the book: There are many varieties of vote buying with different causes and consequences. Many of these consequences are damaging to democracy and society. The success of contemporary efforts to reform vote buying have been at best mixed.

These conclusions also reveal that much work remains to be done. Because vote buying appears under many guises, there is much we still do not understand about its multiple causes and consequences. This book offers a variety of tools, categories, hypotheses, and empirical findings in our search for answers, but in doing so it also raises new questions to be investigated. Vote buying is a widespread but enigmatic practice that yields its secrets only slowly.

Notes

1. Buying voting credentials is a nonviable option in the Philippines, for there is no single document or form of identification that voters are required to produce when voting, and poll workers often do not request to see any form of identification at all.

2. On the distinction between manipulation and mobilization, see Chapter 1, especially Tables 1.1 and 1.2.

3. I thank Chin-Shou Wang and Charles Kurzman for providing me the vote totals and actual bonus amounts upon which these calculations are based.

4. There were thirty-six gubernatorial races in 1990. The data on which this figure is based—from the Gubernatorial Campaign Database, http://www.unc.edu/~beyle/guber.html—are available for twenty-six of these races. The cost per vote is for the general election only, and thus excludes primary and runoff expenses. Details on this database can be found in Jensen and Beyle 2003.

5. See, for instance, Moon and Robinson 1998, 145; Rawnsley 2003, 769; *Taipei Times* 2005.

Bibliography

Acemoglu, Daron, and James A. Robinson. 2001. "A Theory of Political Transitions." *American Economic Review* 91: 938–963.

Agence-France Press. 1996. "Candidates Alleged to Pay 10,000 Dollars to Buy Votes." October 7.

Aldrich, John H. 1995. *Why Parties? The Origin and Transformation of Political Parties in America.* Chicago: University of Chicago Press.

Alvarez, Michael. 1997. *Information and Elections.* Ann Arbor: University of Michigan Press.

Ames, Barry. 1995. "Electoral Strategy Under Open-List Proportional Representation." *American Journal of Political Science* 39, 2: 406–433.

———. 2001. *The Deadlock of Democracy in Brazil.* Ann Arbor: University of Michigan Press.

Ammar Siamwalla. 1997. "Can a Developing Democracy Manage Its Macroeconomy? The Case of Thailand." In *Thailand's Boom and Bust.* Bangkok: Thailand Development Research Institute.

———. N.d. "Why Do Voters Elect Corrupt Politicians? Towards a Theory of Representative Kleptocracy." Working paper.

Anand Panyarachun. 2001. "Good Governance in Asia: Choice or Necessity." Speech given at the third Asian Development Forum, Bangkok, June 13, 2001. http://www.adb.org/documents/events/2001/adf2001/anand_panyarachun.asp.

Anderson, Benedict. 1990. "Murder and Progress in Modern Siam." *New Left Review* 81: 33–48.

Anderson, Margaret Lavinia. 2000. *Practicing Democracy: Elections and Political Culture in Imperial Germany.* Princeton: Princeton University Press.

Anek Laothamatas. 1997. Interview with Allen D. Hicken. Bangkok, September 11.

Ansolabehere, Stephen, and James M. Snyder Jr. 2002. "Party Control of State Government and the Distribution of Public Expenditures." Cambridge: Massachusetts Institute of Technology. Unpublished manuscript.

Anusorn Limmanee. 1995. *Political Business Cycles in Thailand, 1979–1992: General Election and Currency in Circulation.* Research report. Bangkok: Institute of Thai Studies, Chulalongkorn University.

Aparicio, Ricardo. 2002. "La magnitud de la manipulación del voto en las elecciones federales del año 2000." *Perfiles Latinoamericanos* 20: 79–100.

Argersinger, Peter H. 1987. "From Party Tickets to Secret Ballots: The Evolution of the Electoral Process in Maryland During the Gilded Age." *Maryland Historical Review* 82, 3: 214–255.

Arghiros, Daniel. 1993. "Rural Transformation and Local Politics in a Central Thai District." PhD diss., Hull, England, University of Hull.

———. 1995. "Political Structures and Strategies: A Study of Electoral Politics in Contemporary Rural Thailand." Occasional Paper no. 31. Hull, England: University of Hull, Centre for South-East Asian Studies.

———. 2000. "The Local Dynamics of the 'New Political Economy': A District Business Association and Its Role in Electoral Politics." In *Money and Power in Provincial Thailand,* edited by Ruth McVey. Honolulu: University of Hawaii Press.

Assembléia Legislativa do Estado do Piauí. 1998. *Manual do deputado: Regimento interno e constituição do estado do Piauí.* 2nd ed. Teresina: Mesa Diretora da Assembléia Legislativa do Estado do Piauí.

Austen-Smith, David. 2000. "Income Redistribution Under Proportional Representation." *Journal of Political Economy* 108: 1235–1269.

Auyero, Javier. 1999. "'From the Client's Point(s) of View': How Poor People Perceive and Evaluate Political Clientelism." *Theory and Society* 28, 2: 297–334.

———. 2000. "The Logic of Clientelism in Argentina: An Ethnographic Account." *Latin American Research Review* 35, 3: 55–81.

Bacani, Teodoro C., Jr. 1992. *Church in Politics.* Manila: Bacani's.

Bagehot, Walter. 2001 [1867]. *The English Constitution.* Cambridge: Cambridge University Press.

Baland, Jean-Marie, and James A. Robinson. 2003a. "Electoral Corruption and Public Policy." Unpublished manuscript.

———. 2003b. "Land and Power." CEPR Discussion Paper no. 3800. http://www.cepr.org.

Banégas, Richard. 1998. "Marchandisation du vote, citoyenneté et consolidation démocratique au Bénin." *Politique Africaine* 69, 1: 75–88.

Banfield, Edward C., and James Q. Wilson. 1963. *City Politics.* New York: Vintage.

Banyat Tansaneeyavej. 1992. "Eyes on the Prizes." *Bangkok Post,* March 19.

Bates, Robert H. 1981. *Markets and States in Tropical Africa.* Berkeley: University of California Press.

Bauer, Arnold J. 1975. *Chilean Rural Society from the Spanish Conquest to 1930.* Cambridge: Cambridge University Press.

———. 1995. "Landlord and Campesino in the Chilean Road to Democracy." In *Agrarian Structure and Political Power: Landlord and Peasant in the Making of Latin America,* edited by Evelyne Huber and Frank Safford. Pittsburgh: University of Pittsburgh Press.

Bautista, Maria Cynthia Rose Banzon. 2001. "People Power 2: 'The Revenge of the Elite on the Masses'?" In *Between Fires: Fifteen Perspectives on the Estrada Crisis,* edited by Amando Doronila. Pasig: Anvil.

Bava, Weng. 1998. "How Partisan Poll Watching Is Transformed into an Indirect Vote Buying." Chapel Net: Christian Action for Peaceful and Meaningful Elections. http://members.tripod.com/~chapelnet/weng1.html.

BBC News. 2001. "Violence at Kenya Polls." January 12. http://news.bbc.co.uk/1/hi/world/africa/1114130.stm.

———. 2003. "Mafia Turns to 3G Video Phones." May 16. http://news.bbc.co.uk/go/pr/fr/-/2/hi/technology/3033551.stm.

Becerra, Ricardo, Pedro Salazar, and José Woldenberg. 2000. *La mecánica del cam-*

bio político en México: Elecciones, partidos y reformas. Mexico City: Cal y Arena.

Bensel, Richard. 2004. *The American Ballot Box: Law, Identity, and Voting, 1850–1868.* New York: Cambridge University Press.

Berry, Albert, and William R. Cline. 1979. *Agrarian Structure and Productivity in Developing Countries.* Geneva: International Labour Organization.

Binswanger, Hans P., Klaus Deininger, and Gerschorn Feder. 1995. "Power, Distortions, Revolt, and Reform in Agricultural Land Relations." In *The Handbook of Development Economics,* vol. 3, edited by Jere R. Behrman and T. N. Srinivasan. Amsterdam: North-Holland.

Birch, Sarah. 2005. "Electoral Systems and Electoral Corruption." University of Essex. Unpublished manuscript.

Bloom, David E., Patricia H. Craig, and Pia N. Malaney. 2001. *Study of Rural Asia,* vol. 4, *The Quality of Life in Rural Asia.* Oxford: Oxford University Press.

Bondoc, Jarius. 2000. "It's Not Just Erap, It's the System." *Philippine Star,* April 1.

Borisova, Yevgenia. 2000. "And the Winner Is? Part 2." *Moscow Times,* September 9.

Borwornsak Uwanno and Wayne Burns. 1998. "The Thai Constitution of 1997: Sources and Process." *Thailand Law Journal.* http://members.tripod.com/asialaw/articles/constburns1.html.

Bosco, Joseph. 1992. "Taiwan Factions: Guanxi, Patronage, and the State in Local Politics." *Ethnology* 31: 157–183.

———. 1994. "Faction Versus Ideology: Mobilization Strategies in Taiwan's Elections." *China Quarterly* 137: 28–62.

Bourdieu, Pierre. 1984. *Distinction: A Social Critique of the Judgement of Taste.* Cambridge: Harvard University Press.

Brusco, Valeria, Marcelo Nazareno, and Susan C. Stokes. 2002. "Does Poverty Erode Democracy? Evidence from Argentina." Working paper. October.

———. 2004. "Vote Buying in Argentina." *Latin American Research Review* 39, 2: 66–88.

Buchanan, James, and Gordon Tullock. 1962. *The Calculus of Consent.* Ann Arbor: University of Michigan Press.

Burgwal, Gerrit. 1995. *Struggle of the Poor: Neighborhood Organization and Clientelist Practice in a Quito Squatter Settlement.* Amsterdam: Center for Latin American Research and Documentation.

Caciagli, Mario, and Frank P. Belloni. 1981. "The 'New' Clientelism in Southern Italy: The Christian Democratic Party in Catania." In *Political Clientelism, Patronage and Development,* edited by S. N. Eisenstadt and R. Lemarchand. Beverly Hills: Sage.

Cain, Bruce, John Ferejohn, and Morris Fiorina. 1987. *The Personal Vote: Constituency Service and Electoral Independence.* Cambridge: Harvard University Press.

Calderón-Alzati, Enrique, and Daniel Cazés. 1996. *Las elecciones presidenciales de 1994.* Mexico City: La Jornada/Centro de Investigaciones Interdisciplinarias en Humanidades, Universidad Nacional Autónoma de México.

Callahan, William A. 2000. *Pollwatching, Elections and Civil Society in Southeast Asia.* Burlington, Vt.: Ashgate.

———. 2002. "The Ideology of Vote-Buying and the Democratic Deferral of Political Reform." Paper presented at the conference "Trading Political Rights: The Comparative Politics of Vote Buying," Center for International Studies, Massachusetts Institute of Technology, Cambridge, August 26–27.

Callahan, William A., and Duncan McCargo. 1996. "Vote-Buying in Thailand's Northeast: The July 1995 General Election." *Asian Survey* 36, 4: 376–392.

Câmara Legislativa do Distrito Federal. 1998a. *Memória da Câmara Legislativa do DF: 1A e 2A legislaturas.* Brasília: Gráfica da Câmara Legislativa do Distrito Federal.

———. 1998b. *Regimento Interno da Câmara Legislativa do Distrito Federal.* Brasília: Gráfica da Câmara Legislativa do Distrito Federal.

Caramani, Daniele. 2004. *The Nationalization of Politics: The Formation of National Electorates and Party Systems in Western Europe.* New York: Cambridge University Press.

Carey, John M. 1996. *Term Limits and Legislative Representation.* New York: Cambridge University Press.

Carey, John M., and Matthew Soberg Shugart. 1995. "Incentives to Cultivate a Personal Vote: A Rank Ordering of Electoral Formulas." *Electoral Studies* 14, 4: 417–439.

Caro, Robert. 1990. *Means of Ascent.* New York: Knopf.

Castro, José Luis. 1941. *El Sistema Electoral Chileno.* Santiago: Editorial Nascimento.

Cauhy, Jorge. 1999. Interview with Scott W. Desposato.

Cazés, Daniel, et al. 1996. *Memorial de las elecciones de 1994: Testimonios de observadores.* Mexico City: La Jornada/Centro de Investigaciones Interdisciplinarias en Humanidades, Universidad Nacional Autónoma de Mexico.

Central Depository Unit. 2002. "Ghasia Watch: CDU Report on Electoral Violence in Kenya, January–December 2002." Nairobi.

Chang, Eric C. C., and Miriam A. Golden. Forthcoming. "Electoral Systems, District Magnitude and Corruption." *British Journal of Political Science.*

Chang, Mau-Kuei, and Chun-Chue Chen. 1986. "Relations Between Modernization, Local Factions, and Turnout in Local Elections: A Reexamination of Liberalism" [in Chinese]. In *Symposium of Conference on Voting Behavior and Electoral Culture.* Taipei: Chinese Political Science Association.

Chao, Yung-Maou. 1997. *Change and Characteristics of Taiwan's Local Politics* [in Chinese]. Taipei: Hanlu.

Chaowana Traimas. 1998. *Basic Data on 66 Years of Thai Democracy* [in Chinese]. Bangkok: Institute of Public Policy Studies.

Chen, Ming-Tong, and Yun-Han Chu. 1992. "Regional Oligopoly, Local Factions, and Provincial Assembly Elections" [in Chinese]. *Proceedings of the National Science Council* 3: 77–97.

Cheng, Kuen-Shan, Ye-Li Wang, and Yun-Tsai Chen. 2000. *Analysis of the Causes of Vote Buying, and the Study of How to Prevent It* [in Chinese]. Taipei: Ministry of Justice.

Christensen, Scott, et al. 1993. *Thailand: The Institutional and Political Underpinnings of Growth.* Washington, D.C.: World Bank.

Chu, Yun-Han. 1989. "Oligarchy and the Authoritarian Political System" [in Chinese]. In *Monopoly and Exploitation,* edited by Wu Chongji. Taipei: Taiwan Research Foundation.

———. 1994. "SNTV and the Evolving Party System in Taiwan" [in Chinese]. *Political Science Review* 22: 33–52.

Chubb, Judith. 1982. *Patronage, Power, and Poverty in Southern Italy: A Tale of Two Cities.* New York: Cambridge University Press.

Cialdini, Robert B. 1984. *Influence: The New Psychology of Modern Persuasion.* New York: Quill.

Cleary, Matthew. 2003. "Electoral Competition and Democracy in Mexico." PhD diss., University of Chicago.

Coelho, Ana Cládia. 2000. "'Oposição se faz com dois, três, cinco ou dez,' afirma Leal Júnior." *Meio Norte,* March 5.

Cohen, Joshua. 1998. "Democracy and Liberty." In *Deliberative Democracy,* edited by Jon Elster. New York: Cambridge University Press.

Collier, David, and Steven Levitsky. 1997. "Democracy with Adjectives: Conceptual Innovation in Comparative Research." *World Politics* 49: 430–451.

Collins, William, et al. 2000. "Impact Survey of Voter Knowledge and Awareness." Occasional Paper no. 7. Phnom Penh: Center for Advanced Study.

Connors, Michael. 1999. "Political Reform and the State in Thailand." *Journal of Contemporary Asia* 29, 4: 202–226.

Constitution of the Kingdom of Thailand, B.E. 2540. 1997. Bangkok: Office of the Council of State.

Coppedge, Michael. 1993. "Parties and Society in Mexico and Venezuela." *Comparative Politics* 25: 253–274.

Cornelius, Wayne A. 2002. "La eficacia de la compra y coacción del voto en las elecciones mexicanas de 2000." *Perfiles Latinoamericanos* 20: 11–32.

———. 2004. "Mobilized Voting in the 2000 Elections: The Changing Efficacy of Vote Buying and Coercion in Mexican Electoral Politics." In *Mexico's Pivotal Democratic Elections: Candidates, Voters, and the Presidential Campaign of 2000,* edited by Jorge I. Domínguez and Chappell Lawson. Stanford: Stanford University Press.

Coronel, Leandro V. 2001. "Discovering the Poor." *Philippine Daily Inquirer,* May 19.

Coughlin, Peter J. 1992. *Probabilistic Voting Theory.* New York: Cambridge University Press.

Cox, Gary W. 1987. *The Efficient Secret: The Cabinet and the Development of Political Parties in Victorian England.* New York: Cambridge University Press.

———. 1997. *Making Votes Count.* Cambridge: Cambridge University Press.

Cox, Gary W., and J. Morgan Kousser. 1981. "Turnout and Rural Corruption: New York as a Test Case." *American Journal of Political Science* 25, 4: 646–663.

Cox, Gary W., and Mathew D. McCubbins. 1993. *Legislative Leviathan.* Berkeley: University of California Press.

———. 2001. "Political Structure and Economic Policy: The Institutional Determinants of Policy Outcomes." In *Structure and Policy in Presidential Democracies,* edited by Stephan Haggard and Mathew D. McCubbins. New York: Cambridge University Press.

Cox, Gary W., and Frances M. Rosenbluth. 1993. "The Electoral Fortunes of Legislative Factions in Japan." *American Political Science Review* 87: 577–589.

———. 1996. "Factional Competition for the Party Endorsement: The Case of Japan's Liberal Democratic Party." *British Journal of Political Science* 26: 259–269.

Cox, Gary W., and Michael F. Thies. 1998. "The Cost of Intraparty Competition: The Single, Nontransferable Vote and Money Politics in Japan." *Comparative Political Studies* 31, 3: 267–291.

———. 2000. "How Much Does Money Matter? 'Buying' Votes in Japan, 1967–1990." *Comparative Political Studies* 33, 1: 37–57.

Croissant, Aurel, and Jörn Dosch. 2001. "Parliamentary Elections in Thailand, March 2000 and January 2001." *Electoral Studies* 22: 153–193.

Cruz-Coke, Ricardo. 1984. *Historia Electoral de Chile, 1925–1973.* Santiago: Editorial Jurídica de Chile.

Cullinane, Michael. 1993. "*Burgis* Projects in the Post-Marcos Era." *Pilipinas* 21: 74–76.

Dahl, Robert. 1971. *Polyarchy: Participation and Opposition.* New Haven: Yale University Press.

———. 1987. *Democracy and Its Critics.* New Haven: Yale University Press.

Dardé, Carlos. 1996. "Fraud and Passivity of the Electorate in Spain, 1875–1923." In *Elections Before Democracy,* edited by Eduardo Posada-Carbo. New York: St. Martin's.

de Quiros, Conrado. 2001. "Tongues on Fire." *Philippine Daily Inquirer,* May 1.

de Villa, Henrietta T. 1992. "Faith and Fire, the PPCRV Way: A Post Election Report of the Parish Pastoral Council for Responsible Voting (PPCRV) to the Catholic Bishops Conference of the Philippines (CBCP) and to the Commission on Elections (COMELEC) 25 July 1992." Mimeo.

Deininger, Klaus, and Lyn Squire. 1996. "A New Data Set Measuring Income Inequality." *World Bank Economic Review* 19, 3: 565–591.

Desposato, Scott W. 2001. "Institutional Theories, Societal Realities, and Party Politics in Brazil." PhD diss., University of California–Los Angeles.

———. 2005. "Correcting for Small Group Inflation of Roll-Call Cohesion Scores." *British Journal of Political Science* 35, 4: 731–744.

Diaz-Cayeros, Alberto, and Beatriz Magaloni. 2003. "The Politics of Public Spending (II): The Programa Nacional de Solidaridad (PRONASOL) in Mexico." Stanford: Stanford University, Department of Political Science. Unpublished manuscript.

Dixit, Avinash, and John Londregan. 1996. "The Determinants of Success of Special Interests in Redistributive Politics." *Journal of Politics* 58, 4: 1132–1155.

Douglas, Mary. 1966. *Purity and Danger: An Analysis of Concepts of Pollution and Taboo.* New York: Praeger.

Downs, Anthony. 1957. *An Economic Theory of Democracy.* New York: Harper and Row.

Durkheim, Emile. 1984 [1893]. *The Division of Labor in Society.* New York: Free Press.

Eisenstadt, S. N., and Luis Roniger. 1984. *Patrons, Clients and Friends: Interpersonal Relations and the Structure of Trust in Society.* New York: Cambridge University Press.

Eisenstadt, Todd A. 2003. *Courting Democracy in Mexico: Party Strategies and Electoral Institutions.* New York: Cambridge University Press.

Epstein, Richard A. 1985. "Why Restrain Alienation?" *Columbia Law Review* 85: 970–990.

Espina, Rene. 2001. "Minding Other People's Business." *Manila Bulletin,* May 20.

Fairbairn, B. 1997. *Democracy in the Undemocratic State: The German Reichstag Elections of 1898 and 1903.* Toronto: University of Toronto Press.

Fearon, James. 1999. "Electoral Accountability and the Control of Politicians: Selecting Good Types Versus Sanctioning Poor Performance." In *Democracy, Accountability, and Representation,* edited by Adam Przeworski, Susan C. Stokes, and Bernard Manin. New York: Cambridge University Press.

Ferejohn, John A. 1974. *Pork Barrel Politics: Rivers and Harbors Legislation, 1947–1968.* Stanford: Stanford University Press.

———. 1986. "Incumbent Performance and Electoral Control." *Public Choice* 50: 5–25.

Fiorina, Morris P. 1981. *Retrospective Voting in American National Elections.* New Haven: Yale University Press.

Foucault, Michel. 1979. *Discipline and Punish: The Birth of the Prison.* New York: Vintage.

Fox, Jonathan. 1994. "The Difficult Transition from Clientelism to Citizenship: Lessons from Mexico." *World Politics* 46: 151–184.

Fox, Jonathan, and Luis Hernández. 1995. "Lessons from the Mexican Elections." *Dissent* 42, 1: 29–33.

Fredman, L. E. 1968. *The Australian Ballot: The Story of an American Reform.* East Lansing: Michigan State University Press.

Frykman, Jonas, and Orvar Löfgren. 1987. *Culture Builders: A Historical Anthropology of Middle-Class Life.* Translated by Alan Crozier. New Brunswick, N.J.: Rutgers University Press.

Gallin, Bernard. 1968. "Political Factionalism and Its Impact on Chinese Village Social Organization in Taiwan." In *Local-Level Politics: Social and Cultural Perspectives,* edited by Marc J. Swartz. Chicago: Aldine.

Gay, Robert. 1994. *Popular Organization and Democracy in Rio de Janeiro: A Tale of Two Favelas.* Philadelphia: Temple University Press.

———. 1999. "The Broker and the Thief: A Parable (Reflections on Popular Politics in Brazil)." *Luso-Brazilian Review* 36, 1: 49–70.

Geddes, Barbara, and Arturo Ribero Neto. 1992. "Institutional Sources of Corruption in Brazil." *Third World Quarterly* 13, 4: 641–661.

Gerber, Alan S. 1994. "Four Essays on the Effects of Political Institutions." PhD diss., Massachusetts Institute of Technology.

Gerber, Alan S., and Donald P. Green. 2000. "The Effects of Canvassing, Telephone Calls, and Direct Mail on Voter Turnout: A Field Experiment." *American Political Science Review* 94, 3: 653–663.

Gil, Frederico G. 1966. *The Political System of Chile.* Boston: Houghton Mifflin.

Girling, John L. S. 1981. *Thailand: Society and Politics.* Ithaca: Cornell University Press.

Gist, Genevieve B. 1961. "Progressive Reform in a Rural Community: The Adams County Vote-Fraud Case." *Mississippi Historical Review* 48, 1: 60–78.

Golden, Miriam A. 2003. "Electoral Connections: The Effects of the Personal Vote on Political Patronage, Bureaucracy and Legislation in Postwar Italy." *British Journal of Political Science* 33: 189–212.

Golden, Miriam A., and Eric C. C. Chang. 2001. "Competitive Corruption: Factional Conflict and Political Malfeasance in Postwar Italian Christian Democracy." *World Politics* 53: 588–622.

Gonçalves, Robert John. 1997. "Elites políticas: O caso Piauiense." *Serviço Social e Contemporaneidade* 1, 1.

———. 1998. "Tradicional e moderno na política nacional e a permanência da oligarquia no Piauí." Unpublished manuscript.

———. 1999. Interview with Scott W. Desposato. Teresina, Piauí, May.

Graham, Richard. 1990. *Patronage and Politics in Nineteenth Century Brazil.* Stanford: Stanford University Press.

Grofman, Bernard, et al., eds. 1999. *Elections in Japan, Korea, and Taiwan Under the Single Non-Transferable Vote: The Comparative Study of an Embedded Institution.* Ann Arbor: University of Michigan Press.

Grossman, Gene M., and Elhanan Helpman. 2001. *Special Interest Politics.* Cambridge: Massachusetts Institute of Technology Press.

Hanham, Henry J. 1959. *Elections and Party Management: Politics in the Time of Disraeli and Gladstone.* London: Longmanns.

Hasen, Richard L. 2000. "Vote Buying." *California Law Review* 88: 1323–1371.

Heckelman, Jac C. 1995. "The Effect of Secret Ballot on Turnout Rates." *Public Choice* 82, 1–2: 107–124.

Hedman, Eva-Lotta. 1998. "Whose Business Is It Anyway? Free and Fair Elections in the Philippines." *Public Policy* 2, 3: 145–170.

———. 1999. "Mapping the Movement: NAMFREL in Six Philippine Cities." *South East Asia Research* 7, 2: 189–214.

Heise González, Julio. 1982. *Democracia y gobierno representativo en el período parlamentario: Historia del poder electoral.* Santiago: Ediciones Universitaria.

Hernández Carrochano, David. 2003. "Los intermediarios en la compra de voto en México." Mexico City: Facultad Latinoamericana de Ciencias Sociales. Unpublished manuscript.

Hewison, Kevin. 1996. "Emerging Social Forces in Thailand: New Political and Economic Roles." In *The New Rich of Asia: Mobile Phones, McDonalds, and Middle-Class Revolution,* edited by Richard Robinson and David S. G. Goodman. New York: Routledge.

Hicken, Allen D. 2002. "Parties, Pork and Policy: Policymaking in Developing Democracies." PhD diss., University of California–San Diego.

———. 2003. "Parties, Parliaments, and Pork: Budgetary Politics in Thailand and the Philippines." Presented at the annual meeting of the Midwest Political Science Association, Chicago, April.

Hicken, Allen D., and Yuko Kasuya. 2003. "A Guide to the Constitutional Structures and Electoral Systems of East, South, and Southeast Asia." *Electoral Studies* 22, 1: 121–151.

Ho, Chin-Ming. 1995. "The Vote Buying Phenomenon and Its Effect: An Analysis of the Second Legislative Election in Kaohsiung City" [in Chinese]. *Political Science Review* 6: 109–144.

Hofileña, Chay Florentia. 2001. "Gambling on Politics." *Newsbreak,* April 4: 17–20.

Hoppen, K. Theodore. 1984. *Elections, Politics, and Society in Ireland, 1870–1980.* Oxford: Clarendon.

Huang, Jung-Yue, ed. 1997. *Nongovernmental Judicial Reform White Paper* [in Chinese]. Taipei: Institute of National Policy Research.

Ibana, Rainier. 1996. "Epilogue: Ordinary People in Everyday Life." In *[De]Scribing Elections: A Study of Elections in the Lifeworld of San Isidro,* by Myrna J. Alejo, Maria Elena P. Rivera, and Noel Inocencio P. Valencia. Quezon City: Institute for Popular Democracy.

INEGHI (Instituto Nacional de Estadística y Geografía). 1994. *Estadística histórica de México.* Vol. I. Mexico City.

Jacobs, J. Bruce. 1980. *Local Politics in a Rural Chinese Cultural Setting: A Field Study of Mazu Township, Taiwan.* Canberra: Contemporary China Center, Australian National University.

Jensen, Jennifer M., and Thad Beyle. 2003. "Of Footnotes, Missing Data, and Lessons for 50-State Data Collection: The Gubernatorial Campaign Finance Data Project, 1977–2001." *State Politics and Policy Quarterly* 3, 2: 203–213.

Kamol Hengkietisak. 2002. "Money Rules." *Bangkok Post,* July 7.

Karlan, Patricia. 1994. "Not by Money but by Virtue Won? Vote Trafficking and the Voting Rights System." *Virginia Law Review* 80: 1455–1475.

Katz, Richard. 1985. "Preference Voting in Italy: Votes of Opinion, Belonging, or Exchange." *Comparative Political Studies* 18: 229–249.

———. 1986. "Intraparty Preference Voting." In *Electoral Laws and Their Political Consequences,* edited by B. Grofman and A. Lijphart. New York: Agathon.

Kaufman, Robert E. 1967. "The Chilean Political Right and Agrarian Reform: Resistance and Moderation." Political Study no. 2. Washington, D.C.: Institute for the Comparative Study of Political Systems.

———. 1972. *The Politics of Land Reform in Chile, 1950–1970: Public Policy, Political Institutions, and Social Change.* Cambridge: Harvard University Press.

Kerkvliet, Benedict J. 1991. "Understanding Politics in a Nueva Ecija Rural Community." In *From Marcos to Aquino: Local Perspectives on Political Transition in the Philippines,* edited by Benedict J. Kerkvliet and Resil B. Mojares. Honolulu: University of Hawaii Press.

King, Daniel E. 1996. "New Political Parties in Thailand: A Case Study of the Palang Dharma Party and the New Aspiration Party." PhD diss., University of Wisconsin–Madison.

King, Daniel E., and Jim LoGerfo. 1996. "Thailand: Towards Democratic Stability." *Journal of Democracy* 7, 1: 102–117.

Kishlansky, Mark A. 1986. *Parliamentary Selection: Social and Political Choice in Early Modern England.* New York: Cambridge University Press.

Kitschelt, Herbert. 2000. "Linkages Between Citizens and Politicians in Democratic Polities." *Comparative Political Studies* 33, 6–7: 845–879.

Knaub, Gilbert. 1970. *Typologie juridique de la fraude électorale en France.* Paris: Dalloz.

Knoke, David. 1990. *Political Networks: The Structural Perspective.* New York: Cambridge University Press.

Kochin, Michael S., and Levis A. Kochin. 1998. "When Is Vote Buying Wrong?" *Public Choice* 97: 645–662.

Koole, Ruud. 1989. "The 'Modesty' of Dutch Party Finance." In *Comparative Political Finance in the 1980s,* edited by Herbert E. Alexander. New York: Cambridge University Press.

Kornblith, Miriam. 2002. "The Politics of Vote Trading in Venezuela." Paper presented at the conference "Trading Political Rights: The Comparative Politics of Vote Buying," Center for International Studies, Massachusetts Institute of Technology, Cambridge, August 26–27.

Kunicova, Jana, and Susan Rose-Ackerman. 2005. "Electoral Rules as Constraints on Corruption." *British Journal of Political Science* 35, 4: 573–606.

Laakso, M., and R. Taagepera. 1979. "Effective Number of Parties: A Measure with Application to West Europe." *Comparative Political Studies* 12: 3–27.

Landé, Carl H. 1965. *Leaders, Factions, and Parties: The Structure of Philippine Politics.* New Haven: Yale University Press.

Laquian, Aprodicio, and Eleanor Laquian. 1998. *Joseph Ejercito "Erap" Estrada: The Centennial President.* Quezon City: College of Public Administration, University of the Philippines.

Lehoucq, Fabrice. 2002. "Can Parties Police Themselves? Electoral Governance and Democratization." *International Political Science Review* 23, 1: 29–46.

———. 2003. "Electoral Fraud: Causes, Types, and Consequences." *Annual Review of Political Science* 6: 233–256.

Lehoucq, Fabrice, and Iván Molina. 2002. *Stuffing the Ballot Box: Fraud, Electoral Reform, and Democratization in Costa Rica.* New York: Cambridge University Press.

Lerner, Daniel. 1958. *The Passing of Traditional Society: Modernizing the Middle East.* New York: Free Press of Glencoe.

Levitsky, Steven. 2003. *Transforming Labor-Based Parties in Latin America: Argentine Peronism in Comparative Perspective.* New York: Cambridge University Press.

Lijphart, Arend. 1994. *Electoral Systems and Party Systems: A Study of Twenty-seven Democracies, 1945–1990.* Oxford: Oxford University Press.

Likhit Dhiravegin. N.d. "Democratic Development in Thailand." Unpublished manuscript.

Lin, Chia-Lung. 1998. "Paths to Democracy: Taiwan in Comparative Perspective." PhD diss., Yale University.

Lindbeck, Assar, and Jörgen Weibull. 1987. "Balanced-Budget Redistribution as the Outcome of Political Competition." *Public Choice* 52: 272–297.

Lintott, Andrew. 1990. "Electoral Bribery in the Roman Republic." *Journal of Roman Studies* 80: 1–16.

Lizzeri, Alessandro, and Nicola Persico. 2001. "The Provision of Public Goods Under Alternative Electoral Incentives." *American Economic Review* 91: 225–245.

LoGerfo, James P. 2000. "Beyond Bangkok: The Provincial Middle Class in the 1992 Protests." In *Money and Power in Provincial Thailand,* edited by Ruth McVey. Honolulu: University of Hawaii Press.

Loveman, Brian. 1976. *Struggle in the Countryside: Politics and Rural Labor in Chile, 1919–1973.* Bloomington: University of Indiana Press.

———. 2001. *Chile: The Legacy of Hispanic Capitalism.* 3rd ed. New York: Oxford University Press.

Madison, James, Alexander Hamilton, and John Jay. 2000 [1788]. *The Federalist.* Edited by William R. Brock. London: Phoenix.

Mainwaring, Scott. 1997. "Multipartism, Robust Federalism, and Presidentialism in Brazil." In *Presidentialism and Democracy in Latin America,* edited by Scott Mainwaring and Matthew Soberg Shugart. New York: Cambridge University Press.

———. 1999. *Rethinking Party Systems in the Third Wave of Democratization: The Case of Brazil.* Stanford: Stanford University Press.

Mainwaring, Scott, and Timothy Scully, eds. 1995. *Parties and Party Systems in Latin America.* Stanford: Stanford University Press.

Mainwaring, Scott, and Matthew Soberg Shugart, eds. 1997. *Presidentialism and Democracy in Latin America.* New York: Cambridge University Press.

Manin, Bernard. 1997. *Principles of Representative Government.* Cambridge: Cambridge University Press.

Marantzidis, Nikos, and George Mavrommatis. 1999. "Political Clientelism and Social Exclusion: The Case of Gypsies in the Greek Town of Sofades." *International Sociology* 14, 4: 443–456.

Markoff, John. 1999. "Where and When Was Democracy Invented?" *Comparative Studies in Society and History* 41, 4: 660–690.

Martins, Wilson. 1999. Interview with Scott W. Desposato. Piauí, Brazil.

Mayhew, David R. 1974. *Congress: The Electoral Connection.* New Haven: Yale University Press.

McCargo, Duncan. 1998. "Alternative Meanings of Political Reform in Contemporary Thailand." *Copenhagen Journal of Asian Studies* 13: 5–30.

———. 2002. Thailand's January 2001 General Elections: Vindicating Reform?" In *Reforming Thai Politics,* edited by Duncan McCargo. Copenhagen: Nordic Institute of Asian Studies.

McGuire, Martin C., and Mancur Olson. 1996. "The Economics of Autocracy and Majority Rule." *Journal of Economic Literature* 34: 72–96.

McKean, Margaret, and Ethan Scheiner. 2000. "Japan's New Electoral System: La plus ça change . . ." *Electoral Studies* 19, 4: 447–447.

McKelvy, Richard D. 1976. "Intransitivities in Multidimensional Voting Models and Some Implications for Agenda Control." *Journal of Economic Theory* 12: 472–482.

McVey, Ruth, ed. 2000a. *Money and Power in Provincial Thailand.* Honolulu: University of Hawaii Press.

———. 2000b. "Of Greed and Violence, and Other Signs of Progress." In *Money and Power in Provincial Thailand,* edited by Ruth McVey. Honolulu: University of Hawaii Press.

Milesi-Ferretti, Gian Maria, Roberto Perotti, and Massimo Rostagno. 2002. "Electoral Systems and Public Spending." *Quarterly Journal of Economics* 117: 609–657.

Millar Carvacho, René. 1981. *La elección presidencial de 1920: Tendencias y prácticas políticas en el Chile parlamentario.* Santiago: Ediciones Universitaria.

Molinar, Juan. 1991. *El tiempo de la legitimidad: Elecciones, autoritarismo, y democracia en México.* Mexico City: Cal y Arena.

Moon, Eric P., and James A. Robinson. 1998. "Taiwan's 1997 Local Elections: Appraising Steps in Democratization." *American Journal of Chinese Studies* 5: 131–146.

Mozaffar, Shaheen, and Andreas Schedler. 2002. "The Comparative Study of Electoral Governance." *International Political Science Review.* 23, 1: 5–27.

Mulder, Niels. 1997. *Inside Philippine Society: Interpretations of Everyday Life.* Quezon City: New Day.

Munro, Dana Gardner. 1918. *The Five Republics of Central America.* New York: Oxford University Press.

Murashima, Eiji. 1987. "Local Elections and Leadership in Thailand: A Case Study of Nakon Sawan Province." *Developing Economies* 25: 363–385.

Nelson, Michael H. 1998a. "Analysis of 'Thai Society' in Times of Globalization: Some Preliminary Remarks." December. Unpublished manuscript.

———. 1998b. "Central Authority and Local Democratization in Thailand." Studies in Contemporary Thailand no. 6. Bangkok: White Lotus.

———. 1999. "Analysis of 'Thai Society' in Times of Globalization: Some Preliminary Remarks." Bangkok: Faculty of Political Science, Chulalongkorn University. Unpublished manuscript.

———. 2000. "The Senate Elections of March 4, 2000 (etc., etc.)." *KPI Newsletter* 1, 3: 3–7.

———. 2002. "Thailand's House Elections of 6 Jan. 2001: Thaksin's Landside Victory and Subsequent Narrow Escape." In *KPI Yearbook.* Nothaburi, Thailand: King Prajadhipok Institute.

Newsweek. 2001. "Thailand: Moment of Glory?" January 15.

Newsweek Online. 2003. "Why Dean Is Still the Democrat to Watch." http://stacks.msnbc.com/news/910604.asp?0cv=kb10&cp1=1.

Ockey, James. 1991. "Business Leaders, Gangsters, and the Middle Class." PhD diss., Cornell University.

———. 1999. "Creating the Thai Middle Class." In *Culture and Privilege in Capitalist Asia,* edited by Michael Pinches. New York: Routledge.

———. 2000. "The Rise of Local Power in Thailand: Provincial Crime, Elections, and the Bureaucracy." In *Money and Power in Provincial Thailand,* edited by Ruth McVey. Honolulu: University of Hawaii Press.

O'Gorman, Frank. 1989. *Voters, Patrons and Parties: The Unreformed Electoral System of Hanoverian England, 1734–1832.* Oxford: Oxford University Press.

———. 1992. "Campaign Rituals and Ceremonies: The Social Meaning of Elections in England, 1780–1860." *Past and Present* 135: 79–115.

O'Leary, Cornelius. 1962. *The Elimination of Corrupt Practices in British Elections, 1868–1911.* Oxford: Clarendon.

Olivares-Cunana, Belinda. 2001. "Students Should Help Educate Voters." *Philippine Daily Inquirer,* March 13.

Olson, Mancur. 1965. *The Logic of Collective Action: Public Goods and the Theory of Groups.* Cambridge: Harvard University Press.

Organic Law on the Election of Members of the House of Representatives and Senators, B.E. 2541 (1998), with Amendments. 1998. Thailand. http://www.ect. go.th/english/laws/organiclawelection.html.

Orr, Graeme. 2003. "Dealing in Votes: Regulating Electoral Bribery." In *Realising Democracy: Electoral Law in Australia,* edited by Graeme Orr, Bryan Mercurio, and George Williams. Annandale, Australia: Federation.

Parish Pastoral Council for Responsible Voting. 1996. "5th Foundation Anniversary Celebration: PPCRV National Conference, October 18–19, 1996—Conference Report." Mimeo.

Party Interviews. 1999. Allen D. Hicken interviews with officials from Thai political parties. Bangkok, January–June.

———. 2000. Allen D. Hicken interviews with officials from Thai political parties. Bangkok, March.

Pasuk Phongpaichit and Chris Baker. 2002. *Thailand: Economy and Politics.* Malaysia: Oxford University Press.

Pasuk Phongpaichit, Nualnoi Treerat, Yongyuth Chaiyapong, and Chris Baker. 2000. "Corruption in the Public Sector in Thailand: Perception and Experience of Households." Bangkok: Political Economy Center, Chulalongkorn University.

Patiño, Patrick I. 1998. "The Color of Money: Elections and Big Business." *Conjuncture* 10, 1 (April): 12–15.

Pearce, David W., ed. 1992. *The MIT Dictionary of Modern Economics.* Cambridge: Massachusetts Institute of Technology Press.

Pérez Yarahuán, Gabriela. 2002. "Social Programs and Electoral Competition: The Political Economy of the Mexican National Fund for Social Enterprises." Documento de Trabajo DAP no. 123. Mexico City: Centro de Investigación y Docencia Económica (CIDE).

Persson, Torsten, and Guido Tabellini. 1999. "The Size and Scope of Government: Comparative Politics with Rational Politicians." *European Economic Review* 43: 699–735.

———. 2000. *Political Economics: Explaining Economic Policy.* Cambridge: Massachusetts Institute of Technology Press.

———. 2003. *The Economic Effects of Constitutions.* Cambridge: Massachusetts Institute of Technology Press.

Persson, Tortsen, Guido Tabellini, and Francesco Trebbi. 2001. "Electoral Rules and Corruption." Working Paper no. 8154. Cambridge, Mass.: National Bureau of Economic Research.

———. 2003. "Electoral Rules and Corruption." *Journal of the European Economic Association* 1: 958–989.

Petras, James, and Maurice Zeitlin. 1968. "Agrarian Radicalism in Chile." *British Journal of Sociology* 19: 503–531.

Pfeiffer, Silke. 2004. "Vote Buying and Its Implication for Democracy: Evidence from Latin America." In *Global Corruption Report 2004.* Sterling, Va.: Transparency International.

Philippine Daily Inquirer. 2002. "'Jueteng' Return Driven by 2004 Polls." October 7.

———. 2003a. "President Orders: 'Go After Politicians Behind Kidnaps.'" October 31.

———. 2003b. "Solon Sees Link Between Bank Heists, 2004 Polls." September 14.

Pinches, Michael. 1996. "The Philippines' New Rich: Capitalist Transformation Amidst Economic Gloom." In *The New Rich of Asia: Mobile Phones, McDonalds and Middle-Class Revolution,* edited by Richard Robinson and David S. G. Goodman. New York: Routledge.

Pinto-Duschinsky, Michael. 1981. *British Political Finance, 1830–1980.* Washington, D.C.: American Enterprise Institute for Public Policy Research.

———. 2002. "Financing Politics: A Global View." *Journal of Democracy* 13, 4: 69–86.

Popkin, Samuel L. 1991. *The Reasoning Voter: Communication and Persuasion in Presidential Campaigns.* Chicago: University of Chicago Press.

Posada-Carbó, Eduardo. 2000. "Electoral Juggling: A Comparative History of the Corruption of Suffrage in Latin America, 1830–1930." *Journal of Latin American Studies* 32: 611–644.

Powell, John Duncan. 1970. "Peasant Society and Clientelist Politics." *American Political Science Review* 64, 2: 411–425.

Prawase Wasi. 2002. "An Overview of Political Reform Issues." In *Reforming Thai Politics,* edited by Duncan McCargo. Copenhagen: Nordic Institute of Asian Studies.

Przeworksi, Adam, Michael E. Alvarez, José Antonio Cheibub, and Fernando Limongi. 2000. *Democracy and Development: Political Institutions and Well-Being in the World, 1950–1990.* New York: Cambridge University Press.

Pulse Asia. 2001. *Ulat ng Bayan Survey.* June 15–26. Quezon City, Philippines.

Putnam, Robert D. 1993. *Making Democracy Work: Civic Traditions in Modern Italy.* Princeton: Princeton University Press.

Rabinowitz, George, and Stewart McDonald. 1989. "A Directional Theory of Issue Voting." *American Political Science Review* 83: 93–121.

Rafael, Vicente L. 2001. "Dirty Words." *Philippine Daily Inquirer,* July 24.

Ramseyer, J. Mark, and Frances McCall Rosenbluth. 1993. *Japan's Political Marketplace.* Cambridge: Harvard University Press.

Rawnsley, Gary D. 2003. "An Institutional Approach to Election Campaigning in Taiwan." *Journal of Contemporary China* 12, 37: 765–779.

Reed, Steven R. 1994. "Democracy and the Personal Vote: A Cautionary Tale from Japan." *Electoral Studies* 13, 1: 17–28.

Regan, D. T. 1971. "Effects of a Favor and Liking on Compliance." *Journal of Experimental Social Psychology* 7: 627–639.

Rigger, Shelley Elizabeth. 1994. "Machine Politics in the New Taiwan: Institutional Reform and Electoral Strategy in the Republic of China on Taiwan." PhD diss., Harvard University.

———. 1999a. "Grassroots Electoral Organization and Political Reform in the ROC on Taiwan and Mexico." In *The Awkward Embrace: One-Party Domination and Democracy,* edited by Hermann Giliomee and Charles Simkins. Amsterdam: Harwood Academic.

———. 1999b. *Politics in Taiwan: Voting for Democracy.* London: Routledge.

———. 2002. "Weighing a Shadow: Toward a Technique for Estimating the Effects of Vote-Buying in Taiwan." Paper presented at the conference "Trading Political Rights: The Comparative Politics of Vote Buying," Center for International Studies, Massachusetts Institute of Technology, Cambridge, August 26–27.

Rohter, Larry. 2003. "Argentine Moves Against Police Corruption." *New York Times,* November 17.

Romero, Paolo, and Sheila Crisostomo. 2003. "Lawmaker: One-fourth of Public Officials Funded by Drug Barons." *Philippine Star,* June 26.

Rusk, Jerrold G. 1974. "The American Electoral Universe: Speculation and Evidence." *American Political Science Review* 68, 3: 1028–1049.

Salem, Gérard. 1992. "Crise urbaine et contrôle social à Pikine: Bornes-fontaines et clientélisme." *Politique Africaine* 45: 21–38.

Samuels, David J. 1999. "Incentives to Cultivate a Party Vote in Candidate-Centric Electoral Systems: Evidence from Brazil." *Comparative Political Studies* 32, 4: 487–518.

———. 2002. "Pork-Barreling Is Not Credit-Claiming or Advertising: Campaign Finance and the Sources of the Personal Vote in Brazil." *Journal of Politics* 6, 3: 845–863.

Schady, Norbert. 2000. "The Political Economy of Expenditures by the Peruvian Social Fund (FONCODES), 1991–1995." *American Political Science Review* 94, 2: 289–304.

Schaffer, Frederic Charles. 1998. *Democracy in Translation: Understanding Politics in an Unfamiliar Culture.* Ithaca: Cornell University Press.

———. 2002a. "Disciplinary Reactions: Alienation and the Reform of Vote Buying in the Philippines." Paper presented at the conference "Trading Political Rights: The Comparative Politics of Vote Buying," Center for International Studies, Massachusetts Institute of Technology, Cambridge, August 26–27.

———. 2002b. "Might Cleaning Up Elections Keep People Away from the Polls? Historical and Comparative Perspectives." *International Political Science Review* 23, 1: 69–84.

———. 2004. "Vote Buying in East Asia." Cambridge: Center for International Studies, Massachusetts Institute of Technology. Unpublished manuscript.

———. 2006. "Democracy at Risk: The Hidden Costs of Clean Election Reform." Unpublished manuscript.

Schedler, Andreas. 2000. "Mexico's Victory: The Democratic Revelation." *Journal of Democracy* 11, 3: 5–19.

———. 2002a. "The Menu of Manipulation." *Journal of Democracy* 13, 2: 36–50.

———. 2002b. "Vote Buying: Concepts and Frames." Paper presented at the conference "Trading Political Rights: The Comparative Politics of Vote Buying," Center for International Studies, Massachusetts Institute of Technology, Cambridge, August 26–27.

———. 2004. "'El voto es nuestro': Como los ciudadanos mexicanos perciben el clientelismo electoral." *Revista Mexicana de Sociología* 66, 1: 61–101.

———. Forthcoming. "Mapping Contingency." In *Political Contingency: Studying the Unexpected, the Accidental, and the Unforseen,* edited by Ian Shapiro and Sonu Bedi. New York: New York University Press.

Schmidt, Steffen W. 1977. "The Transformation of Clientelism in Rural Colombia." In *Friends, Followers, and Factions: A Reader in Political Clientelism,* edited by Steffen W. Schmidt, Laura Guasti, Carl H. Landé, and James C. Scott. Berkeley: University of California Press.

Scott, James C. 1969. "Corruption, Machine Politics, and Political Change." *American Political Science Review* 63, 4: 1142–1158.

———. 1972a. *Comparative Political Corruption.* Englewood Cliffs, N.J.: Prentice-Hall.

———. 1972b. "Patron-Client Politics and Political Change in Southeast Asia." *American Political Science Review* 66: 91–113.

Scully, Timothy R. 1992. *Rethinking the Center: Party Politics in Nineteenth and Twentieth Century Chile.* Stanford: Stanford University Press.

Seymour, Charles. 1915. *Electoral Reform in England and Wales: The Development and Operation of the Parliamentary Franchise, 1832–1885.* New Haven: Yale University Press.

Sharma, Rakes. 2003. "Attitudes and Expectations: Public Opinion in Ukraine 2002." Washington, D.C.: International Foundation for Election Systems.

Shugart, Matthew Soberg, and John M. Carey. 1992. *Presidents and Assemblies: Constitutional Design and Electoral Dynamics.* Cambridge: Cambridge University Press.

Shugart, Matthew Soberg, and Daniel L. Nielson. 1999. "Constitutional Change in Colombia: Policy Adjustment Through Institutional Change." *Comparative Political Studies* 32, 3: 313–341.

Shugart, Matthew Soberg, and Martin P. Wattenberg, eds. 2001. *Mixed-Member Electoral Systems: The Best of Both Worlds?* Oxford: Oxford University Press.

Silva, Manuel Carlos. 1994. "Peasants, Patrons, and the State in Northern Portugal." In *Democracy, Clientelism, and Civil Society,* edited by Luis Roniger and Ayse Günes-Ayata. Boulder: Lynne Rienner.

Silverman, Sydel F. 1977. "Patronage and Community-Nation Relationship in Central Italy." In *Friends, Followers, and Factions: A Reader in Political Clientelism,* edited by Steffen W. Schmidt, Laura Guasti, Carl H. Landé, and James C. Scott. Berkeley: University of California Press.

Snyder, James M., Jr., and Michael M. Ting. 2001. "An Informational Rationale for Political Parties." *American Journal of Political Science* 46, 1: 90–110.

Social Weather Stations. 2002. *National Survey.* August 24–September 8. Quezon City, Philippines.

Sombat Chantornvong. 1993. *Luaktang Wikrit: Panha Lae Thang Ok* [Thai Elections in Crisis: Problems and Solutions]. Bangkok: Kobfai.

———. 1997. Interview with Allen D. Hicken. Bangkok, September 11.

———. 1999. Interview with Allen D. Hicken. Bangkok, March 23.

———. 2000. "Local Godfathers in Thai Politics." In *Money and Power in Provincial Thailand,* edited by Ruth McVey. Honolulu: University of Hawaii Press.

———. 2002. "The 1997 Constitution and the Politics of Electoral Reform." In *Reforming Thai Politics,* edited by Duncan McCargo. Copenhagen: Nordic Institute of Asian Studies.

Somroutai R. Sapsomboon. 2002. "Concern over Interference." *The Nation,* January 2.

———. 1999. Interview with Allen D. Hicken. Bangkok, February 25.

Speck, Bruno Wilhelm, and Cláudio Weber Abramo. 2001. Transparêcia Brasil/Ibope Survey, summary report. São Paulo: Transparêcia Brasil.

Stigler, George. 1975. *The Citizen and the State.* Chicago: University of Chicago Press.

Stokes, Donald. 1966. "Spatial Models of Party Competition." In *Elections and the Political Order,* edited by Angus Campbell, Philip E. Converse, Warren E. Miller, and Donald E. Stokes. New York: Wiley.

Stokes, Susan C. 2001. *Mandates and Democracy: Neoliberalism by Surprise in Latin America*. New York: Cambridge University Press.

———. 2005. "Perverse Accountability: A Formal Model of Machine Politics with Evidence from Argentina." *American Political Science Review* 99, 3: 315–325.

Suchit Bongbongkorn. 1999. Interview with Allen D. Hicken. Bangkok, February 25.

Summerhill, William. 1995. "A Note on Some Economic Consequences of Electoral Reform in Imperial Brazil." Los Angeles: University of California, Department of History. Unpublished manuscript.

Sydnor, Charles S. 1984 [1952]. *Gentlemen Freeholders: Political Practices in Washington's Virginia*. Westport: Greenwood.

Taipei Times. 2005. "Anti-Vote-Buying Drive Gets Credit for 'Clean' Election." December 5.

Tam, Waikeung. 2003. "Clientelist Politics in Singapore: Selective Provision of Housing Services as an Electoral Mobilization Strategy." Chicago: University of Chicago, Department of Political Science. Unpublished manuscript.

Tasker, Rodney, and Shawn Crispin. 2001. "On an Electoral Collision Course." *Far Eastern Economic Review,* January 11: 22–23.

Teixeira, Tomaz. 1985. *A Outra Face da Oliguarquia do Piauí (Depoimento)*. 2nd ed. Fortaleza: Stylus Comunicações.

Tétreault, Mary Ann. 2000. *Stories of Democracy: Politics and Society in Contemporary Kuwait*. New York: Columbia University Press.

Thornton, Laura. 2000. "Combating Corruption at the Grassroots: The Thailand Experience, 1999–2000." National Democratic Institute for International Affairs.

Times of London. 2000. "Betting Alters the Odds in Close Taiwan Election." March 15.

Tirol, Stella. 1992. "The Art of Cheating." *Manila Standard,* May 8–9.

Tordesillas, Ellen. 1998. "The Operator." *Investigative Reporting* 4, 1–2: 76–79.

Transparency International Armenia. 2003. "Parliamentary Elections and Vote Buying: Phone Survey."

Tusell, Javier. 1969. *Sociología electoral de Madrid, 1903–1931*. Madrid: Editorial Cuadernos para el Diálogo.

———. 1991. "El sufragio universal en España (1891–1936): Un balance historiográfico." *Ayer* 3: 13–62.

Valenzuela, Arturo. 1977. *Political Brokers in Chile: Local Government in a Centralized Polity*. Durham, N.C.: Duke University Press.

———. 1978. *The Breakdown of Democratic Regimes: Chile*. Baltimore: Johns Hopkins University Press.

van de Walle, Nicolas. 2002. "'Meet the New Boss, Same as the Old Boss?' The Evolution of Political Clientelism in Africa." Unpublished manuscript.

Varela-Ortega, José, ed. 2001a. *El poder de la influencia: Geografía del caciquismo en España (1875–1923)*. Madrid: Marcial Pons/Centro de Estudios Políticos y Constitucionales.

———. 2001b. *Los amigos políticos: Partidos, elecciones y caciquismo en la restauración*. Madrid: Marcial Pons/Junta de Castilla y León, Consejería de Educación y Cultura.

Wang, Chin-Shou. 2001. "The Dilemmas of Clientelism: Electoral Mobilization of Clientelism in Taiwan, 1993." Carolina Papers: Democracy and Human Rights no. 1. Chapel Hill: Center for International Studies, University of North Carolina.

———. 2004. "Democratization and the Breakdown of Clientelism in Taiwan, 1987–2001." PhD diss., University of North Carolina–Chapel Hill.

Wang, Chin-Shou, and Charles Kurzman. Forthcoming. "Dilemmas of Electoral Clientelism: Taiwan, 1993." *International Political Science Review.*

Wilson, James Q. 1961. "The Economy of Patronage." *Journal of Political Economy* 69: 369–380.

Wu, Chung-Li, and Chi Huang. 2004. "Politics and Judiciary Verdicts on Vote Buying Litigation in Taiwan." *Asian Survey* 44, 5: 755–770.

Wu, Nai-Teh. 1987. "The Politics of a Regime Patronage System: Mobilization and Control Within an Authoritarian Regime." PhD diss., University of Chicago.

Yang, He-Lun. 1995. "Shuei-De Shiu Said, 'The Courts Are Owned by the Ruling Party'" [in Chinese]. *The Journalist,* July 23–29: 25.

Yang, Wen-San. 1994. "Application of the Randomized Response Method: The Estimation of Vote Buying in Taiwan" [in Chinese]. In *The Social Image of Taiwan,* edited by Chin-Chun Yi. Taipei: Sun Yat-Sen Institute.

The Contributors

Jean-Marie Baland is an economist at the Research Center in Development Economics, and a professor at the Facultés Universitaires Notre Dame de la Paix in Namur, Belgium. He has written on many topics in the field of development economics, including child labor, common property resources, and informal solidarity networks.

Scott W. Desposato is assistant professor of political science at the University of California at San Diego. His general research interests include democratic institutions, campaigning, mass behavior, and political methodology. Specific projects have examined redistricting in the United States, electoral rules and federalism in Brazil, party switching by politicians, and statistical methods for studying legislatures. His latest project, for which he has received a National Science Foundation award, examines the determinants and impacts of negative campaigning across different institutional settings.

Allen D. Hicken is assistant professor of political science and faculty associate at the Center for Southeast Asian Studies and Center for Political Studies at the University of Michigan. He studies political institutions and policymaking in developing countries, with a focus on Southeast Asia. He has carried out research in Thailand, the Philippines, Singapore, and Cambodia. He is currently working on a book titled *Building Party Systems: Elections, Parties, and Coordination in Developing Democracies.*

Charles Kurzman is associate professor of sociology at the University of North Carolina at Chapel Hill and author of *The Unthinkable Revolution in Iran.* He is working on a book on the sad fate of new democracies around the world in the early twentieth century titled *Democracy Denied, 1905–1915.*

Fabrice Lehoucq is a research professor in the Division of Political Studies at the Centro de Investigación y Docencia Económicas (CIDE) in Mexico City. He is the author of four books, the most recent of which is *Stuffing the Ballot Box: Fraud, Electoral Reform, and Democratization in Costa Rica,* coauthored with Iván Molina. He has also written numerous articles in the fields of institutional analysis, electoral politics, and political economy. He is currently at work on a book titled *Political Institutions, Instability, and Democratic Performance in Latin America.*

James A. Robinson is professor of government at Harvard University. His main research interests are the study of the creation, persistence, and change of institutions, and their impact on development with particular reference to Africa and Latin America. He recently published a book with Daron Acemoglu titled *Economic Origins of Dictatorship and Democracy.* He is now coediting *An Economic History of Colombia in the Twentieth Century.*

Frederic Charles Schaffer is lecturer on social studies at Harvard University and research associate at the Center for International Studies at the Massachusetts Institute of Technology. He studies electoral fraud, electoral administration, and the political culture of elections. Among the countries in which he has conducted research or election assessments are Iraq, Haiti, Senegal, and the Philippines. He is author of *Democracy in Translation: Understanding Politics in an Unfamiliar Culture.* Currently he is completing a book titled *Democracy at Risk: The Hidden Costs of Clean Election Reform.*

Andreas Schedler is a research professor and head of the Division of Political Studies at the Centro de Investigación y Docencia Económicas (CIDE) in Mexico City. He also cochairs the Committee on Concepts and Methods of the International Political Science Association. His current research focuses on the dynamics of electoral authoritarianism in the world since 1980.

Susan C. Stokes is John S. Saden Professor of Political Science at Yale University. Her most recent book, coauthored with Matthew Cleary, is *Democracy and the Culture of Skepticism: Political Trust in Argentina and Mexico.* Her current research interests include the transition from clientelism to programmatic politics, and the acquisition of political identities in new democracies.

Chin-Shou Wang is assistant professor in the Department of Political Science and the Graduate Institute of Political Economy, National Cheng Kung University, Taiwan. He is currently working on a book titled *Revolt from the Bottom: Judicial Independence Reform in Taiwan.*

Index

About the Book

Often regarded as a phenomenon of earlier times and backward places, vote buying has made an impressive comeback in recent decades—primarily as a by-product of democratization. *Elections for Sale* offers the first comprehensive analysis of this widespread but ill-understood practice.

The authors systematically explore a series of key questions: What exactly is vote buying? What are its underlying causes? Why does it occur in some places, but not in others? How does it affect political and economic development? Can it be educated or legislated away? Their work presents new theoretical insights, as well as fresh empirical evidence from Asia and Latin America.

Frederic Charles Schaffer is lecturer on social studies at Harvard University and research associate at the Center for International Studies at the Massachusetts Institute of Technology. He is author of *Democracy in Translation: Understanding Politics in an Unfamiliar Culture*.